Yale Broadway Masters

ALSO IN THE SERIES

Richard Rodgers, by GEOFFREY BLOCK

FORTHCOMING

Irving Berlin, by JEFFREY MAGEE

Leonard Bernstein, by CAROL OJA

George Gershwin, by LARRY STARR

John Kander and Fred Ebb, by JAMES LEVE

Jerome Kern, by STEPHEN BANFIELD

Frank Loesser, by THOMAS L. RIIS

Cole Porter, by PATRICK O'CONNOR

Sigmund Romberg, by WILLIAM A. EVERETT

ANDREW LLOYD WEBBER

JOHN SNELSON

With a Foreword by

GEOFFREY BLOCK, *General Editor*

YALE UNIVERSITY PRESS   NEW HAVEN & LONDON

Published with assistance from the Kingsley Trust Association Publication Fund established by the Scroll and Key Society of Yale College.

Frontispiece: Andrew Lloyd Webber (photo: John Swannell).

Posters and record jackets pictured on pages 11, 12, 14, 23, 35, 43, 44, 48, 50, 52, 62, 63, 74, 128, 142, 192, 196, and 201 designed by Dewynters. Photography for *The Phantom of the Opera*, Mexico, pages 84, 85, 86, 100, 107, 112, and 120, Fernando Aceves and Juan Carlos Equihua.

Designed by James J. Johnson and set in Electra Roman types by Tseng Information Systems, Inc.
Printed in the United States of America by R. R. Donnelley and Sons.

Library of Congress Cataloging-in-Publication Data

Snelson, John.
Andrew Lloyd Webber / John Snelson ; with a foreword by Geoffrey Block, general editor.
p.   cm. — (Yale Broadway masters)
Includes bibliographical references (p.   ) and index.
ISBN 0-300-10459-6 (cloth : alk. paper)

1. Lloyd Webber, Andrew, 1948–   Criticism and interpretation.   2. Musicals—History and criticism.   I. Block, Geoffrey Holden, 1948– .   II. Title.   III. Series.
ML410.L78S64   2004
782.1′4′092—dc22   2004004311

A catalogue record for this book is available from the British Library.

The paper in this book meets the guidelines for permanence and durability of the Committee on Production Guidelines for Book Longevity of the Council on Library Resources.

10   9   8   7   6   5   4   3   2   1

For Doreen and Henry

Contents

Series Foreword, by Geoffrey Block   ix

Acknowledgments   xi

CHAPTER 1.   Aspects of Life   1

CHAPTER 2.   Telling Tales: A Survey of the Shows   20

CHAPTER 3.   Pop, Rock, and Classical: First Elements of a Style   55

CHAPTER 4.   "Who Are You, Strange Angel?": Multiple
                        Personalities in *The Phantom of the Opera*   77

CHAPTER 5.   "I'm Ready for My Close-Up":
                        Lloyd Webber on Screen   123

CHAPTER 6.   "Memory": Musical Reminiscences in Lloyd Webber   157

CHAPTER 7.   "Now and Forever": Canons and Challenges   183

List of Works by Andrew Lloyd Webber   213

Notes   221

Bibliography   247

Permissions   249

General Index   255

Index of Lloyd Webber's Works   263

Series Foreword

Geoffrey Block, GENERAL EDITOR

Before Andrew Lloyd Webber, one must turn to the historic Broadway invasion of Arthur Sullivan's music and W. S. Gilbert's words and stories in the late 1870s and early 1880s (*H.M.S. Pinafore, The Pirates of Penzance, The Mikado*) to find a British theater composer who so consistently conquered American popular culture. From the New York arrival of *Jesus Christ Superstar* in 1971 to the present, the sun has yet to set on the Lloyd Webber era either on Broadway or in London's West End. *Evita, Joseph and the Amazing Technicolor Dreamcoat, Starlight Express,* and *Sunset Boulevard* all enjoyed considerable popular acclaim from the late 1970s to the mid-1990s, and in 1997, one Lloyd Webber show, *Cats,* surpassed the record of *A Chorus Line* for longest-running Broadway show. Lloyd Webber's megahit eventually lost its ninth lives in New York and London after eighteen years (1982–2000) and twenty-one years (1981–2002), respectively. Meanwhile, *The Phantom of the Opera* (London, 1986; New York, 1988) continues its spectacular run on both sides of the pond.

Alongside extraordinary and continuous popularity, Lloyd Webber has suffered a divided and often negative critical response, especially in the American media, and the hostility of neglect in the academy. Consequently, despite phenomenal commercial successes on Broadway, in the West End, and in other international markets, Lloyd Webber has not received the kind of serious and balanced scholarly and critical attention a figure of his cultural importance merits. John Snelson's *Andrew Lloyd Webber* is the first book to comprehensively explore the development of the composer's musical and dramatic language and his professional career. Snelson's study also offers a rich and wide-ranging examination of *The Phantom of the Opera* and Lloyd Webber's multifaceted relationship with film.

Snelson, a British music and theater historian and the commissioning editor for musical theater and for popular, light, and pop music for the revised *New Grove Dictionary of Music*, readily acknowledges the critical controversies that almost invariably surround his subject. Individual chapters critique the unorthodox origins of several Lloyd Webber shows as pop or rock albums and the composer's controversial use of preexistent musical materials, what Snelson refers to as "shades of gray" (pastiche, allusion, modeling, and borrowing). Perhaps most provocatively, Snelson addresses Lloyd Webber's challenge to the hegemony of Broadway traditions and the privileging of originality in the crafting, understanding, and evaluation of a musical in the postmodern world. Snelson offers a musical and dramatic paradigm that will help readers discover how a Lloyd Webber musical speaks in a language that frequently resides outside the traditional Broadway boundaries of Kern, Rodgers and Hammerstein, and their progeny (including Sondheim). In the process he delivers an explanation as well as spirited advocacy on behalf of Lloyd Webber's popular yet often critically maligned work.

Acknowledgments

The impetus for this volume was provided when Harry Haskell at Yale University Press wrote to me with the suggestion; he was instrumental in getting the book off the ground and well under way, and I am most grateful for his formative contributions and later detailed observations.

The project became possible when Lord Lloyd-Webber gave his kind cooperation through his Really Useful Group, whose assistance at every point has been valuable and unquestioning. In particular, David Robinson, head of music licensing, has been unfailingly helpful in providing information, arranging permissions, and generally pointing me in the right directions. Caroline Skidmore kindly dug out large piles of orchestral scores and lent me the desk space to study them. Later in the process, Marie Curtin helped with images and checked the manuscript for factual details, and Carolyn Sims and Rosie Hills attended to some finishing touches.

There are several biographies of Lloyd Webber, but there is very little study of the works themselves in print. Consequently, my initial thoughts ranged far and wide, before the finite length of the book imposed its restrictions. I am particularly grateful to David Cullen and his wife, who were generous with time and hospitality; I wish that the final form had allowed for more of his material to feature.

No book of academic investigation is created in a vacuum. Providing a main supply of oxygen, Geoffrey Block has been the most assiduous of series editors, offering detailed views at each stage of the preparation, from early drafts through to final edited text. I have also had the ongoing advice and support of many friends and colleagues; they willingly read substantial sections or complete versions of the developing book and contributed many invaluable observations on form, argument, and detail. John Tyrrell, with whom I have shared many evenings at both musicals and operas, was his usual forensic self and a constant source of encouragement; to him I owe much, not least for some timely metaphorical cups of tea by e-mail or telephone. Bill Everett gave a much-valued, objective, and knowledgeable voice as the chapters rolled out, while Stephen Banfield likewise provided valuable thoughts at key moments. Kate Daubney and Angela Eyre brought the perspectives of film and genre studies to their comments; René Weis preached a timely lesson of persistence and went beyond any call of friendship by reading the final version on a beach in a heat wave in the South of France. Gregory Dart requires a special mention: our highly enjoyable discussions over afternoon teas provoked many useful themes for later chapters, and it is to him that I am indebted for the ornithological observations. Maria Lord suspended her natural instincts in the cause of my cause, instead bringing her expert editorial eye to bear most helpfully. As with all my writings and researches, the British dimension has been assisted by its constant advocates, Rexton Bunnett and John Muir, always generous with time and archival material, and constantly reinforcing of the value of such a project as this. The staff of the Theatre Museum in Covent Garden were helpful as ever as I plundered their box files and collated their cuttings.

As the ideas and chapters gave way to the nuts and bolts of publishing, the staff at Yale University Press came into their own. Larisa Heimert took over with enthusiasm after Harry Haskell had moved on, while Keith Condon was patient with pushing me the right way through the niceties of scheduling and administration. I consider myself especially fortunate that Dan Heaton edited the final manuscript: his knowledge, interest, and judicious interventions helped the reader, while his constant witty asides helped me. In the final stages, Neil Casey at Note-Orious Productions Ltd, London, made his usual fine job setting the music examples on Sibelius.

At The Royal Opera House, Rebecca Erol, Liz Watkins, Kate Bettley, and Áine Sheil have put up with my occasional distractions and diversions as the project has progressed; in Hackney, Tina Jones has lived with the ongoing dramas and loud background music from the basement for longer than I am sure seemed reasonable.

But the book is dedicated to two people in particular. Throughout not just this project but the unexpected directions of my life, my mother has been constantly supportive. She began going to see Lloyd Webber shows before I did, in fact, and only at occasional moments in the writing of this book has brought up the amusing irony of one unexpected conjunction worthy of astrological significance (she more than anyone knows and appreciates what it is). Henry Wilson has accompanied me to many musicals over the past few years, and this book provided the excuse for a few more; his observations from a different perspective are always provocative, and his continual encouragement of my endeavors always makes a difference. He has had to live with the book's (and occasionally my) brooding presence, but without his forbearance as I ran through recordings, pored over papers, and peered at computer screens, it would not have been completed at all.

Andrew Lloyd Webber

Andrew Lloyd Webber (photo: John Swannell).

 CHAPTER 1

Aspects of Life

ANDREW LLOYD WEBBER IS THE MOST PROMINENT FIGURE IN MUSI-
cal theater of his generation.[1] A household name throughout the
world, he can boast a series of pop-chart successes and lengthy stage
runs over a long career that must be the envy of most of his contemporaries.
An awareness of his works is essential to the study of the musical, for he has
become central to our understanding of the art form, both in its history from
the late 1960s onward and in its identity as a genre.

By any measure of commercial success, Lloyd Webber is also a "Broadway master." *Cats* holds the records for the longest-running musical both on
Broadway and in London's West End; seen throughout the world, in some
three hundred cities and more than eleven languages, it has taken in a gross
of more than $2 billion and has been watched in the theater by more than
fifty million people, in addition to those who have enjoyed it through recorded versions. *The Phantom of the Opera* seems likely to equal that record;
at the time of writing (2004) the Broadway and West End productions had
achieved runs of sixteen and seventeen years, respectively. *Starlight Express*,
when it closed in London in 2002, held the record for the second-longest-
running musical in the West End, although about half of the show's estimated 16.5 million audience members saw productions elsewhere. When
we add the international successes of *Joseph and the Amazing Technicolor
Dreamcoat, Jesus Christ Superstar, Evita,* and *Sunset Boulevard,* the portfolio is an astonishing one.[2]

What is more, from the opening of *Evita* in 1979 to 2004 there has always
been a Lloyd Webber show running on Broadway, for most of that time two

Andrew Lloyd Webber with the casts of his six concurrent shows running in the West End in 1991, the first time such a record had been achieved. © 1991 The Really Useful Group Ltd.

concurrently, and for several periods three (table 1.1). In the West End, the opening of *Jesus Christ Superstar* in 1972 marked the start of a continuous presence of Lloyd Webber shows through to the time of writing; often during that span there have been four concurrent Lloyd Webber shows, and in both 1991 and 1997 six were playing simultaneously.[3] The number of Lloyd Webber productions worldwide has been staggering: during 1982, for example, *Evita* could be seen in Australia, Spain, Mexico, Greece, New Zealand, Japan, and Germany, in addition to London, New York, or on one of three overlapping U.S. tours and one in Britain. In 1995 you could have seen *The Phantom of the Opera* in Basel or Osaka, *Jesus Christ Superstar* in Melbourne or Prague, *Cats* in Tokyo or Milan, *Sunset Boulevard* in Frankfurt or Toronto. Even China has been added to the Lloyd Webber atlas.[4]

Such record-breaking runs show that Lloyd Webber's works have done more than catch the mood of a time or pick up on fads. Even his failures have survived longer in the public's consciousness than some composers' hits. But commercial success and popular appeal are not the only arbiters

Table 1.1. Concurrent Runs of Lloyd Webber Shows

Shows as running on January 1 of each given year, with opening dates. For productions/companies that toured or played extended runs in a series of venues, the place and first night of the residency relevant to January 1 is given; where this is different from the start of the tour, the date and place of the first engagement of that series are given in parentheses.

1983

West End	*Evita*	June 21, 1978
	Cats	May 11, 1981
	Song & Dance	April 7, 1982
Broadway	*Evita*	September 15, 1979
	Joseph	January 27, 1982
	Cats	October 7, 1982
U.K. tour	*Joseph*	(London, December 23, 1981)

1989

West End	*Cats*	May 11, 1981
	Starlight Express	March 27, 1984
	Phantom	October 9, 1986
Broadway	*Cats*	October 7, 1982
	Starlight Express	March 15, 1987
	Phantom	January 26, 1988
Austria	*Phantom*	December 12, 1988
Bochum (Germany)	*Starlight Express*	June 7, 1988
Canada tour	*Cats*	January 1, 1989 (Toronto, March 1985)
Nagoya (Japan)	*Cats*	November 23, 1988 (Tokyo, November 11, 1988)
Tokyo	*Phantom*	April 22, 1988 (Tokyo, March 22, 1988)[a]

1991

West End	*Cats*	May 11, 1981
	Starlight Express	March 27, 1984
	Phantom	October 9, 1986
	Aspects of Love	April 17, 1989
Broadway	*Cats*	October 7, 1982
	Phantom	January 26, 1988
	Aspects of Love	April 8, 1990
Bochum (Germany)	*Starlight Express*	June 7, 1988
Chicago[b]	*Phantom*	June 2, 1990
Hamburg	*Phantom*	June 29, 1990
Los Angeles	*Phantom*	May 31, 1989
Melbourne	*Phantom*	December 8, 1990
Nagoya (Japan)	*Phantom*	December 12, 1990 (Tokyo, April 22, 1988)
Stockholm	*Phantom*	October 27, 1989

continued

Table 1.1. Continued

1991

Toronto	*Phantom*	September 20, 1989
Vienna	*Phantom*	December 21, 1988 [c]

1997

West End	*Cats*	May 11, 1981
	Starlight Express	March 27, 1984
	Phantom	October 9, 1986
	Sunset Boulevard	July 12, 1993
	By Jeeves	July 2, 1996
	Jesus Christ Superstar	November 19, 1996
Broadway	*Cats*	October 7, 1982
	Phantom	January 26, 1988
	Sunset Boulevard	November 17, 1994
Basel	*Phantom*	October 12, 1995
Basingstoke (U.K.)	*Aspects of Love*	December 5, 1996
Bochum (Germany)	*Starlight Express*	June 7, 1988
Brisbane	*Phantom*	October 31, 1996
Budapest	*Aspects of Love*	November 4, 1996
Chicago	*Joseph*	November 3, 1996 (West Point, January 31, 1995)
Cincinnati	*Phantom*	December 12, 1996 (Seattle, December 3, 1992)
Detroit	*Phantom*	October 17, 1996 (Chicago, June 2, 1990)
Dublin	*Aspects of Love*	August 26, 1996
Frankfurt	*Sunset Boulevard*	December 8, 1995
Fukuoka (Japan)	*Phantom*	May 19, 1996 (Tokyo, April 22, 1988)
Las Vegas	*Starlight Express*	September 14, 1993
Leatherhead (U.K.) [d]	*Joseph*	December 17, 1996
Melbourne	*Sunset Boulevard*	October 26, 1996
Minneapolis	*Sunset Boulevard*	December 28, 1996 (Denver, June 28, 1996)
Sacramento	*Cats*	December 30, 1996 (Rochester, N.Y., March 2, 1995)
San Francisco	*Phantom*	December 12, 1993
Vancouver	*Sunset Boulevard*	November 21, 1996 (Toronto, October 15, 1995)
Washington	*Whistle Down the Wind*	December 12, 1996

[a] This production opened in Tokyo, played for several months in Osaka, then returned to Tokyo. It ran for eleven years continuously in Japan, visiting Tokyo (six times), Osaka (three times), Nagoya (twice), Sapporo, and Fukuoka.

[b] This U.S. company opened in Chicago in June 1990, then played continuously throughout the United States until its final engagement in Cincinnati on October 13, 2001.

[c] The production opened at the Theater an der Wien in 1988 and transferred to the Raimund in June 1990.

[d] This was the opening engagement for a U.K. tour that played continuously until January 5, 2002.

of importance: to be a "Broadway master" requires more than an impressive number of zeros after the dollar sign and long queues at the box office. The title implies that the creative artist has brought something more lasting to the genre, something that has influenced how the musical is conceived and perceived. How have Lloyd Webber's works changed the history of musical theater over the past decades? Why have the man and his works provoked such extremes of critical response? Has he been pioneering and innovative, challenging how we view the musical, or merely a mirror of what was already happening, his ability that of capitalizing on the ideas of others? However one answers those questions, Lloyd Webber's career demands serious attention, and such questions are explored through the following chapters. First, a summary of events in the life of Andrew Lloyd Webber will provide a chronological framework for the discussion of the shows to follow.

1948–79: Creating Superstars

Andrew Lloyd Webber was raised in London's South Kensington in a home of constant music. His father, William Southcombe Lloyd Webber, was a professional organist and composer who taught at the Royal College of Music; his mother, Jean Hermione Webber (née Johnstone), was a noted piano teacher who counted John Lill among her pupils; and his younger brother Julian was to become an internationally famous concert cellist.[5] Andrew's earliest shows were written for his toy theater and presented with the assistance of Julian to an audience of his parents and guests; his first published compositions were a set of six miniatures numbered Op. 1, entitled *The Toy Theatre*, published in *Music Teacher* magazine in 1959. Trips to the West End in the company of his Aunt Violet nurtured his passion for musical theater. He had a short concentration span and an even shorter fuse, but more important, he was intelligent and talented. Having become a pupil at Westminster Underschool for boys in 1961, he went on to join Westminster School proper as a day boy. The next year he won the Challenge scholarship, which paid his fees but also required that he become a boarder at the school, even though it was only a short distance from his home.

Lloyd Webber took part in shows for his house at school, writing songs, directing, and playing. In 1963 he managed to gain a short-lived contract with the Noel Gay Organisation, a music publisher to which he had sent some material. Although this came to nothing of itself, an approach to Decca yielded an early demonstration recording, "Make Believe Love," which brought Lloyd Webber to the attention of Desmond Elliott, a literary agent and the publisher of Arlington Books. Timothy Miles Bindon Rice, an aspiring pop lyricist, had sought Elliott's advice on a suitable composer with whom to work. Rice wrote to Lloyd Webber and they agreed to give it a try.[6] Andrew had won a scholarship to Magdalen College, Oxford, to study history, a subject about which he had shown a great passion from early on.[7] But he lasted only a single term, starting in October 1965, before requesting a sabbatical in order to pursue his musical interests.

For a time, Rice moved into a room in the flat of Andrew and Julian's grandmother, next door to the Lloyd Webbers.[8] Rice worked in the daytime as a management trainee at EMI Records while Lloyd Webber studied at the Royal College of Music. In 1966 Lloyd Webber and Rice began work on a musical, *The Likes of Us*, about the founding of the children's homes established in Britain by Dr. Barnardo in the nineteenth century. Their lyricist was another client of Elliott's and an ex-Barnardo child, Leslie Thomas, who later gained fame as a novelist. Sustained by a modest deal with Southern Music, they wrote the show, although it never reached the stage. Their second collaboration was more auspicious, written in response to a request from music teacher Alan Doggett for a short piece for his choir at Colet Court School in Hammersmith, London. Based on the Old Testament story of Joseph and his brothers, the "pop cantata" *Joseph and the Amazing Technicolor Dreamcoat* was first performed on March 1, 1968, to an audience of parents. It featured only the essential outline of the longer piece that is now well known but was sufficiently promising that Bill Lloyd Webber arranged for a second performance at the Methodist Central Hall, Westminster, where he was organist. In a slightly expanded version, with the accompaniment augmented by the rock band the Mixed Bag, the performance on May 12 caught the attention of the pop critic Derek Jewell. His review in the *Sunday Times* a week later brought the piece wider commercial attention; Novello published the cantata, Decca recorded it, and another performance was arranged for St. Paul's Cathedral, London, at the invitation of the Dean.

Through *Joseph*'s success, Lloyd Webber and Rice became a couple of bright young things in London; they even set up their own company, New Ventures Theatrical Management. Their next project was *Come Back Richard, Your Country Needs You*, a musical about King Richard the Lionheart set during the Crusades; although a short version was given a stage airing and some work was done on an album, only a title single was released.[9] *Come Back Richard* continued the catchy pop of *Joseph*, albeit in more traditional

vein, adopting the conventions of the "number" musical, with songs interpolated into a book. Some of its music was later recycled by Lloyd Webber,
and the uncompleted show provided the basis of the idea for Rice's collaboration with Stephen Oliver, *Blondel* (1983).[10]

New Ventures Management, with manager Sefton Myers and his associate David Land, was to shepherd the writing team through the main stages
that launched their next work, *Jesus Christ Superstar.* The title song was first
heard on a single, released in November 1969, and thanks to advance publicity that included a live performance on David Frost's television show in
Britain, the record sold well enough in Britain to persuade Lloyd Webber
and Rice to finish the work. The whole album, dramatizing the final days
in the life of Christ, was recorded between March and July 1970, and released in October, first in England, then to considerably greater success in
America. The cast included the unknown Yvonne Elliman as Mary Magdalene, Murray Head (who had been featured on the single release) as Judas,
and Ian Gillan of the rock group Deep Purple as Jesus. The show's money-
making potential was recognized by the impresario Robert Stigwood, and
the next step involved a scale of management which someone like him could
provide; as Rice puts it, "Robert never thought big—he thought massive."[11]

Consequently, on October 12, 1971, *Jesus Christ Superstar* was staged at
the Mark Hellinger Theatre, New York, in an excessively fashioned version
produced by Stigwood and directed by Tom O'Horgan (known from *Hair*).
Critics didn't know what to make of the extravagant and camp staging, but
the album's popularity helped ensure a respectable run to June 1973.[12] Following the New York success it was restaged in the Universal Amphitheater,
Universal City, California, opening on June 28, 1972. The cast included Ted
Neeley (Jesus), Carl Anderson (Judas), and Yvonne Elliman (Mary Magdalene), all of whom played the same roles in the film made that year by the
Robert Stigwood Organization on location in Israel, and released in 1973.[13]
It was not until August 9, 1972, that London saw *Jesus Christ Superstar*, in a
production by Jim Sharman which removed a lot of O'Horgan's Broadway
excesses and was nearer Rice and Lloyd Webber's vision.[14]

By the age of twenty-four, Lloyd Webber had achieved with Rice and
Jesus Christ Superstar an internationally successful album, stage versions
on Broadway and in the West End, and a film version in production. He
was also now married to his first wife, Sarah Jane Tudor Hugill, having met
her at a party in Oxford in 1970, when she was still studying for her final
school exams. Throughout their marriage Sarah Jane was to be the depend-

able organizer of domestic life, a steady support to Andrew's fast-rising star, but never herself keen to be in the public eye.[15] The theatrical follow-up to *Jesus Christ Superstar* actually came from the earlier *Joseph and the Amazing Technicolor Dreamcoat*; interest in its staging had been aroused both by the popularity of *Superstar* and by its attendant religious theme. A version of *Joseph* presented at the Edinburgh Festival in September 1972 by the Young Vic company was later given in London at the Roundhouse, and then in the West End at the Albery Theatre, initially as part of a double bill with a "prequel" to the events of the show, *Jacob's Journey*. (The addition demonstrated by contrast just how good *Joseph* was.) *Joseph* ran for 243 performances in the West End and became a piece that almost every child in the United Kingdom came across through its many amateur presentations, which undoubtedly played a part in the successful revival and tours in the 1990s, an age at which adults could introduce their children to something remembered from their own school days. Its mutable pop styles have also played a large part in its continued appeal, as I shall explain in Chapter 3. In the early 1970s Lloyd Webber had his first contact with film composition, writing the scores for two thrillers: *Gumshoe* (1972), primarily set in Liverpool and presented in a style which parodied Raymond Chandler, and Frederick Forsyth's *The Odessa File* (1974). But this was to be a digression in the medium—one that, for reasons explained later, Lloyd Webber did not pursue.

Financially successful, Lloyd Webber was able in 1973 to purchase a large country manor in Hampshire, Sydmonton Court House; he was also able to cultivate his love of fine art with the beginnings of what was ultimately to become the finest private collection of pre-Raphaelite paintings in the world. His gourmet tastes could equally be indulged—he is a noted wine connoisseur and in the 1990s wrote a restaurant review column—and an interview in 1972 reported him as having sent his wife to Cordon Bleu school. Something of the essential difference between Rice and Lloyd Webber comes through in the detail of this bit of frivolous journalism: whereas Lloyd Webber's recipe for the readers was "Sauce Bernaise à la Andrew," Rice's was "Eggy Bread" (as "Pain perdu à la Tim").[16] In creative terms, Rice's contemporary edge and wry humor complemented the broad romanticism of Lloyd Webber's tendencies: the warmth of Rice's work could be brought out by Lloyd Webber, while the more pointed and direct of Lloyd Webber's work was sharpened by Rice. It was only after they ceased working together that Lloyd Webber's more expansive and indulgent musical style was allowed to develop and even dominate his music.

In his next stage work, Lloyd Webber abruptly changed direction. He had begun to work with Rice on a musicalization of P. G. Wodehouse's famous upper-class comic creations in his novels set in aristocratic Britain of the late 1920s and early 1930s; but the collaboration faltered. Instead of dropping the idea, Lloyd Webber wrote it with the playwright Alan Ayckbourn. The central characters were the young idiot socialite Bertie Wooster and his suave and ever-resourceful butler, Jeeves, while the show's plot was principally based on one of the best novels of the series, *The Code of the Woosters*. A calamitous tryout in Bristol was followed by a no-less-appalling West End run at Her Majesty's Theatre: thirty-eight performances, opening on April 22, 1975, and closing on May 24. This big and public failure was to have significant effects on how Lloyd Webber approached future shows, the most important of which was the founding of his annual Sydmonton Festival to try out new material before it was launched into full production. The failure of *Jeeves* also prompted his return to collaboration with Rice, whose imagination had been sparked after hearing a radio documentary about the life of Eva Perón, wife of President Juan Perón of Argentina. Work progressed quickly enough that by April of 1976 tapes of material for *Evita* were presented at the Sydmonton Festival; in November the concept album was released on the MCA label, along with the singles "Don't Cry for Me, Argentina" (sung by Julie Covington) and "Another Suitcase in Another Hall" (sung by Barbara Dickson).[17]

But it took some time for *Evita* to reach the stage, and between the release of the album and the world premiere in the West End, Lloyd Webber had formed his Really Useful Company and seen the birth of his first child.[18] He was also working on other ideas. The most significant of these was the set of variations on the theme of Paganini's A-minor caprice, written for his brother Julian (as the result of a wager on a soccer match) and integrating solo cello with rock band; unsurprisingly, it was called *Variations*. First performed at Sydmonton in 1977, it was eventually released on disk early in 1978 and also performed in full on London Weekend Television's *The South Bank Show*; an early statement of the main theme in *Variations* was adopted as that program's theme tune, and has thus been heard regularly on British television ever since. *Evita* eventually began rehearsals for its first stage version at the start of May 1978, and publicity had raised public interest to fever pitch by the time of its opening at the Prince Edward Theatre in London's West End on June 21. It received a critical reception of extremes, from adoration to hatred, a pattern common to later Lloyd Webber works and the man himself. To provoke simultaneously such a broad range of opinions—and repeatedly, too—shows that important nerves are being touched, that something needs investigating. Nor have the criteria used to judge his works always been the most appropriate for the shows' shifting forms and intentions. Question: When is a musical not a musical? Answer: When it's by Lloyd Webber. As a result of his inclusive style, a greater diversity of contexts and aesthetic concerns are raised by his body of work than by most others in musical theater, and no judgment on the merits of the Lloyd Webber repertory can take as its sole yardstick the familiar stances common in assessing musical theater. Here, for example, pop, rock, and film will later emerge as important areas of direct relevance to the creation of the stage shows.

Evita ran in London for 2,900 performances to August 2, 1986, overlapping with *Jesus Christ Superstar* for two years and later with *Song & Dance* literally just round the corner at the Palace Theatre. The compound success in the United Kingdom of *Joseph and the Amazing Technicolor Dreamcoat*, *Jesus Christ Superstar*, *Variations*, and *Evita*, along with the American success of the second of these, all by the time Lloyd Webber had turned thirty, was beginning to be a problem for some commentators, especially as the composer was neither comfortable nor adept at dealing with the press. To add to this impressive list, in 1979 *Evita* opened in the United States and won six Tony Awards, including those for Best Musical and Best Score, ensuring a Broadway run of nearly four years.[19]

1980–89: Dance and Change Partners

Evita was the last commercial show that Lloyd Webber and Rice wrote together.[20] Although neither of them ruled out the possibility of another joint work, nothing materialized. Lloyd Webber's response was a new piece on a much smaller scale, the song cycle *Tell Me on a Sunday*, written with another of Britain's leading lyricists, Don Black.[21] This collaboration with Black was to prove the most enduring of Lloyd Webber's frequent changes of lyricist: Black worked on *Aspects of Love* and *Sunset Boulevard* and wrote additional material for revisions of *Starlight Express* and *Whistle Down the Wind*.[22] *Tell Me on a Sunday* was given a concert performance on January 28, 1980, at the Royalty Theatre in London and televised on February 12;

The iconic *Cats* eyes. © 1981 The Really Useful Group Ltd.

it was staged just over two years later, on April 7, 1982, as the first part of *Song & Dance*, where its song was paired with dances set to the earlier *Variations*. *Song & Dance*, in fact, provided the third of a hat trick of shows in London. To *Evita* had also been added *Cats*, launched at the New London Theatre on May 11, 1981, a surprisingly successful combination of the poetry of T. S. Eliot, Lloyd Webber's music, and appropriately feline choreography by Gillian Lynne. In the same year, Lloyd Webber repeated on Broadway this record of three concurrent shows, with *Joseph and the Amazing Technicolor Dreamcoat*, *Evita*, and *Cats*, which opened there on October 7.

Major changes came in the wake of such prominent and international success. Domestically, Lloyd Webber's first marriage broke up in 1982 as a result of his affair with the singer and dancer Sarah Brightman.[23] He and

Song & Dance on Broadway, 1985. © 1985 The Really Useful Group Ltd.

his wife legally separated on July 26, 1983, their marriage—by now with two children—having lasted twelve years; in October, Brightman obtained a divorce from her husband.[24] Business expansion saw Lloyd Webber, through his Really Useful Company, buy a half-share of the Palace Theatre (he bought the rest in 1986), marking the start of a theater portfolio that was to make him the most significant theater co-owner in the West End by the start of the next century. He was an astute businessman from an early age, watching the small print in the contracts and taking a keen interest in the balance sheets, and theatrical ownership and production were natural extensions of his interest in shows.[25] With the hit songs, the stage shows, the business interests, and the money, Lloyd Webber inevitably became a "personality," and his name a theatrical brand.

Starlight Express, a follow-up to *Cats* in style and form, reinforced this idea. The work, prompted by a steam train journey undertaken by Lloyd Webber with his children, had begun as an idea to adapt the "Thomas the Tank Engine" children's stories by the Rev. W. Awdry. (James the Red Engine of the stories was the grumbling "really useful" engine that gave Lloyd Webber's company its name.) By the time of its opening in London early in 1984, a small-scale piece for children involving only a few actors had grown, via director Trevor Nunn's suggestion of roller skates, to an extraordinary scale: "Andrew's New Train-Set (and it cost £2 million)" was just one journalistic line that pointed to the mismatch of idea and end form.[26] The show opened in London on March 27 at the Apollo Victoria Theatre. A gala preview five days earlier had been notable for the attendance of The Queen, to whom Sarah Brightman was presented as the wife of the composer: she and Andrew had married that morning.

Acting as his muse through her clear soprano voice, Brightman herself performed in the next two of Lloyd Webber's works. The first was *Requiem*, a setting of the mass, dedicated to Bill Lloyd Webber: not only had he set an example through his own involvement with sacred music as composer and organist, but he had died in October 1982, just a few weeks after the New York opening of *Cats*. The loss of both a parent and a source of musical advice and support was acutely felt by Andrew, and although the idea for a choral memorial work of a more personal and private nature had been around for a while (as a response to events linked to the violence of Northern Ireland in particular), it was his father's death which seems most directly to have prompted its creation. The Lloyd Webber name could now ensure a celebrity first performance: Lorin Maazel conducted, while the solo parts were sung by Plácido Domingo, Brightman, and the boy soprano Paul Miles-Kingston, when the work was given its premiere at Saint Thomas Episcopal Church in New York on February 24, 1985. It was broadcast on British television in the Omnibus series and received its British premiere in Westminster Abbey (just across the square from the Bill Lloyd Webber's Central Hall, Westminster) on April 21.

The next work for Brightman was *The Phantom of the Opera*, a musical setting of Gaston Leroux's famous novel which brought renewed lyricism to Lloyd Webber's style. The publicity machine was now well honed to create an "event": the trailing of the new show with a couple of songs released as pop singles (Steve Harley and Sarah Brightman in the title song, Cliff Richard and Brightman in "All I Ask of You"); the "name" casting with Michael Crawford, already a famous television comic actor in Britain, as the

The cover design for the single of the title song of *The Phantom of the Opera.*
© 1986 The Really Useful Group Ltd.

Phantom; the long buildup to increase public expectation. All contributed
to a spectacular launch at Her Majesty's Theatre in London's Haymarket
on October 9, 1986, after which the work and Hal Prince's production were
lauded by the press.

By the mid-1980s, when the success of the earlier shows had brought with
them a growing business empire of increasing power, Lloyd Webber was able
to explore new areas and see them through to presentation. The sheer scale
of the Really Useful Company's interests in the global entertainment industry, focused on the works of one man's music and theatrical vision, inevitably
made the commercial dimension dwarf that of the aesthetic. In 1986 business became even more of a driving force when the company was floated
on the London stock market as the Really Useful Group plc. The risk to investors, if any, lay in the prospects of any subsequent Lloyd Webber shows,
yet the share issue did not attract the keen corporate response that had been
expected. Instead, most of the applications were from private investors; and
this paralleled the growing split between an institutional academic distaste
for the man and his works and the individual support from the ticket buyers
in theaterland. Lloyd Webber's personal fortune was amassing substantially,
with a reported £9 million profit from the launch of the Really Useful Group
at the start of the year, and in June he bought, for a reported £3 million,

the estate of some 1,200 acres that surrounded Sydmonton Court House. Invoking the images of critical disdain, mass appeal, and personal wealth that have so frequently coincided in Lloyd Webber, the West End producer Thelma Holt later said: "The British have never been generous about success. The spirit of envy is alive and well in the arts, as it is everywhere else." [27]

The Broadway production of *Starlight Express* opened at the Gershwin Theatre on March 15, 1987; revised from its London version, it was not well received and ran only until January 8, 1989. The next Broadway opening of one of Lloyd Webber's works fared dramatically better: *The Phantom of the Opera* opened at Broadway's Majestic Theatre on January 26, 1988, and at the time of writing is still running. Comparison of their Broadway fates heightens both *Phantom*'s success and *Starlight*'s failure. *Starlight*'s style of pop, rock, and gospel pastiche contrasted with the more fluid, classically referenced, and motivic style of the music of *Phantom* (explored in detail in Chapter 4) and of Lloyd Webber's next show. *Aspects of Love* was adapted from a novella of domestic musical chairs by David Garnett, and a version by Lloyd Webber in collaboration with Trevor Nunn had been given as a "cabaret" at the Sydmonton Festival in 1983, some of the music finding its way into *Phantom*. When it was given again at Sydmonton in 1988 the lyrics were by Charles Hart, who had collaborated on *Phantom*, and Don Black; the West End production opened at the Prince of Wales Theatre on April 17, 1989.[28]

The completion of *Aspects of Love* as a stage work at this particular time seems to reflect on Lloyd Webber's own personal circumstances. Of the writing of *The Phantom of the Opera*, Maria Björnson commented: "Andrew knows about [unrequited love]. That is absolutely how he felt about Sarah. She never gave him the whole of herself and I'm sure that is what also bred this need to write this musical. If they had been truly happy, we would never have had *Phantom*." [29] As a further stage of emotional maturation, *Aspects of Love* fits as an introverted work about Lloyd Webber, containing as it does the youthful Alex (impetuous, ambitious Lloyd Webber) and the sophisticated and culturally educated bon viveur George (oenophilic and gastronomic Lloyd Webber among his art collection). But the story is also about the women moving through George and Alex's lives. Lloyd Webber had divorced his first wife to marry Sarah Brightman; she in her turn drifted away from him; and it was in the year following *Aspects of Love* that he divorced her in order to marry his third wife, Madeleine Gurdon. It is difficult to escape the conclusion that the appeal of *Aspects of Love* as a story at this particular time was a reflection on the whole process of divorce, remarriage, and the concomitant changing of lifestyles and shifting responsibilities that Lloyd Webber had undergone. This is not to suggest that it was a work born of some conscious emotional angst, but the themes of the work and the emotional understanding that they required had resonances with Lloyd Webber's life experiences by the late 1980s: he had matured into an understanding of Garnett's novella.

1990–2002: Much More Than a Sunset

A newspaper article kicked off the 1990s in its heading thus: "Lloyd Webber's good fairy runs out of stardust magic. The golden boy of musical theatre looked increasingly isolated in a one-man show last week. His marriage broken, his future uncertain . . ."[30] It has never been wise to second-guess Lloyd Webber, and the decade which began with the listing of such woes in fact brought a new marriage, the birth of his third and fourth children, the acquisition of more London theaters, three new musicals, a major feature film, the further expansion of his art collection to a status of world importance, his knighthood in 1992, and finally his elevation to the peerage in 1997.

First, there was marriage. On November 5, 1990, Lloyd Webber was divorced from Sarah Brightman; they were already separated and he had begun a new relationship with Madeleine Astrid Gurdon, a businesswoman in her own right and an accomplished horsewoman. Within a few hours of the divorce, Andrew had announced his engagement to Madeleine, and they married on February 21, 1991. After the new marriage came the new show. The idea for a stage musical adaptation of Billy Wilder's Hollywood classic, *Sunset Boulevard*, had been around for some considerable time. In 1976, at the time of *Evita*, Hal Prince (who at that time owned the stage rights) discussed it with Lloyd Webber; then in 1979 Lloyd Webber and Don Black developed some ideas for it, including the song "One Star," whose melody was later used for "Memory" in *Cats*. Other projects took precedence, but by 1990 *Sunset Boulevard* was back on the main creative agenda. In September 1992 a complete performance was given of the new musical at the Sydmonton Festival, featuring Patti LuPone as Norma Desmond and Kevin Anderson as Joe Gillis; both played the same roles in the West End when the show finally opened on July 12, 1993.[31] Between the Sydmonton performance and the opening of *Sunset Boulevard*, *Starlight Express* was given a face-lift in London (first seen on November 23, 1992), with an altered plot and five new songs; "Next Time You Fall in Love," with lyrics by Don Black, gave the show the classy, catchy ballad it had previously lacked. At about the same time, the Really Useful Group bought a half-share in the Adelphi Theatre, where *Sunset Boulevard* was to be staged. The American production opened on December 9 at the Shubert Theater, Los Angeles, on Hollywood's doorstep rather than on Broadway, and so brought the show back to its film roots, reinforcing this reflexivity with the casting of Glenn Close as Norma Desmond. Changes were made for the Los Angeles version, darkening the mood and restructuring certain scenes—notably the first scene in the film studio—and these alterations were in turn introduced into the London production on April 11, 1994.

With Lloyd Webber now forty-seven, his Really Useful Group was set for a record profit of £46.2 million, a staggering reversal of the condition of some four years previous. Dissatisfied with its operation as a public company, in 1990 Lloyd Webber had bought back a controlling proportion of its shares. Managing Director Patrick McKenna made comparisons between RUG and Disney in the *Wall Street Journal* when expressing the new company vision: "We want to see this thing grow into a dynamic, large, powerful entertainment company."[32] In June 1996 Lloyd Webber bought back the 30 percent of Really Useful holdings that had previously been sold to Polygram as part of the deal for the stock market flotation of the company. As with his shows, he did not wish to be answerable to anyone but himself. With this came an entrepreneurial confidence that spread into film, his plans including the production of a stage version of *A Star Is Born* (even announcing that he may build a new theater for it in London if no suitable one was free), alongside broader aspirations: "I'm taking on Hollywood. The point had come where I'd done, amazingly, more shows in the theatre than Rodgers and Hammerstein, I just thought that if I do another stage show now, I might go a bit stale. I thought it would be a bit of an adventure to do something different."[33]

Film projects included treatments for *Starlight Express* and *Aspects of Love*, the long-running proposal for a film version of *The Phantom of the Opera*, and the film of *Evita*, released in December 1994, which won both an Academy Award and Golden Globe for Best Original Song (the newly added "You Must Love Me"), along with Golden Globes for Best Musical and Best Actress in a Musical or Comedy (Madonna). By contrast to the warm reception of the film of *Evita*, Lloyd Webber's next new stage show,

Whistle Down the Wind, opened on December 12, 1996, at the National Theatre, Washington, D.C., as part of a six-week tryout before an intended transfer to Broadway the following spring; in the event, it closed on February 8, 1997, and the Broadway run never began. The show was later revised for the West End, where it opened on July 1, 1998, and ran until January 6, 2001.

Whistle Down the Wind told the story of three children in a Louisiana town who believed that they had discovered the returned Christ. Its claustrophobic and menacing side strongly contrasted the purely inconsequential period fantasy of *By Jeeves*, which opened at the Stephen Joseph Theatre in Scarborough on May 1, 1996, the theater associated with the playwright Alan Ayckbourn, who was again author of the book and the lyrics. Reworked from the disastrous *Jeeves* of 1975, it now had a tighter plot, some new songs, and a pared-down staging of extemporized props and scenery to suit the theater-in-the-round format of the auditorium. It played in the West End for seven and a half months, opening at the Duke of York's Theatre on July 2, 1996, then transferring on October 3 to the Lyric. The closure of *By Jeeves* on February 22, 1997, was the first of three in rapid succession, with *Sunset Boulevard* closing on Broadway on March 22 and then in the West End on April 5. But it was also the year that *Cats* became the longest running show in Broadway's history, having already set a similar West End record. *Cats* eventually closed on Broadway on September 10, 2000, after an eighteen-year run. Other impressive statistics of 1997 included the £3.69 million raised by the auction of Lloyd Webber's wine cellar at Sotheby's in London, while the extent of his personal wealth, now estimated at some £550 million, was thrown into relief by such purchases as Picasso's *Angel Fernández de Soto* at a reported cost of £18 million. This was also the year in which he became a life peer of the realm as the Baron Lloyd-Webber of Sydmonton, and on February 16, 1997, he was invested into the House of Lords in Britain's parliament. The House of Lords has not become a comfortable retreat, however, and the rest of the century and just beyond brought a further expansion of his theatrical holdings. On January 9, 2000, the Really Useful Group, in partnership with Bridgepoint Capital, bought out the Stoll Moss theater group at a cost of some £87 million. This left the new Really Useful Theatre Company in possession of the freeholds or leases of another ten West End theaters, and a total list comprising the Adelphi (co-owned with James Nederlander), Apollo, Cambridge, Duchess, Garrick, Gielgud, Her Majesty's, London Palladium, Lyric, New London, Palace, Queens, and the Theatre Royal, Drury Lane.

The Beautiful Game was the first new work of a new decade, indeed a new millennium, and the last Lloyd Webber musical to be considered in this book. Recognition of the persistence of Lloyd Webber in the musical theater repertory came through in the immediate critical response to the show when it opened at the Cambridge Theatre, London, on September 26, 2000. Lloyd Webber could not be dismissed as populist by virtue of The Beautiful Game's subject matter—the story was one of love and violence across the sectarian divide in Northern Ireland—and his sheer staying power despite decades of divided critical responses in the press seemed to have produced even a grudging acceptance among erstwhile hostile commentators. It ran for just short of a year, closing on September 1, 2001. This was only nine months after the closure in the West End of Whistle Down the Wind, some four months before the closure of Starlight Express, and about eight months before the last performance of Cats, on May 11, 2002, its twenty-first birthday. Although By Jeeves had opened at the Helen Hayes Theatre on Broadway on October 28, 2001, its announced initial run of sixteen weeks was curtailed on December 31, 2001. By the middle of 2002 only The Phantom of the Opera remained in the West End and on Broadway.

Despite these recent closures, the story is one of undeniable success. Over some thirty-five years Lloyd Webber has demonstrated talent, instinct, inspiration, and shrewdness in a sustained and winning combination. Individuality and collaboration, originality and adaptation, high art and popular appeal, aesthetic aims and business tactics: in what proportions these various qualities have been combined in Lloyd Webber—both man and works—has been addressed continually in popular writings on him. And such views have often become entrenched through repetition and unchallenged acceptance. In what follows, the emphasis is on the works themselves, exploring approaches that suggest not only a far more complex repertory than has often been acknowledged, but also one whose importance lies probably as much in its totality as in any single work.

 CHAPTER 2

Telling Tales: A Survey of the Shows

THE NAME ANDREW LLOYD WEBBER IMMEDIATELY CONJURES UP an image clear enough in many minds to be used as an adjective— he is of iconic status to the modern musical. But the works themselves are less susceptible to a group definition than the totemic evocations of a "Lloyd Webber show" might suggest. If anything, this repertory has an underlying restlessness, a resistance to simple categorization that has made its discussion difficult. The subjects, settings, and scales of these shows have been wide ranging, and their presentational formats have adapted to match. Creative relationships have been driven by the needs of the individual show, and so, rather than sustaining a single writing partnership, collaborations have constantly changed. His musical eclecticism has defied prediction, with new combinations and juxtapositions of influences a central part of his technique, with the result that rock, pop, film, opera, and religion in combination have created a kaleidoscopic tapestry of intergenre references. Teasing out these many strands is a fascinating exercise that challenges the common perspective: there is more complexity in and between the shows than the Lloyd Webber musical theater brand would suggest.

Yet beneath such complexity there is a fundamental paradox: Lloyd Webber appears to have made his impact for doing the unexpected and innovative as part of a gradual reassertion of the conventional. The youth who left scholarship study in history to write pop songs has become a British Lord— the rock rebel has become the latter-day member of the Establishment. This is seen in the shows themselves, which move from the no-book musicals of the early works to the book musicals of the later ones. But maybe this should not be so much of a surprise, for his journey from Westminster School in London to the House of Lords in the Palace of Westminster was not so far. Geographically it was a matter of crossing one road. Ideologically, it has encompassed the creative dilemma in which the need to express individuality through novelty vies with a desire for acceptance through canonical values. Metaphorically, the journey has been of a rich variety, not just within the Lloyd Webber repertory, but around the genre of the musical itself. And if the destination seems to have been one familiar from the inception of the journey, the landscape has been made more interesting through the detours taken to reach it.

Tim Rice and the Pop-Song Biography

Given his family background and upbringing, it would have seemed likely for Lloyd Webber to become a classical musician; his experiences with his toy theater and trips to the West End would have seemed to make the lyric stage another option. Yet the chosen medium of his first commercial foray into music was through pop—after all, it was easier to place an individual song in the pop market than to mount an entire show. In 1963, while Lloyd Webber was still at school, Decca prepared a demonstration recording of "Make Believe Love" from *Play the Fool,* one of his Westminster School shows.[1] The song was typical of mid-1960s pop rather than of the musical: untheatrical in its lyrics (by Lloyd Webber), and pop-based in its harmony and repeating, assertive hook that declaimed the song title. By requiring Lloyd Webber to construct contained, catchy works in strophic style, the format of the pop song provoked a conciseness and a directness that were to serve his entire output. In 1966, when Lloyd Webber began collaborating with Tim Rice in earnest, they worked on several pop songs, Rice's primary medium. Indeed, Rice and Lloyd Webber had pop songs recorded and released, including "Down Thru' Summer" and "I'll Give All My Love to Southend," both recorded as a single by Ross Hannaman, whom Rice had encountered while working on her debut recording at EMI. There were several such numbers from the Rice–Lloyd Webber stable in the late 1960s, yet it was not through them that the composer and lyricist became successful, but through a work that began with a substantially different profile.

Instead of secular pop, the new work was from a biblical text and was intended to be performed as a cantata by schoolchildren. Such a description of *Joseph and the Amazing Technicolor Dreamcoat* implies a move away from the pop single toward something less commercial and more "worthy." Yet the work demonstrated its origins from the opening song, "Jacob and Sons," which neatly establishes the setting and story ("Way, way back, many centuries ago, not long after the Bible began"), through to the closing "Any Dream Will Do": this was polished pop writing—words and music—which caught the ear and stayed there. As the pop critic Derek Jewell wrote in his review in the *Sunday Times* a week after the revised second performance, "Throughout its 20-minute duration it bristles with wonderfully singable tunes. It entertains. It communicates instantly, as all good pop should. And it is a considerable piece of barrier-breaking."[2] The flair for communication which Jewell identified is found in the best of Lloyd Webber, and the visceral rather than cerebral thrill of Lloyd Webber's approach to musical theater was to become a regular source of comment: in the youthful works it was communication and "barrier breaking," while in the later ones it has been considered shallow and populist. Familiarity has obscured some of the freshness and innovation that marked this early Rice–Lloyd Webber collaboration, and the surprise and scale of *Joseph*'s success from unlikely beginnings is a useful reminder of the strength of its appeal.

With their next fully realized project, *Jesus Christ Superstar*, the biblical source for the telling of events in a single character's life was taken much further, and both musically and dramatically the advance from *Joseph* was great. By way of its chosen medium, the work was again appealing to a commercial music, although moving away from archetypal 1960s pop. The preliminary single had the gospel-rock title song of the A side in strong contrast to a B side of the elegiac "John 19:41," whose dense string writing evoked the English textures of Elgar. Together the two tracks neatly marked the inclusive range of styles for which Lloyd Webber would become known. Although the "Superstar" single failed to sustain its initial impact, through unexpected popularity in a Dutch gay bar it became a top-selling single in the Netherlands. Other factors also helped the work's promotion. Presaging the publicity machine that has become associated with Lloyd Webber's shows, the project was kept in the public eye with a spurious newspaper report that John Lennon had been approached to play Christ in the performance at St. Paul's Cathedral, and then by the search for "unknowns" to feature on the album instigated by Brian Brolly, the head of MCA-UK, who had bought an option on the complete album. A similar "search for a star" was later undertaken for the stage title role of *Evita*—one that resulted in Elaine Paige's casting—and which also seems reminiscent of the "Who will play Scarlett?"

Jesus Christ Superstar, 1971. © 1971 The Really Useful Group Ltd.

auditions for *Gone with the Wind*. Elements of the *Superstar* promotion were also seen in a nonstop stream of subsidiary press releases for the *Evita* stage production, including those describing the large sum of money spent on refurbishing the Prince Edward Theatre for the show. Even *Superstar*'s initial release of a single as a means of testing the ground before embarking on a major project can be viewed as a forerunner of the single releases used subsequently to promote later Lloyd Webber shows and create a substantial box-office advance.[3] There is no denying that Lloyd Webber has an innate flair for business, but he was particularly fortunate in that his earliest successful projects presented examples of such techniques and demonstrated at first hand their effectiveness.

From the late 1960s on, certain quarters of the established church had begun to encourage the promotion of a more ecumenical, charismatic, and evangelical approach to worship in order to tap into youth culture. Thus the earlier combination in *Joseph and the Amazing Technicolor Dreamcoat* of religion and contemporary pop culture had chimed with the mood of a Christian church which was increasingly espousing more progressive forms of musical and literary expression as part of this drive toward a less stuffy image. At the same time, pop had gradually absorbed a spiritual element as the ideas of the hippie movement spread. Light pop in the service of a Bible story to be performed by schoolchildren was seen as part of these tendencies, bringing something secular to the sacred and vice versa, to the benefit of both. Rock, however, with its more rebellious stance toward society and the frequently overpowering energy of its delivery, was a different matter. Pop was comforting, rock was a threat. And it was rock that came to the fore when the album of *Jesus Christ Superstar* was finally released in October 1970, first in England, then in America. The adoption of a rock basis for *Superstar* was considerably more loaded than the comfortable tunes of *Joseph* and it prompted complaint, especially in the United States. The use of rock was thought by some to debase the story of the last days of Christ; the show's focus on Judas and its conclusion with the Crucifixion rather than the Resurrection also aroused misgivings.

If *Superstar* did not fit the pattern of a devotional work at all comfortably, neither did it behave like a musical. With its origins in the rock concept album rather than the stage show, and through its use of a well-known story, many of the typical narrative concerns of the musical were of significantly less importance than usual: a series of musical scenes presented a drama of attitudes and responses rather than action. Musically, this threw into much sharper relief Lloyd Webber's developing propensity for dramatic juxtapositions of styles, used in *Jesus Christ Superstar* to portray the various factions of the story as well as its central characters.

Jesus Christ Superstar had grabbed attention through Lloyd Webber's inventive musical style—a combination of classical, pop, rock, and musical theater influences—and through the wordplay of Rice's lyrics, which combined contemporary idiom and historic events. In their common cross-genre attitudes, Rice and Lloyd Webber were well matched. Lloyd Webber's character—which through its magnification in the media was increasingly to usurp the acknowledgment of his achievement and of the works themselves—was already in evidence. In an interview conducted shortly before the West End opening of *Superstar* he was described as having "a seriousness of purpose and a determination to succeed which are highly impressive, if somewhat formidable and slightly disconcerting in one so young."[4]

Lloyd Webber's two film scores of the early 1970s, *Gumshoe* and *The Odessa File*, are interesting for their indications of future elements of Lloyd Webber's show music; both of these, along with earlier pop numbers, were useful stores of musical ideas for future development. Indeed, self-borrowing is one Lloyd Webber technique that needs considering in relation to the more general questions of musical borrowing his work has provoked. *Gumshoe* provided several themes and motifs more familiar from his later shows, the most prominent of which became the title song of *Sunset Boulevard*. *The Odessa File* featured solo cello, played by Julian Lloyd Webber, and rock ensemble; it was an experimental ground that was soon to lead to *Variations*. In its turn, this became the "dance" part of *Song & Dance*. Little of the composed score of *The Odessa File* found its way onto the soundtrack of the film, so it is not surprising that some of its material, along with ideas from *Gumshoe*, were incorporated into *Evita*.[5] Furthermore, Tim Rice's screenplay for the film version of *Jesus Christ Superstar*, released in 1973, had been rejected in favor of one by Melvyn Bragg, while André Previn supervised and conducted the music; it was clear to Rice and Lloyd Webber during their brief visit to the film unit on location in Israel that they were not needed. The film was not particularly well received, partly because its hippie designs quickly dated but also because of more fundamental problems in translating a rock album to the big screen; that major strand of the relationship between Lloyd Webber and film requires exploration. The cumulative effect of the frustrations caused by O'Horgan's excessive staging of *Jesus Christ Superstar* in New York, lack of input into its film version, and the eradication of large amounts of his *Odessa File* film score explains why Lloyd Webber became determined afterward to retain control over his own material. In 1989 he told Mark Steyn: "I can't write for somebody else's projects, that's why, since *The Odessa File*, I haven't composed for the cinema. . . . We [composers] are collaborative animals. I do, however, like to control what's done with my scores. The composer must dictate the evening because you are, in the end, the dramatist."[6]

It was this desire to control his own ideas that led to Lloyd Webber's collaboration with Alan Ayckbourn on the disastrous *Jeeves*. Unlike *Joseph and the Amazing Technicolor Dreamcoat* and *Jesus Christ Superstar*, *Jeeves* was a conventional book musical with discrete numbers inserted into a comic plot. This was the first time that Lloyd Webber had worked on such a format professionally from concept through to performance, and there were to be problems. First, Ayckbourn's plot was true to Wodehouse, but the convoluted domestic farce suited to the page was overelaborate for the stage. Second, there was an imbalance in the pacing of music and narrative: while the plot desperately needed to forge ahead through its ever more complicated action, the musical numbers did the opposite and slowed down the dramatic pacing. Before Ayckbourn was involved, Rice and Lloyd Webber had been considering updating the story to the 1960s, with Bertie Wooster as a trendy playboy; while this would no doubt have enraged Wodehouse fans, it may have provided something more imaginative than Ayckbourn's approach, which was fatally too faithful to the Wodehouse novels.[7]

But the disaster also led to several positive results for Lloyd Webber, who observed in an interview just a few days after the show's demise that "you must be certain you have the show 100 per cent right before you go into rehearsal."[8] This provoked the founding of the annual Sydmonton Festival at Lloyd Webber's Hampshire home to test material via workshops and tryouts before going into full production. This also strengthened Lloyd Webber's conviction that in musicals "structure is everything," a focus that has undoubtedly contributed to his later successes. The show that Lloyd Webber should have been able to write, the conventional book musical following the Broadway examples such as *South Pacific* and *The Sound of Music* which he had learned in his youth, was the form in which he had demonstrably failed. The process of transferring a dramatic idea from one medium to another had been insufficiently considered. Both issues were to be tackled later. The shows of the 1990s were marked by a gradual return to the book musical, culminating in *The Beautiful Game* in 2000. Changes of medium were more carefully considered for future works, from novel to stage for *The Phantom of the Opera*, for example, and from film to stage with *Sunset Boulevard*. On the occasion when this was not considered—taking the script of the proposed film musical of *Whistle Down the Wind* onto the stage in Washington in 1996 without sufficient reworking—the result was flawed. The sense of unfinished business which *Jeeves* generated for Lloyd Webber, along with his determination never to be bested, meant that the show was eventually reworked (as was *Whistle Down the Wind*), appearing in the West End (1996) and on Broadway (2001)—though to only qualified popular and critical suc-cess. The ghost of Her Majesty's Theatre was laid to rest when *The Phantom of the Opera* took up prolonged residence in 1986.

The life story of Eva Perón had a similar biographical arc to that of Jesus—lowly origin, rise to influence, political threat, and untimely death—and its musicalization as *Evita* also shared with *Jesus Christ Superstar* a rock opera format on a concept album (released in 1976). It was well received, with Derek Jewell—a keen promoter of Lloyd Webber since his *Joseph* ex-perience—calling it "quite simply a masterpiece."[9] Evita did show develop-ment from *Superstar*, especially in the way in which scenes could be just a single song, as with "Another Suitcase in Another Hall" (its music previously that of "Summer Day" from the failed *Jeeves*) and "High Flying Adored" (at one earlier point a pop song called "Down on the Farm"), or extended musical sequences that flowed through complementary and contrasting sec-tions, as in the early encounter between Eva and Magaldi and in "Danger-ous Jade." Still essentially episodic, the drama was stretched around and be-tween the main scenes more than it had been in *Superstar*, while the use of a more extended series of repeating phrases provided a sense of musical co-hesion, even as it raised questions for some of dramatic cohesion in the exact application of these thematic repetitions.[10] The same question of thematic meaning was to arise in relation to later works, most notably *Aspects of Love*.

Evita took some time to reach the stage, and between the release of the album and the world premiere in the West End, Lloyd Webber worked on other ideas. The most significant of these was *Variations*, which brought together Paganini, rock, and classical cello. This is a good example of Lloyd Webber's refusal to give in to the standard categorizations of music—his best work has always been able to adapt and reinterpret influences from a variety of styles, although he has never actively presented himself as a con-scious champion of such developments. With the pop-rock treatment of a classical theme in *Variations*, Lloyd Webber again showed the influence of British progressive rock and also increased the prominence of an ever-present temporal and cultural duality in his work. Of course, *Joseph and the Amazing Technicolor Dreamcoat* and *Jesus Christ Superstar* had dealt with stories from history and established culture viewed through contem-porary eyes, while jumping between pop, rock, and classical (both Roman-tic and modern) musics. *Evita* included the rock of power and authority, Latin sounds for the people, and the angularity of such twentieth-century classical composers as Stravinsky, Prokofiev, and even Britten in the opening "Requiem for Evita." But *Variations* bridged a gap between classical and commercial audiences very directly: more than an exercise in novelty, it was a vibrant and imaginative fusion of ideas.

Evita began rehearsals for its stage version at the start of May 1978. Some tension was caused when the director Hal Prince requested changes from the original recording: he wanted to reduce the rock content, which he believed obscured the lyrics, tended to make the characters seem the same, and also made the show feel dated. Both conductor and musical director wanted to keep as close to the album as possible. Behind this was a pull between the demands of Broadway and those of London, of which Prince seemed particularly conscious. "You say to me Andrew and Tim are doing this for America. But I'm not—I'm doing it for London. That's the paradox. There's a show here which if I wanted to take it to Broadway, they're going to have to change. Andrew and Tim think there's something called American knowhow or some goddamn thing and they want what they wrote dealt with in that way. They're being quite co-operative. The thing is, they're dealing with a phenomenally successful piece of material and they don't feel the need to change it. They may be right—for England."[11]

The adaption of successfully launched West End shows to accommodate different American tastes was to continue through the later works (such as *Song & Dance* and *Cats* for Broadway and *Sunset Boulevard* for Los Angeles), while the concept of a different critical awareness in each country was to prove a recurring irritation. In this respect, Lloyd Webber has frequently trodden on a raw nerve of national as much as genre identity, a factor crucial to later discussions of the musical theater canon.

When *Evita* opened, the critical response was mixed. Michael Billington wrote in *The Guardian* that the show was "audacious and fascinating," with a "beautiful" and "haunting" score.[12] The skeptical and frequently scathing Milton Shulman acknowledged that Rice and Lloyd Webber had "wrought out of such unlikely material another box office hit."[13] John Barber wrote: "The rich score, by Andrew Lloyd Webber, has melodies even more seductive than the famous 'Don't Cry for Me, Argentina' (for instance, 'Another Suitcase'). The book, by Tim Rice, enjoys to the full his heroine's charisma. But he does more. He uses the splendiferous occasion to enquire, covertly, whether leaders must always win popularity by exploiting the greed and naivety of the masses, and whether it is ever possible for them to rise above the corruption inherent in all power. It is this backbone of enquiry that makes *Evita* mature."[14] But there was dissent, from Michael Coveney, for instance, who, while acknowledging that "in terms of presentation the show is breathtaking," continued, "In terms of content it is irredeemably paltry; rarely in my experience as a reviewer has that cliché-worn chasm been so graphically and effectively detailed." [15] The morality—or rather amorality—of the work was questioned, and some viewed the whole edifice as a glorification of Eva Perón, her motives and methods: not so much an enquiry as an endorsement. Bernard Levin in particular laid into it with extraordinary vitriol in his review "The Cracked Mirror of Our Times," calling *Evita* "one of the most disagreeable evenings I have ever spent in my life, in or out of the theatre." [16] He pointed out what he considered the "corruption at the heart of this odious artefact, symbolized by the fact that it calls itself an opera, and has been accepted as such by people who have never set foot in an opera-house, merely because the clichés between the songs . . . are sung instead of spoken and the score includes, among the appropriate 'slow tango feel' and similar expressions, such markings as '*poco a poco diminuendo.*'"

Critical response to *Evita* was not good in New York when the show opened there in 1979. More sparse in its presentation than in London, Hal Prince's work was acclaimed, but not so the musical and dramatic material itself by the "two amoral, barely talented whipper snappers" (as John Simon described them for *New York*). Yet the public response in the tryouts had been positive, the album gained the show further popularity, and its six Tony Awards increased an already prominent profile. It ran for 1,568 performances. The pattern of West End qualified critical reception in the press followed by New York panning, both overtaken by strong public demand, was to become a familiar pattern, and it illuminates Prince's observations on the differing West End–Broadway (or British-American) expectations, at least in respect to newspaper critics.

At the point that effectively marks the end of the Lloyd Webber–Rice partnership, it is worth reflecting on the common genesis of *Joseph and the Amazing Technicolor Dreamcoat, Jesus Christ Superstar,* and *Evita*. All three works began with sound, not image: one pop cantata promoted through a recording, and two rock operas released as concept albums. [17] This was not a conventional training for anyone with aspirations in musical theater. As all these works had been conceived first as unstaged pieces (albeit that *Joseph* had included a brief appearance of a costumed Elvis), their subsequent stage adaptations had to deal with performance material already familiar to the public through recordings. *Jeeves,* the one work by Lloyd Webber which had originated on the live musical theater stage, was a failure. This could suggest

a significant and sustained early influence on Lloyd Webber's entire output: from the start he was obliged to think entirely aurally for his audience
rather than aurally and visually, as with a filmed or staged show. This resulted in a musical language that drew upon bold aural gestures as a form of
visual substitute. Without a visual dimension, his music had an even more
important part to play than in a work conceived for stage presentation, for
it had to create the images and convey the physical movement of the story
as much as portray the underlying emotions and moods of the characters.
For example, the dramatization of strongly opposing individuals or blocks
of society were articulated in clear and contrasting types of music: the disciples, priests, and Romans of *Jesus Christ Superstar* or the ruling aristocracy, the military, and the *descamisados* of *Evita*. The deliberately polarized
styles become the equivalent of the characters' costumes. In itself this created problems for anyone subsequently superimposing a visual dimension
through staging, and in the films of *Jesus Christ Superstar* (1973) and *Evita*
(1994) the need to visualize something so fundamentally aural was to produce responses different in method and, more importantly, in effectiveness,
as I shall show in Chapter 5.

There is a further consequence of Lloyd Webber's characteristic musical eclecticism: by the time of *Evita*, questions of originality began to be
mooted. The inclusion of so many different identifiable musical genres
within the same work seemed to emphasize musical collage as the basis for
Lloyd Webber's musical voice. The novelty lay in the method rather than the
materials. This was reinforced by pastiche: the diversionary and anomalous
Elvis of *Joseph and the Amazing Technicolor Dreamcoat* proceeded to the
Dixieland jazz of Herod in *Jesus Christ Superstar* (honky-tonk piano, "oom-
pah" trombone bass line, stop-time lines), and on to the Latin serenading of
Magaldi in *Evita*. Yet the use of such immediately distinctive sounds, with
their quite specific connotations of period or personality, contributed substantially to the nature of the pictures conjured up by the recordings on their
own: the power and charisma of Pharaoh, the superficiality of Herod, the
smoldering eyes of the seductive tango singer. The music was not just portraying a character, it provided considerably more specific mental images.
Without Tim Rice's storytelling ability in the exploration of character and
in specific moments of verbal wit or poignancy, Lloyd Webber had to find
after *Evita* a new way of using his extrovertly visual musical style in conjunction with stage drama. His initial response was to bypass narrative drama
by adopting variants on the song cycle, and to match big aural images with

even bigger stage ones at the expense of the storytelling. It was not until *The Phantom of the Opera* that he worked out a new accommodation of ear and eye to complement a strong storyline.

Revisiting the Revue

Tell Me on a Sunday, Lloyd Webber's first "post-Rice" work, was the result of a collaboration with the lyricist Don Black. As in all the previous Lloyd Webber dramatic works, it had an essentially episodic structure made up of a set of formally discrete songs that here collectively combined to convey the ups and downs of the relationships of an English girl in America. In this way, it suited Black's ability to provide clear, concentrated images, often encapsulated in a memorable title line; in this case he yielded such examples as the title song, "Capped Teeth and Caesar Salad," and "Take That Look Off Your Face." Presented in 1980 as a song cycle, *Tell Me on a Sunday* was staged just over two years later as the first part of *Song & Dance*, where its song was paired with dances set to the earlier *Variations*. It made for an unusual evening for the musical theater audience, with the two elements polarized rather than integrated: all the song first, then all the dance. It was a physical deconstruction of established elements of the musical, the opposite of the concept of the integrated musical that had come to define the genre. Yet the form had a more pragmatic origin, building on the elements of another show that had begun in a similar way to *Tell Me on a Sunday*, and had at its heart the dance foundation of *Variations*.

Cats was first seen as a simply presented song cycle at the Sydmonton Festival in 1980; it ended up as a visual extravaganza animated by Gillian Lynne's choreography, launched in the West End in 1981. To tie together T. S. Eliot's poetry a linking idea was introduced: by the end of the evening one of the cats depicted would be chosen to ascend to the Heaviside Layer (a cat version of heaven) and be born again into a new life. In fact, this tenuous thread of a plot was subservient to the parade of varied cat characterizations in Eliot's poetry, amplified by the use of contrasting music styles through strutting rock number ("Mr Mistoffelees" and "The Rum Tum Tugger"), quasi-lullaby ("Old Deuteronomy"), and the big show ballad ("Memory"). There were also musical approaches to help cohesion, as in the deliberate orchestration of numbers as either all acoustic or involving electronic sounds, or in an overarching musical structure described here by Lloyd Webber: "Nobody, I hope, notices that the beginning of *Cats* is a

fugue and that the middle of the Jellicle Ball is a fugue and that the resolution comes in a later theme. But for me it's the crucial thing on which
the score depends, just as the whole of *Evita* is based on a tri-tone and goes
round in a complete circle."[18] The combination of source material, dramatic
approach, and anthropomorphic felines was unexpected, and the novelty
of such a gallimaufry undoubtedly contributed to its early success. Beyond
that, it seems to have retained a following through its inherent escapism and
apparent whimsy, even inconsequentiality—especially in the late 1980s and
the 1990s, when so many new musicals seemed especially intent on killing their characters off instead of marrying them off. Also, a level of intense
production on each element of the show meant that the ear and eye were
constantly bombarded with shifting stimuli and changing pace. *Cats* was
about sampling lots of different things, enjoying each in its moment, then
moving on to the next—the recording of the score alone makes the point
very clearly. The show was also about family entertainment, with an underlying message about redemption so general and diffuse, open to so broad a
range of interpretations, that it offended no one or could be simply ignored.
One element did pull it all together, namely its energy in live performance,
a force that communicated itself to the audience and provided a vicarious
thrill in its constant motion, just as *Starlight Express* was to do soon after.
When *Cats* opened in London, it received strong critical endorsement for its
totality of experience as an evening in the theater, although its constituent
elements came in for criticism—Gillian Lynne's choreography was in turn
praised and panned, for example. The overall response was perhaps summed
up best by Robert Cushman's remark "*Cats* isn't perfect. Don't miss it."[19] At
the same time, any prediction of the scale of the show's global and sustained
success would have been met with incredulity; the quirkiness of its subject
matter and presentational style would have seen to that.

A success of some description was needed by Lloyd Webber, who had
borrowed extensively to put money into the production, and the show's failure would have caused him to lose Sydmonton Court. The success was also
to be an important one for the producer with whom Lloyd Webber had
teamed for *Cats*, Cameron Mackintosh. At the time of *Cats*, Mackintosh's
theatrical productions had a checkered history, with the West End disaster of a revival of *Anything Goes* one of his more prominent failures, and a
touring version of *My Fair Lady* a notable success. Like Lloyd Webber, he
was not hidebound by any sense of convention in musical theater, and their
pairing has been one of mutual benefit in coproducing and other related

business. For example, Lloyd Webber co-owns the Palace Theatre, which housed Mackintosh's *Les Misérables* up to March 2004, when it transferred to The Queen's Theatre, itself now a part of the portfolio of Really Useful Theatres: Mackintosh has prime West End theaters for his show, and Lloyd Webber has the sustained annual rental income from a long-running hit. Added to the *Cats* equation was direction by Trevor Nunn, at that stage associated with the subsidized straight theater through his post as artistic director of the Royal Shakespeare Company. Nunn had limited experience with musicals, but after *Cats* he went on to direct *Starlight Express, Les Misérables* (with John Caird), *Sunset Boulevard,* and *Oklahoma!, South Pacific, My Fair Lady,* and *Anything Goes* for the Royal National Theatre. In retrospect, *Cats* can be seen as pivotal through the combination of its creative team and important in the way that a nonstandard mixture of music, movement, and narrative achieved large-scale popular appeal.

Lloyd Webber's next show, *Starlight Express,* continued the approach of *Cats* and so reinforced a particular image of what a "Lloyd Webber musical" was. Characteristics included a lightweight plot that involved some sort of triumph (probably spiritual) over adversity, with punchy songs in derivative styles if not actually pastiches. In addition, the production design went overboard in scale and effects; it dwarfed the performers, who were reduced to ciphers in a slight drama in which the more slow and satisfying development of character had been replaced by the temporary fix of vigorous action. *Starlight Express* was praised for its innovative staging, accepted within the limits of its pastiche-song score, but criticized for its basic story and sometimes absurdly simplistic lyrics. In the clichéd plot, the underdog steam train Rusty loves the glamorous carriage Pearl but must steal her affections away from a rival diesel train, Greaseball (characterized by rock 'n' roll and macho attitude), by winning a race. But the show became hugely popular, second only to *Cats* in the West End. It appealed to both adults and children through lyrics and music that worked on a dual level: children could enjoy the fantasy and the fast-changing novelty of styles along with the repetitive and accessible lyrics; adults could bring a different and more complex level of genre recognition to the music and also pick up on the sexual innuendo employed by Richard Stilgoe in many of his lyrics, for example, the opening number, "Rolling Stock."[20] *Cats, Joseph and the Amazing Technicolor Dreamcoat,* and *Starlight Express* have provided a good night out for the whole family, and the addressing of a different audience from that of many musicals, especially those of the 1980s and early 1990s, has undoubtedly contributed to

a

their sustained success. That particular baton seems now to have passed to
Disney, with its stage versions of the cartoons *Beauty and the Beast* and *The
Lion King,* for example, and picked up by others even more recently in the
West End with the stage adaptation of the fantasy film *Chitty Chitty Bang
Bang.*

   To see *Starlight Express* again in London shortly before it closed early
in 2002 was to appreciate that its format—revue crossed with circus—was
undeniably great fun. It was criticized at the time of its opening for its slight
plot, obvious outcome, and predictably stereotypically "human" trains; after
its 1992 revision, the show still contained no real dramatic tension. But such
complaints missed the point, for the appeal of *Starlight Express* lay in the
individual moment rather than the cumulative effect of its dramatic thrust.
This was reflected musically in discrete numbers of strophic form, pastiched

Music by
ANDREW LLOYD WEBBER   Lyrics by
RICHARD STILGOE
Designed by   Choreographed by   Lighting by
JOHN NAPIER   ARLENE PHILLIPS   DAVID HERSEY
Sound by MARTIN LEVAN   Musical Director DAVID CADDICK
Directed by
TREVOR NUNN
Produced by The Really Useful Theatre Company Ltd.

Opening 27 March 1984
APOLLO VICTORIA THEATRE
17 Wilton Road, Victoria, London SW1 Box Office: 01-828 8665

Designed & Printed by DEWYNTERS LTD. LONDON

b

(a) *Starlight Express* in rehearsal, 1984 (photo: Nobby Clark). (b)
Starlight Express. Both images © 1984 The Really Useful Group
Ltd.

from easily identifiable styles, and insistently repeated rather than gradually developed. The elaborate staging, extravagant costumes, and use of the auditorium itself as a performance arena through its encircling racetrack were reminiscent of similar indulgences at the Folies Bergères in Paris or the shows of Las Vegas, in whose Hilton Hotel *Starlight Express* became a cabaret fixture for more than four years, starting in September 1993. With *Starlight Express*, Lloyd Webber created in essence another *Joseph and the Amazing Technicolor Dreamcoat*, telling a simple story for children through a pop parade. Whereas the novelty in *Joseph* came from the use of pop in a youth work on a biblical theme, in *Starlight Express* it came from contemporary physical and visual trends—respectively, the roller skating and the conspicuous hi-tech stage designs. Lloyd Webber had gone full circle, from discrete pop song to episodic narrative of increasing structural complexity *(Joseph* to *Evita)*, to discrete pop song with minimal dramatic framework *(Cats* and *Starlight)*. For *Starlight Express* Lloyd Webber relied on what was already comfortable and familiar—pastiche numbers and direct pop songs: musically the show was no more than a stopgap. A new direction was needed, and it proved to be one that returned to more interesting and personal characterization, extended his musical range, and moved away from mythic icons and anthropomorphic character clichés toward recognizable people in dramas of a more human scale. Such a change was provoked by his second wife, Sarah Brightman, whose voice—large range, flexible technique, bright tone, and clear diction—provided the catalyst for Lloyd Webber to begin writing in a more expansive and romantic idiom, first with *Requiem* in 1985, and then with *The Phantom of the Opera* in 1986.

Church music had been a part of Lloyd Webber's upbringing, and he had continued to compose sacred pieces for services that formed part of the annual Sydmonton Festival. So *Requiem* was not as unlikely a project as it may have seemed. Indeed, later he wrote a Benedicte for the service blessing of his third marriage that was to reappear in *Sunset Boulevard*, in pretty much the same musical form as "The Lady's Paying" and in a more lyrical treatment as "Surrender." As so often with Lloyd Webber's work, the reviewers were divided over *Requiem*, but the public in Britain took to it, and it was given a Grammy Award in 1986 for Best Classical Composition; the "Pie Jesu," released as a single, climbed to the top of the British singles charts within a matter of weeks. To be sure, the whole work is uneven, and the by now common references to a derivative style—here with Fauré particularly prominent—were invoked. *Requiem* warrants a mention in a book on stage works as an important vehicle for musical change, enabling Lloyd Webber to progress to his next stage show, *The Phantom of the Opera*. It also included specific musical ideas that emerged in *Phantom*. For example, *Requiem*'s opening three-note motif on flutes is now also familiar from *Phantom* as the start to the verse of "Wishing You Were Somehow Here Again," a song which laments the loss of a parent and seeks the strength to move forward. Furthermore, the octave-perfect 5th sparseness of *Requiem*'s opening vocal statement was significantly transmuted through its new context in *Phantom*'s "Think of Me." But beyond the musical contents and structure of *Requiem*, there was also the increasing problem for commentators attempting to reconcile Lloyd Webber's artistic achievement with undeniable commercial success, and this was aggravated further with the addition of the spiritual to the equation:

> The approach of Easter was honoured by the *Gramophone* in a more than usually eclectic way, starting with the hype surrounding Andrew Lloyd Webber's "Requiem." . . . Judging from the record . . . this is as much a commercial as an artistic phenomenon. It borrows, probably unconsciously, from sources as far apart as Puccini, Messiaen and Fauré, but develops few of its ideas beyond two or three bars. It cashes in on every possible marketing angle, including the inevitable single of the pretty choirboy and the composer's wife duetting in a mawkish "Pie Jesu"; and all this is seen as perfectly normal and tolerable by an artistic establishment which dare not let itself seem idealistic or out of touch. And finally, by a supreme poetic justice, the one really striking passage in the work, the Benedictus, slips up because the world-famous tenor flown in at great expense to help sell (sorry, I mean sing) it gets the tricky rhythms wrong.[21]

Sung-Through Stories

The two shows of the late 1980s, *The Phantom of the Opera* and *Aspects of Love*, mark a return to strong storyline and a new exploration of characterization through music. Both shows take novels as their starting points, in contrast to the separate poems of *Cats* or the simple idea of the contrasting trains in a stock plot for *Starlight Express*. Alongside the comparative increase in complexity of their plots, *Phantom* and *Aspects of Love* also describe an increasing interest in a tapestry of musical ideas rather than Lloyd Webber's by now familiar solid blocks of self-contained numbers. This development moved toward the through-composed show, in the opposite direction from the "revue" works. Now the emphasis was not on difference and structural separateness—with contrasting songs juxtaposed for deliberate contrast—but on dissolving such boundaries to create a more seamless whole. This was a return to the clearly delineated musical characterizations which had been such a major feature of the Rice–Lloyd Webber works, but refined to include more subtle layers.

It was no longer possible to see Lloyd Webber as a transient figure whose shows were limited to the rock-crossover trends of the early 1970s. *The Phantom of the Opera* was about to be added to the West End's list of Lloyd Webber shows still running *(Cats, Starlight Express,* and *Evita),* and *Cats* was a major draw on Broadway as well. Lloyd Webber's sustained success was attributed by some to his uncanny anticipation of public taste, confirmed when he defied his immediate track record by going for something more old-fashioned in *Phantom.* In advance of *Phantom,* Lloyd Webber and Hal Prince had talked about what they thought the next trend was going to be, agreeing, "It's got to be . . . romance."[22] As Lloyd Webber said in an interview before its opening in October 1986: "I played the first version of the score to an old theatrical friend who said: 'You've taken one big step backwards towards the world of Rodgers and Hammerstein.' I was delighted because I've always wanted to write for a conventional orchestra and write real love songs and do my own 'Some Enchanted Evening.' I hope it's going to be about slightly old-fashioned theatrical values because it's absolutely imperative the musical now goes back to the direction it was taking during the years of Rodgers and Hammerstein and the best of the Americans."[23]

Unexpected shifts of focus were becoming a conscious part of the Lloyd Webber progression: "I've always wanted to change direction sharply after each score: *Jeeves* was a totally English reaction to the biblical enormity of *Superstar,* and after the Eva Perón story I deliberately chose a totally anonymous heroine for *Tell Me on a Sunday.* It's no good repeating yourself."[24] While this holds true in relation to the subject of each successive show, it does not apply to either their underlying themes or musical approaches. If anything, as Lloyd Webber's work has progressed, the sense of what is distinctive to his style has become more clear, and links rather than differences have become more apparent: apotheosis of the principal character, cross-genre references, and so on are all returning themes.

Phantom's change of direction was made more marked by the elevation of Sarah Brightman not only to center stage but to the center of the very concept. Inspired by her vocal qualities, Lloyd Webber broke into a warmer

and more romantic musical vein and returned to some of the thematic devices that he had begun to experiment with in *Jesus Christ Superstar* and
Evita but from which he had been sidetracked by the essentially revuelike
formats of *Cats* and *Starlight Express*. The show and his own romantic pursuit of Sarah Brightman seem linked, given that he said, "*The Phantom* is
really about this man's obsession with this girl, and nothing will stop him
from getting *to* her." In addition, the confines of a plot that revolved around
two men's battle for the heart of one woman allowed for character motiva-
tions and tensions impossible in the generic worlds of cats and locomotives.
Phantom was a kind of growing up. It was a chance to work toward real
people in real circumstances: "I wanted to write from down here [heart]
rather than up there [head]. . . . Something where I could let the emotion
go."[25] Of course, the story has a strong mythic element, but the focus on the
internal life of recognizable human beings became a crucial element—if to
differing degrees of effectiveness—in shows from *Phantom* on.

After his last commercial collaboration with Lloyd Webber, *Evita*, no
permanent writing partner had arisen to replace Tim Rice. *Cats* had sidestepped the issue with the poetry of T. S. Eliot, and the new writing in
"Memory" was an adaptation by Trevor Nunn of existing ideas by Eliot (Tim
Rice's own suggested lyrics for that song having been rejected by Nunn).
Richard Stilgoe, who wrote the lyrics for *Starlight Express*, began work on
The Phantom of the Opera but did not strike the right romantic tone; he was
replaced by the newcomer Charles Hart, who effectively auditioned for the
role by providing sample lyrics to some of the show's tunes. Lloyd Webber
had begun his career alongside Rice, with their skills and reputations developing simultaneously, so their projects had a shared genesis. Later, lyricists
were brought into Lloyd Webber's existing power base to develop concepts
that began with him alone; Mark Steyn pointedly summarized how "the relationship between music and words degenerates to that of a rich employer
and his hired hand."[26] Lloyd Webber was able to assume a more "executive"
role by defining, dictating, and altering any aspect of his shows to bring them
in line with his own personal vision. As each show was now required to have
its own distinctive tone, the choice of lyricist became something akin to the
choice of performers. The linking features across Lloyd Webber's stage output were to be his vision and his music; this single-mindedness made him a
serial collaborator determined to get the best possible creative team for each
new project. No doubt this has contributed to the reasonable perception
of Lloyd Webber as dominating his partnerships, for his work—as a com-

poser rather than a composer-lyricist—cannot be easily categorized through the usual name format: after Rodgers and Hammerstein or Lerner and Loewe comes Lloyd Webber and Rice/Stilgoe/Black/Hampton/Hart/Elton. But such characterization is made even harder by overlapping influences: Stilgoe and Hart (with a few lines from Mike Batt) for *The Phantom of the Opera*, Hart and Black for *Aspects of Love*, Black and Hampton for *Sunset Boulevard*. In fact, it is only with Tim Rice that there has been a clear sense of sustained musical and lyric character in combination. For example, Stilgoe's technique of pun and other wordplay in *Starlight Express* matched Rice's; but Rice also had a fine sense of the use of anachronism—the language of today in the mouths of people from the past to pointed effect— along with infinitely stronger dramatic contexts to respond to, and so was able to bring a certain wry and often dark quality to his lyrics. No doubt the method of writing itself has played a part in all this, for word has almost always been added to music with Lloyd Webber—as already quoted, "The composer must dictate the evening because you are, in the end, the dramatist." In such a context, it is the sustained writing relationship which allows the lyricist to attune himself to the composer's rhythms, and the repeated appearance of Black suggests some awareness of this need for an element of consistency. In any case, the strong encapsulating images for which Black is particularly known have matched the strong musical images of the focal big numbers. By way of comparison, the one-off collaboration with Ben Elton on *The Beautiful Game* produced lyrics of endless lists and synonyms on generic themes, with much sexual innuendo, suggesting only dimly the individuality of the characters on stage. Stilgoe's lyrics rightly reflected the superficiality of *Starlight Express*, matching its tone as well as its content, but Elton's worked in opposition to the intense and serious subject. The continuing tone in Elton's lyrics was one of verbal quick-fixes in which a repetitive rhetorical structure dominated the dramatic themes: it was difficult to get past the surface to the drama beneath, something that did not need to concern Stilgoe. Through the serial collaborations since his break with Tim Rice, Lloyd Webber has retained his own identity as preeminent in successive writing teams; but where there has been some continuity of lyricist, the works appear to have benefited.

When *The Phantom of the Opera* opened in London in 1986, the expensive imagery was there in Maria Björnson's design, but with a new opulence after the alley fantasy of *Cats* and the hi-tech wheels and metal of *Starlight Express*. The eclectic musical styles were also still there, but brought within a tighter dramatic framework and to more pointed effect. *Phantom* is especially worth consideration for its witty play with genre boundaries across temporal divides, bringing together opera, operetta, and various elements of musical theater to produce a complex group of reflexive comments on the nature of lyric stage. The show's dialogue between theatrical plot and theatrical nature has added a particularly effective subtext of continuing relevance to the work, and no doubt contributed to its richness and sustained appeal. (While I shall in Chapter 4 study this in some detail, in Chapter 7 I shall put such dialogue into a wider context that suggests the prime importance of Lloyd Webber to the musical as a genre.) Of all Lloyd Webber's works first conceived for the stage, *Phantom* is the one whose audience appeal has remained the most enduring—justly so, for it was a work of a new maturity for him in its integration of dramatic and musical structures. Above all, Lloyd Webber's love of melody for its own sake came through, notably with some of his most lyrical music for its protagonist ("The Music of the Night") and his rival ("All I Ask of You"). The effect of writing for Sarah Brightman's voice spilled over into the other characters, and the singing range of the Phantom especially seems to have been written to match hers as Christine, and then parodied in Carlotta.

The American production of *Starlight Express* opened at the Gershwin Theatre in 1987 to poor reviews—maybe the theater's name invoked past American glories and heightened the distance that Lloyd Webber's show was from that "golden era." In 1987 Broadway experienced a "British invasion" through the two West End hits of Lloyd Webber and Stilgoe's *Starlight Express* and Boublil and Schönberg's *Les Misérables*. Each notched a record before opening: *Les Misérables* with a ticket advance of around $11 million and *Starlight* with costs of about $8 million. The transfer to Broadway of the former show was relatively straightforward, while the latter was vastly changed both in staging and plot in the process of transfer, and its opening was postponed several times for technical reasons (as was later to happen with *Sunset Boulevard* in London). *Starlight* also had a large investment from MCA, which was using television to advertise the show to non-Broadway audiences. With such emphases, it was difficult to escape the technical and commercial side of *Starlight*, and it reinforced the growing interpretation of Lloyd Webber as "a businessman first and a musician last."

There was a further factor extrinsic to the content of the Lloyd Webber shows, increasingly tied to perceptions of him and what his works symbolized. When *Evita* had won its six Tony Awards, it was at a time of greater competition from American shows, but by 1987 there were high-profile West End shows succeeding on Broadway with severely diminished local opposition. (It was a geographic reversal of the situation in the West End in the years immediately after World War II, when the term "American invasion" had been used.)[27] Successful West End transfers to Broadway in the mid-1980s aroused concern among practitioners and commentators, manifested in increasing hostility over the next few years to the principal target, Lloyd Webber. Such feelings were heightened by the gradual build-up of a power base essentially vested in Lloyd Webber and Mackintosh: the overlapping, long runs of their shows accumulated to give them such financial power that by 1995 they were prepared to challenge the rules imposed by Broadway unions and face a showdown. For Lloyd Webber and Mackintosh the removal of *Les Misérables*, *Cats*, *The Phantom of the Opera*, and *Sunset Boulevard* from Broadway was hardly desirable, but with productions worldwide and accumulating royalties from copyrights, they were in an extraordinarily strong position; in contrast, the unions were faced with having to bite the hand that fed so many of them. It was a British musical theater invasion—in practice a steady flow of high-profile productions rather than a sudden assault—that threatened some who saw (and still see) the form as an essentially American preserve.[28]

It is unfair, however, to attribute the adverse critical response to *Starlight Express* solely to a sense of nationalistic sour grapes. It was an unsatisfying contrast to the big rolling drama of *Les Misérables*, which had opened three days before it, or, in yet another direction, Sondheim's *Into the Woods*, which opened later the same year. Nor did audiences take to it as enthusiastically as they had *Evita* or *Cats*. More interesting were the preemptive attacks on *The Phantom of the Opera*, anticipating its opening in 1988. It was increasingly unnecessary to deal with a specific show, for Lloyd Webber had become a symbol of an approach to musical theater and to its commercial exploitation that demanded attention. With Sondheim put up as a defining figure at the opposite dramatic extreme, together they have encapsulated for many the fundamental dilemmas of the musical from the 1970s on: how to retain popular appeal in the face of a dissipating sense of a common, vernacular musical language, and how to balance broadly appealing entertainment with dramatic truth. When *Phantom* finally opened at Broadway's Majestic Theatre, hostile reviews focused on it as an expression of consumerism and ostentatious extravagance over serious values. Michael Walsh makes the point that there was a fundamental contrast between the Ameri-

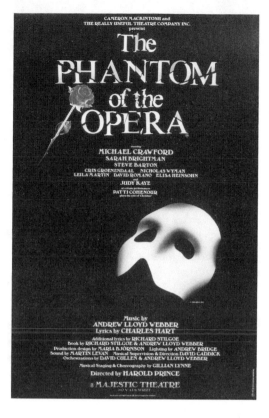

Phantom of the Opera on Broadway. © 1988 The Really Useful Group Ltd.

can and British perspectives. For American critics, the "greed and glitter" of the Reagan years was on the wane. For British analysts, the zeitgeist of the Thatcher years, when overt display of financial accumulation was a sign of inherent worth, was not only on the rise in 1986 when *Phantom* opened in the West End but was still in play when *Phantom* opened on Broadway. Yet the audience response to the show in New York was such that as this book goes to press it is still running at the Majestic, some sixteen years later; it also ran in Los Angeles and San Francisco for over four years each, and national tours ran continually in the United States for the whole of the 1990s and beyond. It has clearly outlived any zeitgeist that may have surrounded its launch, and its fundamental appeal will later be shown to lie in its intrinsic qualities, not just the period of its creation.

Having mastered the theatrical broad brush to his own satisfaction in

Aspects of Love on Broadway, 1990. © 1989 The Really Useful Group Ltd.

shows through *Starlight Express*, Lloyd Webber now proceeded to refine the
detail. And so the more thorough characterizations of *The Phantom of the
Opera* led to the most introspective of all the Lloyd Webber works to date,
Aspects of Love. Like many of Lloyd Webber's projects, it had a long gesta-
tion and development. It was begun in the early 1970s, before *Jeeves*, when
David Garnett's novella had been mooted to Tim Rice for possible film treatment. A version by Lloyd Webber in collaboration with Trevor Nunn had
been given as a "cabaret" at the Sydmonton Festival in 1983, and some of the
music found its way into *Phantom*. When it was given again at Sydmonton
in 1988, it had lyrics by Charles Hart, fresh from his *Phantom* collaboration,
and Don Black. On this second occasion it was also presented in a form that
was remarkably close in music and structure to that finally seen on stage, although some sections of lyrics were subsequently given major rewrites. This

process of fixed musical content and subsequently changed lyrics is an important pointer to Lloyd Webber's approach to the link between character, motif, and structure in *Aspects of Love*: the musicalization of the general emotional subtext has generally taken precedence over any specific moment as articulated through a particular phrase in the lyrics.

As had become common, not just to Lloyd Webber but to the promotion of all musicals in an unpredictable commercial field where high potential gains matched high potential losses, the production was kept in the public eye before its London opening in April 1989. Not only was it the latest Lloyd Webber show, but the casting included the film actor Roger Moore as the urbane and sophisticated George. Moore withdrew after realizing that he was not coping to his satisfaction with the musical side of the role: James Bond in a musical had been a good story, but James Bond withdrawing from the production late in rehearsals was also good publicity. Perhaps most important in the advance publicity for the show was the release before Christmas of Michael Ball's recording of "Love Changes Everything." The stirring anthem, vibrant voice with its final high Bb, and judicious timing put the work in the public mind, and advance bookings guaranteed more than a year's run before the rest of the work had been heard. But to those expecting another *Phantom of the Opera* it was a long evening. *Aspects of Love* was essentially a chamber piece—even its orchestration was of chamber dimensions—and the story of emotional musical chairs played out by a handful of literally interrelated characters was too intimate a concept for a large theater and the values of a big production. More important, the musical portrayal expanded the use of running themes and developed the organic structures of *Phantom* to create a continuous score. In identifying this more organic musical construction and tighter emotional focus on an identifiably human scale, the work was praised for what were viewed as higher artistic aspirations. But this was too much for a public expecting the more consistent, sustained melodic accessibility of *Cats* or *Phantom*, so it remains in the shadow of its predecessors.

Aspects of Love did continue the Lloyd Webber pattern of pulling something unexpected out of the hat. Here, however, it was not so much in the basic musical building blocks, which remain characteristic—the rousing anthem ("Love Changes Everything"), the emotive ballad ("Seeing Is Believing"), the catchy chorus ("Everybody Loves a Hero" and "The Wine and the Dice"), the recycling of earlier material ("Chanson d'enfance")—but in the concentrated and almost obsessive way in which they were manipulated.

There is an uneasy intensity about the piece that is in some ways disturbing, going beyond the ambivalence that an audience is likely to feel for the characters who come out of their changing alliances as not-quite-admirable and not-quite-lovable. To be sure, there is a technical command in evidence that could not have happened without the experience of *The Phantom of the Opera*. (In particular, the interweaving of dramatic action and music from the prologue through to the end of scene 7 is masterly, and analysis in the final chapter will show it to be a technically accomplished and dramatically effective sequence.) In its emotional and musical concentration, *Aspects of Love* provided another focus for theatrical change: just as *Starlight Express* had been at the extreme of the musical-as-glamour-revue, so *Aspects of Love* was at the other extreme of musical-as-opera. The boundaries of the musical as a form were being tested: from "songs but no book" to "book but no songs." The most conventional position—"both book and songs"—which had yielded an early failure in *Jeeves*, became the goal of the next decade.

Screen and Stage

Adverse comment on *Aspects of Love* found its strongest expression when the show opened on Broadway, though it ran for 376 performances, far more than what might have been expected from the response of the newspaper critics. Frank Rich, never a Lloyd Webber enthusiast, wrote: "Though *Aspects of Love* purports to deal with romance in many naughty guises—from rampant promiscuity to cradle-snatching, lesbianism and incest—it generates about as much heated passion as a visit to the bank."[29] Clive Barnes summed up the overall tone of the attacks: "Lloyd Webber has never done well in the *New York Times* . . . but none of the earlier reviews have I think been anything like as tough or dismissive, or even as simply contemptuous, as this storm of civilized and urbane invective against *Aspects of Love*."[30] Charles Bremner amplified the observation: "All but one of New York's theatre critics wielded their axes on *Aspects of Love* after its Broadway opening yesterday, lacerating Andrew Lloyd Webber's musical with a glee that, to some in the composer's camp, smacked of anti-British prejudice."[31] In this chapter it is sufficient to note that in both artistic and commercial senses, Lloyd Webber is the principal British *composer* of musicals after World War I to warrant a place in a series entitled *Broadway Masters*. While there are cases to be made for the pre–World War I composers Sullivan and Monckton, the only other more recent contender, Noël Coward, had a distinctly checkered history in musical theater after his successes of the late 1920s, in both London and New York.[32] In both the United Kingdom and the United States he is probably the best-known English musicals writer of his time, but this has been achieved through his presence as a playwright, actor, writer, and cabaret performer of his own songs, along with his many recordings and memorable film roles. All this was brought together as the embodiment of a certain English sensibility, portrayed especially through the observation and wordplay of Coward's lyrics. In musical terms, his influence today is through his individual songs, but this is disproportionate to the influence of his shows, which remain substantially unknown.[33] For the only other possible British contenders, one needs to go back to P. G. Wodehouse and Guy Bolton, librettists and lyricists mainly for the musicals of Kern, but also some by Gershwin. A single, British-made success with a musical on Broadway has been an occasional and refreshing novelty—Sandy Wilson with *The Boy Friend*, Lionel Bart with *Oliver!* Serial success on a large scale such as Lloyd Webber has achieved is of a completely different order, and again points up Lloyd Webber's challenge to the hegemony of the "American musical."

Critical opprobrium was compounded by further questions of Lloyd Webber's musical integrity, occasioned by two legal cases for plagiarism, one in England in 1991 *(Brett v Lloyd Webber)*, the other in America *(Repp v Lloyd Webber)*; the U.S. case lasted for almost the entire decade, from November 1991 until October 1999.[34] It was a period of increasing litigiousness in such matters in the popular music world as the potential for large payments in compensation drew attention.[35] The unfortunate aspect of such lawsuits is their emphasis of opposition—black and white, right and wrong—with one side as the winner. This polarized attitude has accompanied much of the comment on Lloyd Webber's music that is similar to or apparently copied directly from other works. In some cases the resemblances are undeniable, but there are other factors at work: that of the deliberate interplay of genres is one which will surface later. The verdicts in Lloyd Webber's favor of both cases nonetheless suggest something of the possible shades of gray, for the legal arguments were settled principally on a question of access: Lloyd Webber could not plagiarize material which it was unlikely or impossible that he could have heard. A judgment on the qualitative nature of the asserted plagiarism was thus sidestepped. Seen as a process of blame or exoneration, the issues raised by Lloyd Webber's potential musical borrowing are limited and tend toward the prurient, but when set in a wider context of

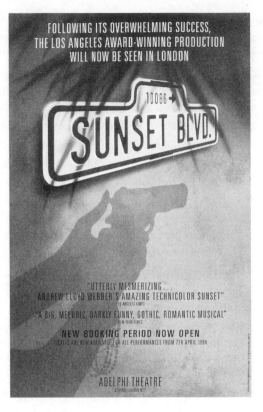

Sunset Boulevard, 1994. © 1994 The Really Useful Group Ltd.

compositional method and subtextual musical narrative, they gain significantly in interest.

When Lloyd Webber's next show, *Sunset Boulevard*, opened in London
in July 1993, his tendency to romanticize his subjects was picked up by several commentators, who identified the adaption from screen to stage as "a
hymn to Hollywood dreams rather than a detached satiric attack on their
ultimate destructiveness."[36] The show also brought further developments
in Lloyd Webber's delineation of atmosphere through music, particularly
strong for Norma, played to acclaim by Patti LuPone, who "starts to sing almost without having bothered to talk: not just one song, but two. That is
when you think what a clever composer Lloyd Webber is: the master of the
slow build-up. The sound of a growingly confident orchestra fills the house
and you are persuaded that the piece can never look back."[37] There was

indeed a confidence to the score, benefiting from a musical intensity developed with *Aspects of Love*, but now applied more fluidly. The music picked
up on particular moments and tied together characterizations as the show
moved easily between dialogue and song, between formal strophic numbers
and freer musicalized sections. It is as though steps were being retraced from
the sung-through, motivic extreme of *Aspects of Love*.

The central feature of the 1995 Sydmonton Festival was a performance
of Lloyd Webber's next and newest musical idea for trial, *Whistle Down
the Wind*, but the medium for the new work was film, not theater. Lloyd
Webber had been developing the idea since seeing a version of the classic
British film from 1961 presented as a stage musical by the National Youth
Music Theatre, of which he was a sponsor. In trying to make the work more
international, the story of three children who mistake an escaped criminal
for the Jesus of the Second Coming was relocated to Louisiana, and the
whole venture shifted up an emotional gear through lyrics by Jim Steinman,
whose reputation rests on his epic outpourings in the field of rock, particularly for Meat Loaf. The Sydmonton audience felt strongly that it should
be a stage work and not a film, and the whole project was reappraised in
this light. And so, to use Lloyd Webber's own words, "the big derailment
occurred." The world premiere was given at the National Theatre, Washington, D.C., in December 1996, but the show was never transferred to Broadway. Lloyd Webber explained that its failure was founded in the transfer
from one medium to another: "Basically our confidence in the material had
meant that we had not addressed one obvious fact: the book was really a
movie script slung onto the stage."[38] But nothing is ever wasted with Lloyd
Webber: tunes are recycled if they don't get their due the first time around,
projects are revised and revived almost as a point of honor, as if Lloyd Webber has continually to prove to himself that he has not lost his touch. With
the show's direction now undertaken by Gale Edwards, who had staged the
original Sydmonton concert, a revised version ran in London from July 1998
to January 2001.

There was an underlying intensity in the revised version, brought about
by a dark subtext to an apparently innocent story; its power at key moments
was due in no small way to the handling of that subtext in music and lyrics
in a more mature fashion than Lloyd Webber's shows had previously demonstrated. And it was unambiguously a book musical, with songs and dialogue alternating; the songs were mostly strophic, and multisectional musical structures were limited principally to climactic scenes near the ends of

By Jeeves, 1996. © 1996 The Really Useful Group Ltd.

the acts. Its form was one of the most conventional of Lloyd Webber's works, and at this point his least challenging for an audience. That it never gained the following of, say, *The Phantom of the Opera* or *Cats* was in part due to its subtext, whose sexual overtones in the relationship between the young girl Swallow and the Man (whether viewed as convict on the run or Jesus Christ) made it difficult to view purely as escapist. It is this all-too-human dimension that points to a significant but slow change in the dramas of the Lloyd Webber repertory, for the characters have become in one sense ordinary people in situations that make them seem extraordinary or intriguing. The overt symbolism of Jesus, Judas, and Mary Magdalene, then Eva Perón, Juan Perón, and Che Guevara, has given way—via the anthropomorphism of *Cats* and *Starlight Express*—to the domestic introversion, even obsession, of Alex, George, and Rose, then Norma, Joe, and Max, before becoming a group of children and townsfolk. The key figures of the stories have gradually approached something related more to everyday life, and the emotional explorations of the drama have gained additional power through their application to characters who are not intrinsically mythic from the outset. The progression was to reach a limit of sorts in *The Beautiful Game*, which has none of the otherworldly ambiguities of the Man of *Whistle Down the Wind* to distract from the realism of characters drawn from the divided community of Northern Ireland.

Lloyd Webber also returned to his previous book musical failure, now reworked with a tighter plot and some new songs as *By Jeeves*. True to the period of its setting (the early 1930s) the show was written with the conventions of a musical comedy: a plot based on marriage, misunderstandings, and social status, and with dialogue to convey the plot alternating with strophic songs for reflection. Some of the problems of the original remained; for example, the music numbers are sparsely interpolated in the first half of the first act, and the framing device employed to make the story appear as a series of reminiscences is cumbersome. But with the opening of *By Jeeves* in London in 1996, after twenty-one years Lloyd Webber finally had an archetypal book musical running in the West End.

Closure

When *The Beautiful Game* was announced as the next Lloyd Webber musical to hit the West End, it eloquently reconfirmed Lloyd Webber's ability to surprise. Central to its story was soccer, an unusual choice for a musical but in one sense an inevitable consequence of Lloyd Webber's enthusiasm for the sport: he had for years been a supporter of Leyton Orient, and of course a bet on the outcome of a soccer match had provoked the composition of *Variations*.

There were two particularly surprising elements to the project. First, the book and lyrics were to be by Ben Elton, first feted as a socialist comedian during the Thatcher years and then as a comic novelist and playwright; his views on the political left were as well known to the public as Lloyd Webber's on the political right. But such an opposition of their worlds proved a creative spur, as Lloyd Webber described it: "With *Whistle Down the Wind* I was feeling that I was repeating myself, and I was fed up with it all. I was bored with musicals. Working with Ben [Elton] has completely made me rethink where I was coming from musically. And this is an original musical.

The Beautiful Game, 2000. © 2000 The Really Useful Group Ltd.

Everything I have ever written before has been based on something else, like a book or a film."[39] Second, the story was set in Northern Ireland, beginning at the time of the sectarian strife in the late 1960s; it followed the maturing of a group of teenagers, connected through a local youth soccer team, to adulthood. The Protestant-Catholic conflict shapes their lives, and the drama plays itself out on the fault line of day-to-day survival, poised between idealism and bigotry. Although Elton described the story in television and newspaper interviews as a universal one of love across the divide—the eternal tragedy of Romeo and Juliet, wherever the geographical location, whatever the opposing factions—the specifics were too near and too recent to be readily escaped. Politics that remained uncomfortably close to home, and about which each member of the West End audience was likely to have ingrained views, did not make for easy musical theater. To be sure, the critical response to the show when it opened at the Cambridge Theatre in September 2000 was generally measured and even generous: Lloyd Webber could not now be dismissed as populist by virtue of the subject matter, and his sheer staying power in spite of the decades of ambiguous critical responses in the press seemed to have produced even a grudging acceptance among previously skeptical commentators.

With its wonderfully inventive use of stylized soccer moves in the choreography, its onstage shooting, and its love story across sectarian boundaries, comparisons with *West Side Story* were inevitable. Robert Carsen's direction in a minimal and uncluttered set was worlds away from the usual visual expectations of a Lloyd Webber show. The cast, as befitted the story, was young and essentially unknown, so no "star" hype came into play. It was probably the most ordinary of Lloyd Webber's musicals, adopting the more restricted scale and the socially aware approach of so many other 1990s musicals. There was no big redemption theme centered on a single strong central character, just a stoic belief in a better future despite the evidence of the present. There was no apotheosis in a final scene, the ambiguity of which could be taken as either a hint for future optimism or the portent of history damningly repeating itself. It was a book musical with clear sections of spoken dialogue for the plot and sung numbers for the amplification of emotion. And at its heart there was something regressive, not just in its music, which was redolent of bottom-drawer material (lots of *Evita* tritones in jagged phrases, for example, or simple tunes in Lloyd Webber's early pop vein), but also in the very concept of the piece, which used long-established approaches to just about every one of its constituent elements.

Then there was sheer theatrical chutzpah. Sir Edward Marsh, an early patron of that greatest of British musical theater showmen, Ivor Novello, is said to have remarked, on reading an apparently unbelievable line or situation in one of Novello's scripts: "Really, Ivor, you simply *can't* say that!" Novello replied: "But the extraordinary thing is, Eddie, I can."[40] And he could. Lloyd Webber's output is noted for a similar talent to find the surprisingly effective in the unlikely or banal, but *The Beautiful Game* does not have this quality. Even "Our Kind of Love," its big ballad and the one released as a promotional pop single, was "Memory" with the notes rearranged (12/8 meter, similar chord progressions, upward key change at the end for some thrilling, high, female belt notes). It was diluted further by its appearance not long before as "The Heart Is Slow to Learn," a number for the proposed sequel to *The Phantom of the Opera*, which was given a public air-

ing in an appropriately Puccinian arrangement by the operatic soprano Kiri
Te Kanawa at the concert in London's Albert Hall to mark Lloyd Webber's
fiftieth birthday.

The closure of *The Beautiful Game* in September 2001 marked the end
of a thirty-year arc of stage shows that began with the first production on
Broadway of *Jesus Christ Superstar* in 1971 and reached its apogee in 1990
with five shows in the West End and three on Broadway running concurrently. There is also closure of a different sense, for *The Beautiful Game* was
a book musical. Having begun with shows that went against expectations
in subject matter, form, and both verbal and musical style, in his last show
to be considered here Lloyd Webber revisited some of the most established
concepts of the genre. Having made his name by exploring the unexpected
in the musical, Lloyd Webber has completed this body of work with an assertion of convention.

 CHAPTER 3

Pop, Rock, and Classical: First Elements of a Style

The big bang with which [Lloyd Webber's] commercial success began was the result of a collision between a middle-class arts background and Sixties rock, when the charm of cheap music had an even greater potency than Noël Coward could have envisaged.
—ALAN FRANKS

DESPITE LLOYD WEBBER'S PREFERENCE FOR A DRAMATIC CON-text for his songs, and despite the descriptions of his early infatua-tion with musical theater (his own toy theater and its shows, his trips with his Aunt Vi to the West End), Broadway or West End musical the-ater is not at the foundation of his music in the earlier shows. Although his name and money have been made most conspicuously through the musi-cal stage, his stylistic origins are more strongly in commercial pop. It was through pop that the cantata *Joseph and the Amazing Technicolor Dream-coat* was endowed with the qualities of freshness and novelty that brought it to wider attention, so launching the careers of Rice and Lloyd Webber. Ele-ments of rock were added to Lloyd Webber's musical vocabulary with *Jesus Christ Superstar*, dominating, but never quite supplanting, the earlier pop styles. Although the melodic lines became more jagged, the rhythms more punchy, and the contrasts more prominent, the need to root the music in memorable melody remained.

From "middle-class arts" came the influence of such twentieth-century composers as Prokofiev and Stravinsky, adding astringency to the pop but blending well with certain aspects of rock. For the aspirations of rock were conflicting, in that its exponents—many of them well-educated, classically trained musicians—wanted at the same time to disturb the musical establish-ment and to secure an artistic respectability generally denied to pop. Even as they broke down musical ties with the past, they wanted to demonstrate their knowledge of them: they wanted to join the club as it was, but also change its rules. Such a description sits well with Lloyd Webber, who is staunchly conservative yet has constantly displayed a flair for novelty, and who is intensely aware of the balance sheet yet cries in response to a fine painting. The negotiation of the boundaries between conformity and innovation, culture and counterculture, runs through the heart of his work, curiously demonstrated in his unusual position as the only Peer of the Realm with chart-topping hit songs. But such juxtapositions were present from the start, when, surrounded by classical musicians (most immediately his father, mother, and brother), he set his sights on musical theater and, more immediately, 1960s pop.

Pop and "Joseph"

In 1967 the singer Ross Hannaman recorded two pop songs by Rice and Lloyd Webber: "I'll Give All My Love to Southend" and "Down Thru' Summer," the A and B sides, respectively, of a single released on the Columbia label.[1] "I'll Give All My Love to Southend" is fast-paced, and the light voice of Hannaman is gradually smothered in an accompaniment of increasing activity; Rice's lyrics stand little chance in the face of the over-produced mix of the recording, a quality also found on the flip side, "Down Thru' Summer." On the B side in particular the influence of the Phil Spector "wall of sound" is apparent as the low timpani accents contrast with a sustained, high string line, punctuated with tambourine off-beats. The song cannot quite sustain this overdramatic presentation, and the voice of Hannaman sinks under the weight of it all. "Down Thru' Summer" has a greater claim to musical fame in the music of Lloyd Webber than its being an early pop work: the vocal melody later became the wonderfully exuberant middle section of "Buenos Aires" in *Evita* ("And if ever I go too far . . .") and the melodic spur to that show's songs "Oh What a Circus" and "Don't Cry for Me, Argentina."[2] In 1969 Hannaman recorded another two songs of Rice and Lloyd Webber: an A side of "Probably on Thursday" backed with "1969." These were more successful as records — if not commercially any great breakthrough — and "Probably on Thursday" shows a much more lyrical approach that accords better with voice and song in an arrangement featuring prominent harpsichord and a country-style acoustic guitar which goes into finger-picking overdrive in the coda.[3] The sounds of this track are lighter, although Spector is again evoked in a strange instrumental break near the end of the song, in which a strong theme on trumpets—apparently related to nothing that has gone before—brings with it a distinctive heavy drum rhythm and that backbeat tambourine again. This out-of-place trumpet tune is an early version of one better known when sung to the words "Give me my coloured coat" (at the end of *Joseph and the Amazing Technicolor Dreamcoat*).

In 1968 Sacha Distel recorded Rice and Lloyd Webber's song "Believe Me I Will" on an MCA album. There is not a lot to say about this song; pleasant enough as it is, it makes little impact. What it does demonstrate, however, is where some of Lloyd Webber's later strong ballads came from. The insipid tune is marked by the short phrases, clear harmonies, and repetitions that were not only typical of the middle-of-the-road pop song for the romantic solo voice of that time, but in a stronger form were the basis of Lloyd Webber's later hugely successful ballads. In 1970 Paul Raven recorded "Goodbye Seattle" for a single release on Decca (in the United States only), a rock 'n' roll song with elements of funk, and with a gospel-style presentation of the refrain for the female backing singers.[4] By contrast, the solo male voice of Raven is uninteresting and often unintelligible; the strength of the song lies entirely in its short refrain (and a most successful hook): "Goodbye Seattle/Thanks for the ride/Goin' home to Boston/You know I tried." It is hardly surprising that Lloyd Webber later used the music of this memorable refrain, wasted on this record, for "Lotta Locomotion" in *Starlight Express*.

None of these songs was particularly successful commercially, but what the music increasingly demonstrates is Lloyd Webber's ability to create a strong and simple hook: an instantly memorable phrase that effectively brands the song. Such a hook is found in the opening of the refrain to "Herod's Song" in *Jesus Christ Superstar*, first released in 1970 as a record album rather than presented as a stage show. The tune (to the lyrics "So, you are the Christ/You're the great Jesus Christ") encapsulates a snappy syncopated rhythm and an immediate sequential use of its rising melodic figure, making it a direct and memorable musical idea. This is reinforced by monosyllabic lyrics with their own repetition at the beginnings and ends of the lines ("You are"/"You're" at the start, "Christ" at the end); these provide a spiky and clear sound to complement and reinforce the structure of the melody. The whole effect is neat, direct, and easy to remember. More important, it is hard to forget. Such a matching of lyrics and music represents, however, the third incarnation of the material. It had previously been "Those Saladin Days" in the briefly aired musical *Come Back Richard, Your Country Needs You*, and prior to that had been a song called "Try It and See," presented as a prospective U.K. entry for the Eurovision Song Contest of 1969, to be performed by Lulu and recorded for demonstration by Rita Pavone.[5] So once more, behind the musical theater number is a stand-alone pop song of the late 1960s. But more interesting in this case, the heritage is apparent in the musical material once it is considered away from its 1920s-influenced arrangement. The bouncy, upbeat melody—one whose short phrases allow so much room for simple and repetitive lyrics—is ideal Eurovision material, and the optimistic outlook implied by the title "Try It and See" is typical of the upbeat and affirmative tone that the contest's winning songs have so often embodied.[6]

That such a forum should be attractive to two British songwriters of the late 1960s is hardly surprising. First, the contest provided a Europe-wide audience: sixteen countries competed in 1969 and the contest was broadcast to them all. Second, it provided a showcase for young songwriters in a period when groups were increasingly writing their own materials, consequently making it harder for nonperforming songwriters to gain adequate commercial exposure; the song contest was—and still is—in essence one of solo singers and singing groups rather than bands, with the songwriters receiving awards. Third, the reputation of the United Kingdom in the contest by the late 1960s was good: in the twelve years of its participation it had regularly been a runner-up and had won in 1967 (Sandie Shaw, with "Puppet on a String"); the contest had given Cliff Richard a huge hit with his 1968 runner-up song, "Congratulations." The British seemed to be on a roll, and so a song in the contest (yet to achieve the level of kitsch it now has) would hardly have harmed the reputations of up-and-coming songwriters. Indeed, the United Kingdom did win in 1969, but Lulu's song was "Boom-Bang-a-Bang" and she had to share first place with three other countries.[7] The pert and perky Eurovision pop of "Try It and See" has its parallel in a Lloyd Webber number also of the end of the 1960s, the final song of *Joseph and the Amazing Technicolor Dreamcoat*, "Any Dream Will Do," which began life as an early Rice and Lloyd Webber (unrecorded) pop song, "I Fancy You."

Pop sounds of the 1960s more generally are clear throughout *Joseph and the Amazing Technicolor Dreamcoat*. It was given its premiere in the first of many incarnations on March 1, 1968, at Colet Court School, London, as a fifteen-minute "pop cantata" to be sung by the school choir. The cantata was slightly extended that May for a concert version given in Central Hall, Westminster, London. As a result of the concert, the work was augmented

and recorded during the summer; the recording was released the following
year. In 1972 the work was successfully staged at the Edinburgh Festival by
the company of the Young Vic, who then transferred it to the Roundhouse
in Camden, London; a recording of this show was released in 1973. A third
recording of the show was released in 1974, incorporating changes to the
Young Vic production included when it transferred successfully to the heart
of the West End (February 1973). In 1991, after a significant history of professional and amateur performances, and a notable long-running tour in the
United Kingdom under the auspices of the theater producer Bill Kenwright,
a large-scale new production was mounted in 1991 at the London Palladium,
with Jason Donovan—the Australian pop singer, teen idol, and television
soap actor—in the title role.[8]

The instrumentation of the first recorded version (1969) is distinctly of
the late 1960s, with the electric organ creeping in and a prominent, over-
bright harpsichord. David Daltrey's Joseph is pleasant but rather light and
bland, very much the voice of the young pop singer of a group rather than of
the popular solo ballad singers of the time. Shades of the tonal qualities of
any number of British or American pop groups of the time are evoked: the
harpsichord and oboe solo in "Joseph's Dreams" (with the assistance of the
triple meter) is evocative of such records as Sonny and Cher's "I Got You
Babe," itself a summary of a classic instrumental texture of a period; the I-IV-
I7-IV [C-F-C7-F] accompanying figures, articulated by 5-6-7♭-6 [G-A-B♭-A]
in the melody over a tonic pedal, is ubiquitous in pop styles of the time and
a pattern that occurs as the opening oboe phrase of the Hannaman single
"Probably on Thursday," but with a natural rather than flattened 7th.

Essentially, the music of *Joseph and the Amazing Technicolor Dreamcoat* reflects what was "in the air" for Lloyd Webber.[9] Thus the construction of pop was reflected in the cantata: in the short melodies, with simple
melodic and harmonic direction, repetitive rhythms, and association with
memorable lyrics. For a truly period pop sound, the number "Go, Go, Go
Joseph," not in the original Colet Court or Westminster Hall versions but
added for the first recording, has the qualities of such British groups as the
earlier Beatles or Manfred Mann and signals how much the contemporary
pop style was a driving force behind the work. This packaging of constrained
musical material into quickly accessible forms fundamentally distinguishes
the best and the most popular of Lloyd Webber's output. He has an ear for
the hook, the catchy idea that lingers beyond the performance, the sound-
branding of pop. The very first phrase of the cantata—stated majestically by

instruments, then sung—is an example of this, both melodically and rhyth-mically; "Close Every Door" has a melody which elevates distinctive pitch groups (arpeggiated triads and especially the "Eastern" effect of 6♭-5 [D♭-C]) above a rhythm essentially of straight crotchets; the hook of "Any Dream Will Do" inverts this, for it is the crotchet rhythm 2-3-4-1 that provides the distinctive anchor for the simple scalic movement of each phrase of the first section of the refrain. The border between naive simplicity and carefully judged restraint is a close one.

The instrumentation of the whole work on this recording has a sense of too much playing with the paint box, as 1960s timbral clichés follow each other in swift succession: high sustained strings, electric organs, high wood-wind fills, animated string sounds with any combination of harp, electric guitar, acoustic guitar, or harpsichord. "Go, Go, Go Joseph" in particular is heard today as a real period piece: its introductory verse in the minor is a jazz waltz; the combination of metallic electric guitar arpeggios and male vocal harmonies on the refrain evoke endless all-male groups of the late 1960s, from the Beatles to the Monkees; its instrumental fade-out provides another indication of how it was intended to tap into a contemporary pop song mar-ket, utilizing the techniques of the recording studio rather than those of live performance.[10] "Any Dream Will Do," the final song, and one that subse-quently became a British pop single in the early 1990s (predominantly for the preteen market), presents itself initially more in the mold of British light music, as the sustained string line, dotted rhythm, and light character evoke elements of Ronald Binge or Ron Grainer: family music for Sunday lunch-time radio.[11] In the song's coda, as the music broadens for the big finish, the stately rhythm returns to a more American sound (Phil Spector again), especially with the tambourine on the last beat of each bar.

Included in the very first short performance of the cantata was an indul-gence indebted to Tim Rice: Pharaoh was written as if he were Elvis Presley, with a neat pun in the title, "Song of the King." In its first version, the song provided Rice with the opportunity to indulge in performance his desire to imitate Elvis; over the life of the piece, it has gradually been expanded to be-come a focal set piece within the work.[12] Musically, it seems to combine the opening of the refrain of Presley's "All Shook Up" (complete with that song's distinctive "uh-uh-huh" at the end of the opening lines of each refrain) with the middle-eight of "Don't Be Cruel" or "Teddy Bear," but the I-IV-V chord patterns derived from the twelve-bar blues—both walking bass and melody are essentially rhythmic articulations of the triads of the chord structure—

are generic. The only overt stylistic parody in the original cantata, it provided a moment of witty diversion by adopting rock 'n' roll from a decade previous.[13] The effect was further compounded by the introductory passage, which describes Joseph appearing before Pharaoh, musically set in epic film mode, with a broad heroic melody in the melodic minor accompanied by big, solid, modal pillars of I minor-VIIb major-I minor [Em-D-Em]: from Charlton Heston to Elvis across the barline.[14]

In short, the way that the work adapted the pop culture—the music of youth—to a religious tale and with such a fresh sound was innovative.[15] It was not a big stage musical, it was a direct piece of pop. For those who have come to know the work only in its most recent manifestations, notably those following the 1991 revival at the London Palladium and its subsequent production in North America (respectively, the Jason Donovan and Donny Osmond versions), the original 1968 version must come as something of a revelation for its evocation of period. Yet it is this very basis in pop music that has provided *Joseph and the Amazing Technicolor Dreamcoat* with the means for its astounding longevity. As pop has changed over the decades, so *Joseph* has been presented in altered forms, with the accompaniments adapted to new instrumentation and new rhythms. The reinvention of the show for each generation reflects the continual reinvention of pop itself. With its essence in the clear melodies and harmonies, and in its lively and direct lyrics (with a few lines occasionally changed here or there to avoid the more dated of the original 1960s phrases), such re-presentations still retain these basic elements and thus the immediacy of its appeal.

By the time of *Joseph*'s second recording (1973), several linked changes had taken place. The work had moved from concert cantata to staged show, and thus the instrumentation was scaled down from a large studio ensemble of pop group and orchestral musicians to a smaller ensemble more manageable for live theater performance. The presentation of the score was subject to informal arrangement as the individual musicians in the band brought the improvisation and embellishment of a pop instrumentalist's performance practice to the core elements of the music's bass + harmony + melody. With the rock combination of drum and electric guitars at its center, the sound of this second version is consequently more earthy. For example, the opening of "Jacob and Sons" on the 1973 recording has heavy, rock-style drumming at the start, with increasingly prominent electric rhythm guitar on the offbeat. The voice of the Narrator is not that of light pop (sometimes wayward in pitch and never full-blooded in tone) but one that is stronger

Joseph, London 1972. © 1972 The Really Useful Group Ltd.

and more commanding, colored with the direct, nasal tone of folk, along with some of its vocal inflections. Indeed, there are many folk-rock elements introduced, such as the male unison sound accompanied by heavy chords at the first utterances of the brothers in "Joseph's Dreams." While harpsichord sounds, limited woodwind, and brass are used, there are longer passages of consistent texture—less of the 1969 "paint-box" production—which strengthen the focus on the dramatic thrust. With the 1974 recording of the West End version, the score had been extended by a further five numbers, three of which were pastiche styles representing rhinestone-cowboy country and western ("One More Angel in Heaven"), French chanson ("Those Canaan Days"), and calypso ("Benjamin Calypso"). While enlivening proceedings with their musical and verbal jokes through parody, their addition

Joseph updated: the Jason Donovan mega-remix single (photo: Michael Le Poer Trench). © 1991 The Really Useful Group Ltd.

did alter the balance of the show by diluting the anachronism of the "Song of the King": it became no longer a number that provided a moment of rock 'n' roll contrast, but part of a more general parade through the world of popular song. Today, *Joseph and the Amazing Technicolor Dreamcoat* creates the impression of a work of pastiche numbers, glued together with linking passages that advance the narrative; in 1969 the "linking passages" constituted the main body of the work, with the fleeting appearance of Elvis as the exception.

This effect of a mini-kaleidoscope of pop genres has been further strengthened by the treatment of other numbers in later versions. To listen to the 1991 rendition of "Go, Go, Go Joseph" is to note just how much the 1960s origins of the show have been lost with time. The 1969 all-male pop group became the faster rhythm-and-blues-influenced chorus of 1973, with additional funky overtones toward the end of the 1974 version. By 1991 the refrain was not the initial exhortation to optimism and action of the previous versions but a *sotto voce* encouragement from the other prisoners around Joseph's cell. Hints of gospel in the early refrains become explicit in an extended end that moves from funk-gospel, through the addition of strong "clap" backbeats and funky drum breaks, into pure, ecstatic 1980s disco for the coda ("Ahead of my time . . .")—complete with clichéd, fast high-hat semiquavers and a descending bass riff of 1-7♭-6-6♭-5 [C-B♭-A-A♭-G]. But the huge changes in style made around the central core material as it evolves to suit changing music fashions show just how this rooting in a pop basis has enabled *Joseph and the Amazing Technicolor Dreamcoat* to remain continually relevant.

Rock and *Jesus*

Where *Joseph and the Amazing Technicolor Dreamcoat* had been a pleasant and ultimately comforting Bible story for children—everything turns out fine in the end, and a jolly sing-along finishes the entertainment—the events of the last days of Jesus Christ required a more subversive music to match the subject matter.[16] With rock often portrayed as a countercultural form of artistic subversion, stressing individual freedom and self-expression, it provided a more dynamic musical basis for a story that came to be presented with an emphasis on social responsibilities and their relationships to political structures in the confronting of the state by one man. To quote one definition: "Rock is about the search for permanence within the free-floating values of the market place. . . . [It] is hierarchical in that it believes in geniuses and heroes."[17] This definition of the musical genre has resonance with the dramatic themes of *Jesus Christ Superstar*. In dropping the Resurrection and stressing the dilemma of Judas, the work moved from religious morality play to a play about morals, thus also open to a secular reading. There could hardly be a happy ending and a toe-tapping finale: the material did not suit pop.

In Britain of the late 1960s, such groups as Led Zeppelin, Deep Purple, the Rolling Stones, and the Who were establishing rock not only as a music of youth but also one of sophistication and aspiration. Deep Purple, for example, combined the amplified sound of raw guitars with a virtuoso skill that could include classical references in instrumental cadenzas.[18] Furthermore, there was an aspiration toward something beyond the strictly commercial, indicated by the rock and orchestral combination of that group's *Concerto for Group and Orchestra* in three movements (1969).[19] Indeed, the progressive rock movement was beginning to gather impetus at the end of the 1960s, with the drawing together of influences from classical repertory into the field of rock: 1970, for example, brought the release of the eponymously titled album *Emerson, Lake & Palmer*, whose tracks included reworkings of Bartók and Janáček, and an organ solo ("Clotho") indebted to Messiaen. Rock was the music of experiment, a bridge between the worlds of classical and pop music, a player in a large commercial field, but at the same time distancing itself from the disposability of pop through virtuosity and individuality. The higher artistic aspirations of rock led to the notion of the album group (which did not additionally release individual tracks out of context as singles) as superior to the singles group (which did). The difference was between a series of tracks to be seen as constituent parts of a single entity and a collection of discrete short pieces; the former approach helped bring the dramatic program into the sphere of the rock album. In 1969, the year before *Jesus Christ Superstar* was recorded and released, the Who released *Tommy*, a rock opera that described the story of a deaf, dumb, and blind boy and his route to full sensual awareness. Conveyed through a series of songs that suggested rather than stated the story, it was a seminal work, one subsequently presented in live performance. From all these contemporary influences, it is easy to see where *Jesus Christ Superstar* found its form. Like *Joseph*, it was a reflection of the times, annexing to a classically informed style hard rock's driving rhythms and riffs, and progressive rock's acceptance of and experimentation with a wide variety of stylistic references.

The gestures of hard rock in *Jesus Christ Superstar* appear most overtly in the many numbers which use rock riffs, for example Judas's songs "Heaven on Their Minds" and "Damned for All Time" and the scene in the temple. Something similar to the first of these examples can be heard on the track "Mandrake Root" from Deep Purple's *Shades of Deep Purple* (1968), in which the tonic repetition on the first beat is countered with an accented 3♭ on the second beat. In the scene in the temple, two riffs (in 7/8) provide the main musical themes: one short descending pattern (through 3♭-2-1 [E♭-D-C]), similar to the first melodic idea in Deep Purple's "Shadows," and one rising pattern (1-2-3♭-5-8 [C-D-E♭-G-C]). Such flattened thirds are typical in hard rock.[20] The reliance of rock on terse, blues-inflected riffs seems in many ways antithetical to Lloyd Webber, who has since become known for his broad-phrased, popular ballads, yet the construction of works from a series of repeating motifs is in one sense a development on a larger scale of his ability to find that defining hook for a song. The rock influence went beyond that of short repeating phrases and affected the foundations of the numbers in their harmonies and bass lines. Hard rock has not relied on the tonic-dominant polarity that permeates much pop, preferring instead either the tonic-subdominant relationship derived from the blues structure or decorative elaborations of the tonic in descending scalic patterns; typical is the descending modal bass pattern 1-7♭ [C-B♭], often extended downward through 6b-5 [Ab-G], heard in *Jesus Christ Superstar* in the "Gethsemane" theme with the lines "But if I die . . ."; a similar bass line can be heard, applied to a ballad in this case, in Led Zeppelin's "Babe, I'm Gonna Leave You."[21]

In addition, *Superstar*'s religious theme itself suggests black gospel, and thus the whole related areas of soul and funk entered the equation. Gospel in particular was behind the show's title song, one which resolutely hammered home a chordal structure built on 4th relationships through its refrain "Jesus Christ, Jesus Christ, who are you, what have you sacrificed?" over a harmonization of I-IV-VIIb-IV-I [C-F-Bb-F-C]; indeed, the melody line itself is essentially the articulation of these triads. With the title of the show linked to such a strong hook, it is not surprising that this number was chosen for single release to promote the work. The affirmative tonic-subdominant relationships of gospel also have parallels with rock, in which the same chord relationship derived from the blues is more strongly privileged than that of tonic-dominant, still at the heart of the pop song. This I-IV underpinning is heard in the final leader-response section of "Simon Zealotes," with its vocal extemporization to color the words "You'll get the power and the glory, forever and ever and ever," while Simon's main verse uses a modal rock descending bass line (1-7b-6b [C-Bb-Ab]).

Gospel and rock also find a meeting ground in vocal style, for both employ melisma and extremes of pitch and tone to convey heartfelt emotion: the gospel-soul indulgences in "Simon Zealotes" are found in the characterizations of Judas and Jesus in particular. The original singer of Jesus was Ian Gillan, the lead vocalist of Deep Purple, and his interpretation ranges from the intimate and subtly inflected (the start and end of "Gethsemane"), through the impassioned melismas in the same number (to the lines "Alright, I'll die/Just watch me die/See how I die") to the controlled rock scream in "Everything's Alright." Murray Head as Judas had no less of a task in ranging from the direct exposition of his first number to the tortured sound—achieved through high tessitura, rough tone, and cut-up phrasing—of his own "I Don't Know How to Love Him" just before his death.

One of the most effective pieces in *Jesus Christ Superstar* is "Everything's Alright," the number in which Mary Magdalene plays the role of conciliator, as Judas and Jesus argue. Part of its effectiveness comes from the way in which so many musical elements are drawn into one scene to elaborate on the characters. The main refrain of the number is a deceptively simple chorus of reassurance, in a lilting 5/4 time, whose melody, based on oscillating thirds and steady repetition, pairs perfectly with Rice's lyrics: "Try not to get worried, try not to turn on to / Problems that upset you, oh, don't you know / Everything's alright, yes, everything's fine." The stress on the first and last two syllables of each bar and the repetitions carried through from the beginning of the phrases ("Try" and "Everything's") convey the reassuring insistence behind Mary's intervention. The music portrays the same spirit through the steady I-IV [E-A] harmonic underpinning and the simplicity of the melodic motif of thirds. The musical presentation of Mary and her refrain is that of a light jazz-rock number, with Yvonne Elliman's vocal style having an expressive lightness, while the female backing singers reinforcing the "Everything's alright" phrase add an element of gospel, hinting at a spiritual reassurance behind Mary's practical reassurance. In contrast, the sections for Judas and Jesus assume a heavier rock instrumentation and vocal embellishments to match, especially in the phrase "You'll be lost and you'll be sorry when I'm gone" at the end of Jesus's section. The tendency of their sections to rise through phrases, with the oscillating thirds now as repeated notes—hammering home a point—bring a growing tenseness to the confrontation between Jesus and Judas. Mary's subsequent interventions are all the more calming as a result, and by the time of the last one the prominent orchestral strings also reinforce her control and calmness with their sustain, in contrast to the aggressive rock of Judas and Jesus. The very long fade-out, which plays with recording balance as though someone was experimenting with the volume sliders, recalls the lengthy ending to the Beatles' "Hey, Jude" and reminds the listener that the recording studio has become an element of the artistic vision.

The presentation of the work as a concept album allowed some dramatic license, most notably—like *Tommy*—in not needing to present a continuous story. Aided by a reasonable assumption that the audience would in any case know the progression of the story, the numbers could focus on particular scenes and moments without the need to have linking dialogue to explain the plot. This did not mean, however, that the construction of drama was not a part of the album. Far from it. The pacing of the tracks created their own momentum—for example, in whether tracks were run abruptly into each other, as in the sudden shift from "Gethsemane" to "The Arrest," or whether long fade-outs were used, as in "Everything's Alright" and "The Last Supper." This latter track also brought in a bit of 1960s psychedelia in the opening accompaniment, a Bach-like organ obbligato—Procol Harum and "A Whiter Shade of Pale" are unavoidable parallels here—and in Rice's lyrical suggestion ("Don't disturb me now I can see the answers/Till this evening is this morning life is fine" and "What's that in the bread? It's gone to my head") that the Apostles are as likely stoned as drunk. Kept within limits on the original recording, the drunkenness (or "doped-ness") has been increasingly played up in later versions, changing a subtle undercurrent to a more obvious foreground role. Also subsequently adapted from its original is "Herod's Song" (the former Eurovision "Try It and See"). Set up on the 1970 recording by an introduction that suggests a more soul-blues style, the move to a vaudeville two-step is a surprise, tempered with a Herod who accommodated the change of style within his existing vocal characteristics; the bouncy style and honky-tonk piano did not undermine Herod musically within the work.[22] With the 1996 recording, the rock singer Alice Cooper played Herod most effectively, his rock delivery also providing the necessary bridge to integrate the number within its surroundings. In the video of 1998, however, the comedian Rik Mayall played up his Herod in a dinner jacket amid a female cabaret lineup but played down the singing; the work was thus removed visually, vocally, and dramatically from the context of the rest of the show. This is another case of musical reinvention for a changed time. But whereas the musical reinvention of *Joseph* was to reflect the changing appeals of pop music and the shifting of styles from contemporary to by now historic, in *Jesus Christ Superstar* the playing-up of the 1920s connection, not only musically, but visually and verbally, merely served to take the song out of the work; it became an amusing diversion, but one that weakened the integrity of the whole.

One element of *Jesus Christ Superstar* that is admirably wrought is its handling of instruments, especially the integration of orchestra with rock group. The early experiment of the Moody Blues with the London Festival Orchestra in *Days of Future Passed* (1967; intended as a demonstration of the reproduction quality of Deramic™ wall-to-wall sound) did not significantly integrate the orchestral and group resources, although the final track, "Nights in White Satin," demonstrated something of the epic sound that could be achieved. String sounds, the most prominent section used alongside the group on this recording, had gained a presence in pop, for example, in the productions by George Martin for the Beatles, while in rock their presence was made possible through the Mellotron.[23] Significantly, Jon Lord commented of his *Concerto for Group and Orchestra* that he "tried to present the Orchestra and Group as you would expect to hear them — as antagonists."[24] *Jesus Christ Superstar* did not do this, its overture demonstrating inventive ways to use rock group, electronic, and orchestral tones in dramatic combinations. Among the many such textures it employed were aggressive string decorative figures or punchy brass triads over an electric guitar riff, and horn solos between recitative-like, punctuating rock chords. The cello in particular was sometimes equated with an electric guitar, as in the instrumental of "Heaven on Their Minds," and the use of rock cello ran through the early 1970s for Lloyd Webber, with the film score to *The Odessa File* and, of course, *Variations*. The versatility of the French horn—an instrument that Lloyd Webber studied in his youth—also ensured its diverse use; particularly distinctive was the integration of its fanfare calls into "Simon Zealotes."

The abrupt contrasting of sound worlds still constituted a fundamental part of Lloyd Webber's approach to dramatization through music and was strongly present in the work. It was an opposition of particular sound qualities, however, rather than the blunt orchestra-group antagonism identified by Lord. The statement of the main "Jesus Christ Superstar" theme for the first time, at the end of the Overture, is one such case, where the broad full orchestra sound breaks in to silence the multilayered (rock group and orchestral) preceding riff section. "Hosanna" sounds wonderfully fresh in its orchestration through woodwind decorative flurries in the chorus, or in Gillan's transparent vocal tone alongside the clear brass with strings and sleigh bells for Jesus's first comments. All this contrasts with the rock-group accompaniment of "This Jesus Must Die" that precedes it, and is heightened by the move from the untidy group singing of the priests (suggesting a rough alliance of individuals) to the unison chorus. Elsewhere, the priests gain further vocal contrast with the beautifully toned and enunciated heavenly choir, most distinctively heard in their "Well done, Judas." All these forms of vocal and textural contrast were to be developed more explicitly in *Evita*.

Classical Concerns

Running alongside the pop of *Joseph and the Amazing Technicolor Dreamcoat* and the rock elements of *Jesus Christ Superstar* was another side of Lloyd Webber which took its aspirations and precedents from twentieth-century classical music. The use of irregular meters (particularly 5/4 and 7/8), accented chords which aggressively emphasize or disturb the sense of meter, and angular melodic lines frequently involving prominent tritones, as well as the juxtaposition of solid textural blocks, contribute to a sound with roots in Stravinsky, Prokofiev, and Shostakovich.[25] In the overture to *Jesus Christ Superstar* (later heard with lyrics as "The Trial Before Pilate"), the brooding opening theme with prominent tritone over a portentous pedal has something of the uneasy quality of the opening bars of Prokofiev's *Cinderella*. The unison melody that follows shortly after has a similar flexibility in line as the Prokofiev, while adopting more Stravinskian rhythms and punctuating, accented chords.[26] As the section winds itself to even greater intensity, something of *Le Sacre du printemps* creeps in through the sheer rhythmic insistence and high woodwind-accented flurries. At the time of the launch of the recording of *Jesus Christ Superstar* in New York, Lloyd Webber mentioned among his influences Stravinsky, whose *Symphony in Three Movements* was "an object lesson for a rock band." Modernistic traits continued through the rock opera, mostly in association with the forces opposing Jesus. The shape and tonal gesture of the *Cinderella*-like theme at the start of the overture also has a parallel later in Caiaphas's lines "Tell the rabble to be quiet/ I anticipate a riot"), where rising arpeggios and contrasting twisting chromatic phrases create fleeting impressions of the score to *Romeo and Juliet*, particularly the famous "Dance of the Knights" in the ball scene. The distinctive chordal accompaniment of "The Dance of the Knights," which alternates heavy bass notes with *pesante* chords, is also heard underpinning Caiaphas's pronouncement; later this effect is even stronger as Jesus is brought before Pilate ("Who is this broken man, cluttering up my hallway?"), with Pilate's status and brutal sarcasm conveyed through the imperious assertiveness of the accompanying chords alongside the chromatic angularity of the melody. The effect of the introduction of the chromatic influences from Prokofiev and Stravinsky in *Jesus Christ Superstar* is an interesting one in that the tritones and semitones of the melodic line never dispel a sense of a tonal center; it is chromatic decoration around a still-clear tonal base. However, the most avant-garde of effects is found in "The Crucifixion," a sound montage initially made up of three main elements: lines spoken by Christ; sustained voices overlapping and shifting to create slowly changing clusters, as in Ligeti's *Lux aeterna* (1966); and free jazz on drums and piano. Later, sliding high string clusters are added, as in early Xenaxis or Penderecki.[27]

If anything tends to distinguish the earlier Lloyd Webber of *Jesus Christ Superstar* and *Evita* from the later Lloyd Webber of *Sunset Boulevard* and *Whistle Down the Wind*, it is a freedom of rhythm. *Joseph and the Amazing Technicolor Dreamcoat* had fun with contrasting meter—for example, in

"Poor, Poor Joseph," with the 5/4 of the sung phrases ("Joseph was taken to Egypt in chains and sold") set against the 5/8 of the instrumental breaks. But these rhythms themselves kept within the bars rather than crossing the bar line, and this tendency to use short repeating units, each of a bar, has continued through much of Lloyd Webber's work. Examples include "Everything's Alright" and "The Temple" *(Jesus Christ Superstar)*, where the link to the nature of the rock riff is most apparent, and the dance of "The Wine and the Dice" *(Aspects of Love)*, which exhibits the same pedigree in a different context. The cross-barline phrasing in 7/8 of "And the Money Kept Rolling In (and Out)" *(Evita)* or the 5/4 of "Married Man" *(Tell Me on a Sunday)* has been atypical. Indeed, Lloyd Webber's whole approach to rhythm tends to be one of simple repetition in mostly quaver and crotchet patterns. A good example of this, written with extreme rhythmic repetition but mitigated to some degree through the rubato it usually receives in performance, is "Too Much in Love to Care" *(Sunset Boulevard)*.

The two film scores that Lloyd Webber wrote, for *Gumshoe* (1971; directed by Stephen Frears) and *The Odessa File* (1974; directed by Ronald Neame), also explored a more classical, twentieth-century language. The first piece of music in *Gumshoe* is contrapuntal and angular; it is a sparse and hard sound to depict the depressing contemporary life of its setting in Liverpool, a world of raw nerves and seldom-concealed aggression. Later, the score employs Ligeti-like sliding string clusters to accompany the appearance of the menacing John Striker (played by Fulton Mackay) at the labor exchange (unemployment office); the night scene at the Atlantis bookshop employs tritones in its bass line counterpointed by accented minor seconds in the brass. Across the score, Lloyd Webber's use of opposing styles to create drama between characters is present in such sound images as the music to accompany the appearance of the Sam Spade advertisement. The effect is largely indebted to 1940s and 1950s film noir (big rising brass chords and high strings) to match the Chandleresque elements of—in the words of the main character, Ginley—"a girl, a gun, and a grand." This contrasts with the more wistful and contemporary theme that marks the missed-the-boat attraction of Ginley (Albert Finney) to his sister-in-law (Billie Whitelaw). That theme first occurs as a short and quiet passage under dialogue when the sister-in-law arrives at Ginley's flat, just after the character Danny has struck him; it is the first lyrical section heard in the score. The theme is stated more prominently, broad and loud in its arrangement, when his sister-in-law sees Ginley off at Lime Street Station. Another noticeable theme accompanies De Vries (referred to as "the fat man") hurrying away from the Red Star Parcel depot at the station; this theme uses the cumulative effect of the repetition of one short phrase, a device heard in *Jesus Christ Superstar* and to be used throughout later Lloyd Webber works, especially in relation to passages in more unusual time signatures. Just as the later pastiche work in *The Phantom of the Opera* in particular was used to intensify the music associated with the central drama of the three main characters, so the diegetic music (music that is actually present and heard in the world of the drama, such as the club band and the radio song) strengthens the drama of the non-diegetic score.[28] The end credits are accompanied by a rock 'n' roll number by Rice and Lloyd Webber, "Baby, You're Good for Me," sung by Roy Young. But the music in *Gumshoe* is minimal, used sparingly to highlight particular moments, seldom given an extended role.

The music in *The Odessa File* is even more limited, and seeing the film leaves the impression that Lloyd Webber merely threw down a few bars to be scattered here and there. In fact, the soundtrack as released on disk fills an album and is texturally revealing. The nondiegetic music uses an ensemble of solo cello (played by Julian Lloyd Webber) and rock group with prominent synthesizer, in frequently contrapuntal writing that tends at times toward fugue; it prefigures both the resources and style of *Variations*. The main musical material for the world of Peter Miller's crusade to avenge an earlier violence is stated in the slow and suspenseful theme that accompanies Miller's reading of Solomon Tauber's diary and in Miller's own theme, which first appears as he decided to pursue Roschmann.[29] Set against this quite distinctive music, as in *Gumshoe*, is the diegetic music of the film. In *The Odessa File* it consists of a military anthem (to represent the Nazi Odessa organization), polka music, and a drinking song—all for the military reunion scene—along with music for a carousel, and a radio song. Unlike "Baby, You're Good for Me" in *Gumshoe*, the song in *The Odessa File* was more successful dramatically, musically, and commercially. Called "Christmas Dream," it is heard right at the start of the film, played on a car radio, when its lyrics of seasonal peace counterpoint news of the shooting of President Kennedy. Recorded by Perry Como, the song provided some limited seasonal success, and exemplified the pop-song catchiness of Lloyd Webber in its simple harmony and distinctive upward semitone slides in the fourth melodic idea of the refrain ("And I hope you believe it too . . ."). In the background to this song Elvis Presley once more lingers: Germanic oom-pah bass, accordion, and bilingual lyrics (English and German) suggest

"Wooden Heart" as an obvious influence, one that Tim Rice has acknowledged.[30]

It is not surprising that Lloyd Webber sought to reuse elements of these scores, given how little of each was used for the films. Both provide a summary of the compartments of his style in the early 1970s (classical and astringent themes, popular song, rock instrumentation, and contrapuntal textures) and a ground for the establishment of ideas for further treatment. Specifically, *Gumshoe* provided *Evita* with a repeated horn phrase, to a melodic pattern of 3b-2-1-2-1 [Eb-D-C-D-C]. In the film this is a short, discrete phrase used, for example, as a form of musical punctuation to add emphasis to Ginley's pointed remark to his brother-in-law, "The only person who knew I was in London was your missus." *The Odessa File* provided *Evita* with melodies from Miller's theme, heard as Evita's early phrase "It's happened at last / I'm starting to get started"; a later theme in the same passage that inspired "The Art of the Possible," added after the album release for the stage show; pointillistic chords heard in both *Variations* and as Alex waits at the station in *Aspects of Love* (scene four), which are heard in the music which underscored the section on Solomon Tauber's Diary. Probably the most obvious reuse of material from either film came in the substitute love theme from *Gumshoe*, now best known as the title song to *Sunset Boulevard*.

Neither of the films seem in retrospect to have been an ideal subject for Lloyd Webber. The broad, melodic tendencies and expansive palettes that occur through the stage shows could find little space in two suspense dramas, each with a sparse, contemporary, and brutal attitude. Thus *Sunset Boulevard* feels to some extent like the big film score Lloyd Webber would like to have written, while *The Odessa File* appears now as a doodling pad for *Variations*, itself the end marker of a stylistic period that began with *Jesus Christ Superstar*. Lloyd Webber and film were not well matched in the 1970s; possibly the emotional indulgence and broad melodies à la Max Steiner from a few decades earlier, or in John Williams territory with Spielberg a decade or more later, would have provided better vehicles. Interesting though they are, these two Lloyd Webber film scores primarily earn their place as transitional works whose experimentation was developed and utilized on stage.

Developing the Style

The musical influences on Andrew Lloyd Webber substantially from outside the musical theater canon have undoubtedly enhanced the popular

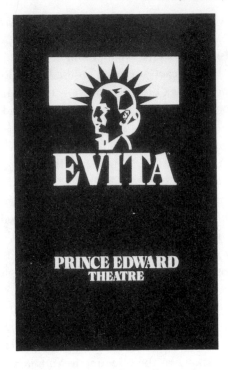

Evita, 1978. © 1978 The Really Useful Group Ltd.

appeal of his works. Effectively, he learned about the pop and rock songs first, and the stage shows came later. Show songs used to be linked to popular music, becoming standards, arranged for dance bands, topping the hit parade; with the advent of pop those symbiotic links of popular standards and shows began to break down. One of the biggest questions for the musical after 1960 has been how to maintain a musical integrity that is progressing rather than fossilizing yet retains widespread popular appeal, all in the face of the shifting and fragmenting styles of pop music and of pop's continual redefinitions as it changes in its relationship to and uses by society. Lloyd Webber's diverse musical interests positioned him well to negotiate this area from the late 1960s through to the late 1980s. *Evita* did much to consolidate the use of rock from *Jesus Christ Superstar* and brought together its various elements more successfully; indeed, it was something of a pop parade, as *Joseph* became, but with a greater stylistic integrity. Military and political scenes got the tough rock ("The Lady's Got Potential," "Dangerous Jade," "A New Argentina," and "And the Money Kept Rolling In (and Out)");

intimate moments were given an easy-listening gloss ("I'd Be Surprisingly Good For You" and "Another Suitcase in Another Hall"); Latin standards provided regional color ("On This Night of a Thousand Stars"); there was the astringent modernism of the more narrative, recitative-based sections; and the show tune was acknowledged through the big belt ballad ("Don't Cry for Me, Argentina").

The potential vocal extravagance of rock provided an undercurrent in *The Phantom of the Opera*, whose title song sought to combine the accessibility of pop with the power of rock, while retaining a strong and flowing melodic line in keeping with the opera of the title. Wide ranging in pitch and tone, the voice of the Phantom had something of the rock vocalist about it—the initial single release of the song before the launch of the London show was recorded by Sarah Brightman partnered by Steve Harley, former lead singer of the group Cockney Rebel. The title song did not provide the most comfortable of stylistic combinations, and rock dropped out of the equation for *Aspects of Love* and *Sunset Boulevard*, whose particular stylistic mixes involved more of the show tune and more of the modernistic. Both these shows also explored more intense musical organization in which arching groups of scenes rather than individual contrasting numbers became an even greater structural focus than they had been in *Phantom*. Both also developed the use of music to characterize the emotional lives of the characters (they are essentially intimate dramas involving few people), too introverted and claustrophobic in *Aspects*, more measured and effective in *Sunset Boulevard*. When rock returned in *Whistle Down the Wind*, it was to stunning effect, with the epic grandeur of "A Kiss Is a Terrible Thing to Waste" and the pulsating insistence of "Tire Tracks and Broken Hearts." But a blurring of musical boundaries had by this stage given way to discrete numbers in discrete styles, the distinctions made even clearer by the use of spoken dialogue. This was rock as the music of a musical play, not the integrated rock of 1970s rock opera. It was also rock of only part of the show, for, just as in *Jesus Christ Superstar* and *Evita*, it was used to characterize only part of the onstage community—rock could not provide a voice for all.

With the removal of any strong narrative in *Cats* and *Starlight Express*, the use of pop and rock became not so much a device for sustained narrative as part of a pop music revue, a chance to use an ability for the catchy melody writing that marked the early pop songs. This ability was less in evidence from *The Phantom of the Opera* through *Sunset Boulevard*, although each show had its share of hook phrases in takeout songs. It returned most noticeably, though, in *Whistle Down the Wind* with the songs for the children: "When Children Rule the World," in particular, was a return to Eurovision pop. In *The Beautiful Game* the laid-back, rhythmic pop of "Don't Like You" or the sentimental lyricism of "Let Us Love in Peace" continued the trend, while rock traits were evidenced in the modal harmony of the numbers of more rebellious tone, such as "Clean the Kit" and the introductory section to "Off to the Party" (beginning with "We're just totally great"). Further still, the modern classical elements increasingly became less obvious, occasionally apparent in the melodic angularity (semitones, tritones, and unexpected leaps) of "The Craic" in *The Beautiful Game* or in that show's more physical musical episodes: the soccer match sequences, for example, or the scenes of politically motivated, violent expression, especially as in "I'd Rather Die on My Feet Than Live on My Knees."

For all the rebalancing of their respective emphases through a succession of works, commercial pop and rock, along with twentieth-century classical influences, have been constant features of Lloyd Webber's output. Pop honed a melodic directness that gave *Joseph and the Amazing Technicolor Dreamcoat* its persisting, easy charm. Rock shaped the more tough and intense sound of *Jesus Christ Superstar* and *Evita*. The modern classics of Prokofiev, Shostakovich, and Stravinsky gave edge and acidity—both melodic and rhythmic—to the whole, vital mix.

 CHAPTER 4

"Who Are You, Strange Angel?": Multiple Personalities in *The Phantom of the Opera*

O N SEPTEMBER 29, 1860, A DECREE WAS DRAWN UP ESTABLISH-
ing the geographical boundaries of a proposed new opera house in
the center of Paris. The subsequent competition for its design attracted more than 170 proposals, and from the final seven entrants chosen
the project was awarded to Charles Garnier. Construction began in 1861
and involved, among other things, the massive task of draining the land,
which in the process created a lake underneath the foundations. The newly
completed opera house was some seventeen stories high, contained a maze
of corridors, rooms, and cellars, and included such innovations as control-
lable gas lighting for stage effects (replaced with electric in 1881). It opened
on January 5, 1875, although the program for the evening had to be altered
when a leading soprano was unable to sing in planned extracts from Gounod's *Faust* or Ambroise Thomas's *Hamlet*. In its various theaters and companies, the Paris Opéra had held a state-ordained, preeminent position in
the cultural life of Paris and of France since the time of Lully. Consequently,
the new Palais Garnier (as the opera house was called) was designed to reflect such importance in its scale and decoration. Even today the grand staircase is an impressive symbol of power and wealth, as much a theatrical set
as those on stage. The auditorium is also spectacular, with a large domed
ceiling from which hangs a vast chandelier whose counterweight fell into
the auditorium in 1896 during a performance of Duvernoy's *Hellé*, killing a
member of the audience.

It is not difficult to see where Gaston Leroux found the inspiration for
his original novel of 1911. The lake, the passages, the falling chandelier, the

Lon Chaney in *The Phantom of the Opera*, 1925, directed by Rupert Julian.
BFI Collections.

stricken prima donna, the staircase as a setting for a masqued ball: all are in
place, requiring only their conjunction with an existing legend of a ghost in
the theater to create *Le Fantôme de l'Opéra*. The story attracted little attention when first published, but with the first film in 1925 (directed by Rupert
Julian), in which Lon Chaney portrayed the disfigured and reclusive composer, it became internationally famous. This seminal film is still gripping
today, with a wonderful sense of mood and strong visual imagery: especially
notable are the original two-color Technicolor scenes that present the Phantom as a striking Red Death at the ball and atop the opera house, his red
cloak billowing in the wind.[1] Films were also made in 1943, 1955, 1960, 1961,
1962, 1974 (updated as a rock musical in Brian De Palma's *The Phantom
of the Paradise*), and 1983. By the time of Lloyd Webber's musicalization of
the novel in 1986, to a book by Lloyd Webber and Richard Stilgoe, and with
lyrics by Charles Hart and Stilgoe (with a few additional lyrics contributed to
the title song by Mike Batt), the story had achieved more the level of myth,

and further screen versions have been made in the musical's aftermath, in 1987 twice, 1989, 1998, and in 1990 as a television miniseries.[2]

The idea for the musical is generally reported as having come from a chance purchase by Lloyd Webber in New York of an English translation of the novel. The story further amplified his interest in the operatic voice and its potential, which his marriage to the singer Sarah Brightman had inspired, and the idea of the show was established. But it is more complicated than that. An existing melodramatic play of the story by Ken Hill was presented in London at the Royal Theatre, Stratford East. Lloyd Webber saw this, thought it might have potential for development, and bought the rights with a view to adding a composite score of period operatic works. Persuaded to write an original, he abandoned the Ken Hill play for a completely new one. Maury Yeston, having secured the American rights to the novel and begun work in 1983, had also written a musical version of the story to a book by Arthur Kopit, called, simply, *Phantom*. Unfortunately for Yeston and Kopit, the rights were in the public domain in the United Kingdom, and in 1986 Lloyd Webber brought his work to the stage first, originally in the West End and then on Broadway nearly two years later; by then the American rights had also entered the public domain. With a regional production of Yeston and Kopit's show (Houston Theatre Under the Stars) and a tour of Ken Hill's piece, it was possible at one point in the early 1990s to see all three versions of *The Phantom of the Opera* in the United States. The relationship between the various writers and their productions has been the subject of much theatrical gossip, whose alleged double-dealings and characterizations of "goodies" and "baddies" are almost worthy of a murder mystery in their own right, although it is unlikely that this is the subject matter Lloyd Webber had in mind for his much vaunted but as yet unproduced "Phantom II" sequel.

The novel *Le Fantôme de l'Opéra* by Leroux (1868–1927) was published in 1911 around an existing tale of a murderous ghost who inhabited the lower depths of the Paris Opéra. Leroux's version is a good story, presented through the framework of a journalistic report thirty years after the event and drawn from newly discovered eyewitness accounts and biographical writings of some of the characters involved.[3] The novel includes scenes of fine Gothic horror—midnight visits to graveyards, secret passages, mysterious notes, unexplained events, and sudden murders—but ultimately leaves no sense of the supernatural, for all incidents are explained logically. The thrill of primal fear is always counteracted with the cool logic of practical explanation. Mysterious letters are delivered through secret trapdoors in walls and floors; secret passages have been constructed by Erik, the Phantom of the title, a former magician and ventriloquist. While in service to the Shah of Samarkand, he had been drawn into political assassinations and torture, finally fleeing the country in fear of his life for knowing too much of the Shah's secrets. He then developed extraordinary skill in mechanical devices and automata in the service of the Sultan of Constantinople before again fleeing the danger his knowledge presented. It was as a building contractor on the construction of Garnier's magnificent new Paris opera house that he gained his knowledge of the place, and was also able to add a few useful adaptations of his own to what became his retreat from the everyday world. By the end of Leroux's novel the rational mind has convincingly explained away the supernatural fear; the epilogue (chapter 27) is appropriately titled "Loose Ends Tied Up." It is the weakness of those interacting with the all-too-human Phantom that has created his power, that of a self-perpetuating myth built on human superstition, credulity, and insecurity.

But there is another dimension to the tale. The Opéra was the center of Parisian society, the place to see and be seen; the sentiments of "Masquerade" at the start of act II of the musical may have been directly inspired by the declaration in Leroux's novel that "In Paris our lives are one masked ball."[4] Not only is it one long party, it is also by implication one in which the truth is constantly kept hidden, in which public and private lives are kept apart. Thus the opera house represents a microcosm of Paris, and the novel peoples it from every walk of life, from the rat catcher in the cellar to the nobility in the boxes. The Phantom's disruption of the life of the opera house is a threat to the fabric of society itself as much as to the Opéra, and through the final defeat of that threat in the novel's tidy ending, we are reassured that the Parisian world is once more in order. The status quo has prevailed and people are still in their rightful social places.

In its many film incarnations since 1925, the story has been subject to all sorts of variations, with the title character portrayed as anything from a vengeful composer whose work has been passed off by an aristocrat as his own (Herbert Lom, 1962) to the Manager's disfigured son (Charles Dance, 1990). Lloyd Webber's musical takes no such liberties, retaining much of the plot and detail of the novel. In an interview at the time of the show's opening in Basel in 1995, Lloyd Webber gave his own evaluation of the novel: "It can't make up its mind if it's a melodrama or a romance or just a very good thriller. Frankly, it's a piece of hokum. But it works."[5] The description can equally be made to fit the musical.

Where the stage version principally differs from Leroux is in tone, constantly subduing the novel's rationalist element: the tricks are never explained, the history of the Phantom as "Erik" is perfunctorily and briefly given very late (in act II) by Madame Giry but hardly stressed, and the fate of the Phantom remains a mystery as he vanishes into thin air at the end. Also, the stage show takes its time to set up the air of mystery surrounding the central characters: act I of the show covers only the first seven of the novel's 28 chapters. Where Leroux's original presents superstition and illusion in order to expose their falseness through reason, the musical elevates mystery, avoids explanation, and invites the suspension of disbelief. It has the air of Gothic writing of the late 1700s and early 1800s rather than the rational and scientific style of the late 1800s, the period of the story itself.[6]

A Strange Affair

The musical begins in 1911 with an auction of items from the Paris Opéra, thirty years after the events of the main story. (See table 4.1 for a list of scenes and musical numbers.) Set on a dim and shrouded stage, an auctioneer moves through a series of lots, all of which relate to the story to follow. Lot 663: a poster for the opera *Hannibal* by Chalumeau, the work which launches the heroine, Christine Daaé, as an opera soloist. Lot 664: a wooden pistol and three skulls from the original 1831 production of *Robert le Diable*—the symbolism of the objects and the work needs no explanation; lot 665: a little music box with a monkey automaton on the top. Lot 666 (an appropriately diabolic number): the great chandelier, symbol of "the strange affair of the Phantom of the Opera."[7] As the dust sheets are removed, the chandelier flickers into (new electrical) life and rises to the top of the auditorium while the title song of the show is played in a full orchestration, an overture that leads the audience back in time to 1881.

A rehearsal for the opera *Hannibal* is interrupted by the arrival of the new managers of the company of the Opéra Populaire, Gilles André and Richard Firmin. They meet the leading tenor Ubaldo Piangi and the diva Carlotta Giudicelli; other characters introduced are the somber ballet mistress, Madame Giry, her daughter Meg (one of the dancers), and Christine Daaé (also a dancer). As Carlotta sings her act III aria ("Think of Me"),

Table 4.1. *The Phantom of the Opera*: Scenes and Music Numbers

---

Prologue
  The Stage of the Paris Opera, 1911[a]
Overture
  ACT I: Paris 1881
Scene 1: *Hannibal*, dress rehearsal

"Think of Me"	Carlotta, Christine, Raoul

Scene 2: After the Gala

"Angel of Music"	Christine, Meg

Scene 3: Christine's dressing room

"Little Lotte"/	Raoul, Christine
"The Mirror" (Angel of Music)	Phantom

Scene 4: The labyrinth underground

"The Phantom of the Opera"	Christine, Phantom

Scene 5: Beyond the lake [the Phantom's lair]

"The Music of the Night"	Phantom

Scene 6: Beyond the lake, next morning

"I Remember"/	Christine
"Stranger Than You Dreamt It"	Phantom

Scene 7: Backstage at the Opera

"Magical Lasso"	Buquet, Meg, Madame Giry, ballet girls

Scene 8: The managers' office

"Notes"/	Firmin, André, Raoul, Carlotta, Giry, Meg, Phantom
"Prima Donna"	Firmin, André, Raoul, Carlotta, Giry, Meg, Phantom

Scene 9: *Il muto*, performance

"Poor Fool, He Makes Me Laugh"	Carlotta and company

Scene 10: The roof of the Opera

"Why Have You Brought Me Here?"/	Raoul, Christine
"Raoul, I've Been There"	Raoul, Christine
"All I Ask of You"	Raoul, Christine
"All I Ask of You" (reprise)	Phantom

Entr'acte
  ACT II: Six months later
Scene 1: The staircase of the opera house, New Year's Eve

"Masquerade"/	Full company
"Why So Silent"	Phantom

Scene 2: Backstage at the Opera

[the history of the Phantom]	Raoul, Giry

Scene 3: The managers' office

"Notes"	André, Firmin, Carlotta, Piangi, Raoul, Christine, Giry, Phantom
"Twisted Every Way"	Christine

Table 4.1. Continued

Scene 4: *Don Juan Triumphant*, rehearsal	
	Christine, Piangi, Reyer, Carlotta, Giry, company
Scene 5: A graveyard in Perros	
"Wishing You Were Somehow Here Again"	Christine
"Wandering Child"/	Phantom, Christine
"Bravo Monsieur"	Phantom, Christine, Raoul
Scene 6: *Don Juan Triumphant*, before the premiere	
	Raoul, André, Firmin, Firemen, Phantom
Scene 7: *Don Juan Triumphant*, performance	
"Here the Sire May Serve the Dam"	Carlotta, Piangi, Passarino, company
"The Point of No Return"	Phantom, Christine
Scene 8: The labyrinth underground	
"Down Once More"/	Phantom, Christine
"Track Down This Murderer"	Full company
Scene 9: Beyond the lake	Christine, Phantom, Raoul, and company

[a] Earlier printed versions of the libretto give 1905.

a backdrop crashes to the stage. The chorus members panic, invoking the name of "the Phantom of the Opera," a ghostlike figure reputedly responsible for the many accidents that happen at the opera house. A message arrives from this "Opera Ghost" instructing the new managers that he is to be paid a monthly salary, and that box number five is to be kept free for him at all times. Carlotta refuses to sing at the gala, and Christine Daaé is put forward as an understudy. She begins to sing the same aria tentatively, but as her confidence increases the scene changes to the night of the gala and her rapturous reception by the audience. The financial sponsor of the new managers, Raoul, the Vicomte de Chagny, applauds her from a box, recognizing her as the girl with whom he used to play when they were children. Back in the dressing room, Christine tells Meg about her unknown teacher, the "Angel of Music" sent from Heaven—as she thinks—by her dead father. Raoul arrives to congratulate her and they briefly reminisce ("Little Lotte"); he is to take her to dinner but first leaves her to change. The Angel of Music appears in the mirror to Christine and, obeying his summons, she passes into a passage revealed as the mirror slides away, and is then led off by him to the depths of the opera house ("The Phantom of the Opera"). Mean-

Christine is called by the Phantom through mirror. © 1999 The Really Useful
Group Ltd.

while, Raoul has returned to find her gone and the room—locked from the
inside—empty.

In the underground lair of the Angel/Phantom, Christine is seduced by
the Phantom's "Music of the Night," an oblique, symbolic love song. He
is "Angel" in the mind of Christine, but "Phantom" according to the song,
which covers their descent below the Opéra. The character has three names:
"the Phantom of the Opera" to those who see the supernatural and diabolic in him, "Opera Ghost" to those to whom he represents a meddlesome
and dangerous blackmailer, and "Angel of Music" to Christine. She faints at
the sight of a waxwork model of herself, dressed as a bride, which suddenly
reaches out to her. Christine is awakened by the Phantom's own composition, on which he is working at the organ; a little monkey music box plays. As
Christine remembers the events that have brought her here, she determines
to discover the face that is hidden behind the mask of her Angel. Catching
him unawares, she pulls off the mask to reveal (to her, but not to the audience at this point) what is clearly a hideous face. She recoils from both his

The journey across the underground lake. © 1999 The Really Useful Group Ltd.

appearance and from the violent outburst her actions provoke. He returns her to the world above ground, the world of the Opéra.

In the managers' office a series of notes bearing demands from the Opera Ghost perplex and antagonize the two managers, as well as Raoul, Carlotta, and Piangi. Madame Giry has received yet another note: the Ghost wants Christine to sing the leading role instead of Carlotta in the next opera, *Il muto*. Carlotta reacts like a stereotypical prima donna, and the managers try to pacify her. The managers want Carlotta; Christine does not want to sing the main role in any case; Raoul is concerned about Christine; Madame Giry interjects prophecies of doom and disaster if the Opera Ghost is not mollified. In the event, *Il muto* takes place with Carlotta in the leading soprano role, but the performance is interrupted by the voice of the Phantom: his box has not been kept free, and the wrong woman is singing. Disturbed by the interruption, Carlotta restarts her aria, but croaking noises come out instead—the Phantom's witty revenge for her calling Christine a "little toad." The implication of hypnosis lurks behind many of the Phantom's tricks, although it is never explicitly referred to in either novel or musical. The ballet from the third act of *Il muto* is brought forward to cover the

Act II: "Masquerade." © 1999 The Really Useful Group Ltd.

confusion, but the shadows of the Phantom keep appearing to disconcert the dancers, and the performance is finally halted as the body of Joseph Buquet, the flyman, falls to the stage, a noose round his neck. To escape the confusion, Christine and Raoul rush to the roof of the opera house, where she tells him of the Angel and her trip to the caverns below the opera house; he declares his love for her ("All I Ask of You"), which is duly requited. The Phantom overhears and declares war on his male rival in love. Back on stage, the performance of *Il muto* has concluded with Christine in Carlotta's role. As the cast bow, the Phantom cuts loose the great chandelier, which crashes onto the stage.

Act II opens with André and Firmin in fancy dress: a masqued ball is taking place, with all the guests assembled round the great staircase ("Masquerade"). The Phantom, dressed as the Red Death, briefly appears and presents the score of his new opera, demanding that it be staged. When pressed by Raoul, Madame Giry tells him that Phantom is a prodigy whose deformities led to his exhibition in a locked cage in a traveling circus; the man escaped and was never found, but she has seen him at the Opéra. The managers are taxed by repeated additional demands from their Opera Ghost but see in the staging of the opera a chance to trap their persecutor and blackmailer. Raoul persuades Christine to help them in setting the trap, for she — and consequently they — cannot be free until the Phantom is caught. This time, it is Raoul who declares war on the Phantom.

Rehearsals do not go well, and an agitated Christine returns to the mausoleum of her father to find some comfort in his memory ("Wishing You Were Somehow Here Again"). The Phantom appears to her in the guise of the Angel of Music once more, but Raoul's arrival interrupts his hypnotic calls to her; defied by Raoul, the Phantom makes the third declaration of war — on Raoul and Christine together. At the first night of the new opera, *Don Juan Triumphant*, the police are in place to catch the Opera Ghost when he eventually appears. While the performance is under way, the Phantom takes the place of Piangi (undetected under the voluminous cloak and hood) so as to play out himself the seduction scene opposite Christine. During the duet ("The Point of No Return"), gradually everyone realizes what has happened, and Christine reveals the Phantom's true face. As the police rush onto the stage to arrest him, he escapes below once more, dragging Christine with him.

Raoul descends after Christine, and a mob prepares to chase after the Phantom. Meanwhile, the Phantom is trying to bully Christine into submission, but she resists. When Raoul reaches the underground lair, he is trapped in a noose, his life to be exchanged for her marriage to the Phantom. Fighting against her impulses, Christine kisses the Phantom, signaling that she places her love of Raoul above her own fate; the symbol of self-sacrifice marks the demise of the Phantom's last hopes that Christine could ever love him, and he crumbles. Releasing Raoul, he tells them both to go quickly but tell nothing of what they have seen: the Phantom wishes his legacy to be that of the myth, not the desperate, all-too-real man. As the first of the mob arrive, the Phantom hides himself under a cloak; Meg Giry enters the lair, looks round, and pulls away the cloak. Nothing is left of the Phantom but his mask.

Dramatically, the story hinges on a series of direct conflicts, which continually redefine Christine's own position in relation to those around her; only late in the story does she make herself an active part of this process of self-definition. Lloyd Webber has reflected this in his score through musical themes (recurring melodies), motifs (essentially individual phrases), and textures which portray various characters, attitudes, and emotions. The material of each of these musical themes and motifs themselves is rarely modified, except through fragmentation, but together they literally play out the dramatic tensions of the work as they are restated and juxtaposed in different combinations. In addition, the orchestration and key structure are also used to strengthen the aural differentiation between these musical ideas. Those expecting something of the weight and ever-shifting fluidity of Wagnerian leitmotifs will be disappointed; the thematic system here is a more blunt tool, but nonetheless an effective one. The apportioning of summary "titles" to the various themes and motifs is a somewhat old-fashioned analytic device, but the way in which the themes are treated by Lloyd Webber as discrete blocks of sound to be reassembled in different patterns—like the bricks of a Lego kit—makes such an approach clear and effective for our purpose in this chapter. The music will be shown to be direct in its manipulation of these musical building blocks, gaining subtlety through the interactions of the material rather than modifications of the material itself. To explore how the musical ideas characterize in sound the tensions of the drama, we must first scrutinize the dramatis personae and their relationships.

The Music of the Day

Of the show's series of contrasting worlds, it is perhaps best to establish at the start the most normal—but equally the most one-dimensional. This is the world of Raoul, Vicomte de Chagny, who combines elements of two characters from Leroux's novel: the socialite, ennobled Philippe Comte de Chagny, and his younger seafaring brother, the shy Raoul. Our musicalized Raoul is one representation of the "real" world of Paris. He is young, wealthy, and handsome; he is romantic, honest, and genuine. He has every hallmark of the conventional hero, with many of the clichés to match: the knight in shining armor in the guise of a vicomte in a tail suit, who rescues his damsel in distress by displaying selfless devotion. That he and Christine will live happily ever after is never in doubt, for this is romantic Lloyd Webber, not cynical Sondheim.

Raoul has the distinction of musically opening the show, with the first lines sung (rather than spoken) by any character, although these are not at the very start of the drama. The prologue opens with the bareness of a dusty stage, the perfunctory ritual of an auction, and a bleakness amplified by the lack of an overture; only the lowering of the house lights marks the start of the show. As the auction of objects from the opera house proceeds, Raoul successfully bids first for the poster of Chalumeau's *Hannibal* (a spurious composer and work invented for the musical) and then for the musical box

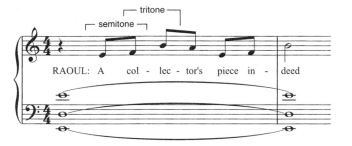

Example 4.1. "A collector's piece indeed" *(The Phantom of the Opera)*

with an automaton in the form of a monkey playing cymbals. The auction-eer sets the device to play, and the simple A major melody of the music box provokes the memories of the elderly Vicomte. To a low, sustained string-like chord (founded on a minor 7th chord, E-G-B-D) on synthesizer he sings of a woman, as yet unidentified, who has described the toy to him: "A col-lector's piece indeed . . . every detail exactly as she said." The melody is a twisting, unsettled one, indistinct in harmony and melodic shape, in con-trast to the clarity of the music box, but it is a musical theme that is to recur frequently when someone is trying to grasp something just slightly out of focus. When Christine wakes up in the Phantom's lair (the start of act I, scene 6), it is with this theme that she reminds herself of what she thought had happened earlier: "I remember there was mist . . . swirling mist upon a vast, glassy lake." It is the effect of people interpreting something heard, read, or remembered not quite clearly enough, and thus distorted in the telling by their own imaginings and the projection of their own feelings. It is a theme that evokes "impressions": voices from the past or the distance, factually uncertain, always communication with a blurred edge at the inter-face of fact and fiction, the real and the imagined, the cool light of reason and the darkness of primitive fear. There is always an uneasy shadow be-hind this Impressions theme, namely the myth of the Phantom, in which legend has taken over from the real; and not surprisingly this theme is not just associated with the Vicomte: others use it, so this is not just his music. A good example occurs at the start of act I, scene 7, as Joseph Buquet de-scribes the face of the Phantom to the ballet girls in a manner calculated to both shock and amuse them: "Like yellow parchment is his skin . . . a great black hole served as the nose that never grew." The unsettling twists of the melody are echoed by a bass ostinato figure, which slowly oscillates between

B♭ and B, conveying yet more uncertainty, more of the unknown of which to be afraid.

It is, in fact, late in act I before there is music that is quite specifically Raoul's. Such music comes only with his love song "All I Ask of You," one of the best-known numbers from the show. The characteristics of the song are what we now think of as typical in a Lloyd Webber ballad, with a wide vocal range (here starting low) and distinctive, large melodic leaps (in this case with a descending major 9th at the start of the refrain, echoed by a descending minor 7th a bar later, reaching the security of the tonic octave in the third bar). It is luxuriantly scored with prominent strings, while horns add an indulgent chromatic phrase for an extra romantic twist in the second refrain. This is the personification in music of Raoul, the idealized romantic hero. He sings this love song to Christine on the roof of the opera house, physically as far from the subterranean lair of the Phantom as possible, for Raoul is of a world external to the Opéra and from a place of light. Although we learn virtually nothing of his life away from the naturally dark internal environment of the theater, his externality is set up through his introduction proper to the audience: as a spectator at a musical show, like themselves. Indeed, the concentration of the musical within the physical confines of the Palais Garnier—Christine's act II visit to her father's mausoleum is the only time someone is seen to step outside the building—adds much to the increasingly intense, even claustrophobic focus that develops around the three central characters. The Opéra does not go out to the world, the world is first drawn in and then absorbed into the community of the Opéra. The process, mirrored in the focus of the show, is one of insistent introversion. Raoul moves from spectator to participant in the internal world of the opera house in romantic pursuit of Christine, and indeed he appropriates theatrical language by adopting the melody of "Prima Donna" to implore Christine in act II to help set the trap for the Phantom. He uses the music that appeals to Christine's newfound status in the world of the opera, and there is not some little element of deliberate flattery in this, for Raoul knows what he wants and means to get it. But there is no indication that he (or, indeed, she) will remain in the operatic world after he has ultimately achieved his conquest of her. Raoul's purpose is to take Christine away; the Phantom's is to keep her at the Opéra. Indeed, on first impression and in so many respects the portrayal of Raoul seems to be as far removed from that of the Phantom as possible; but their apparent polarization will in fact become something more symbiotic as the drama plays itself out.

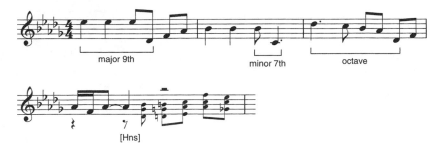

Example 4.2. "All I Ask of You" *(The Phantom of the Opera)*

And what of Raoul's object of desire, the heroine, Christine Daaé? Musically, she appears more fully drawn than her dashing suitor, for she sings many things in many ways. But her music reflects her unique role as the pivot between all the different worlds of the story: the worlds of the opera house (its life and actual operatic performance), of the Phantom and his lair, of the high society Raoul represents, and of Raoul's world of physical love. It is not surprising that she above all of the three main characters is consequently appropriating the music of others, answering them (consciously or otherwise) in their own musical languages. But beyond this, she has learned singing from her "Angel of Music," and her musical language is thus inherently not her own: in any case, as an opera singer she is the emotional conduit of many people—composers, librettists, directors, teachers—as well as, if not before, herself. The story revolves around a young and immature woman, unable to let go of the emotional ties to her father, now deceased, and repeatedly prevented by demonic forces from embracing fully her lover. Thus the entire tale can be viewed as a metaphor for Christine's sexual awakening and maturing, as she is pulled unwillingly from the adolescent relationship of parent-child (the Phantom as "Angel of Music" substituting for her dead father) to that of adult lover with Raoul. In this light, the forces exerted upon Christine by others are dominant, for she has not yet identified her own voice. Such a theory has musical support in one unexpected moment in act II. In order to draw the Phantom out into the open the Phantom's opera *Don Juan Triumphant* is being staged, but police will be waiting to catch the composer when he turns up for the performance. Christine is asked to help in setting the trap. For the first time she must actively choose between, on the one hand, her father, the Angel, and music itself as sublimation of and substitute for sex, or, on the other, her lover, adult romance, and mature

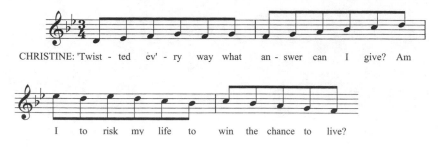

CHRISTINE: 'Twist - ted ev' - ry way what an - swer can I give? Am
I to risk my life to win the chance to live?

Example 4.3. "Twisted" *(The Phantom of the Opera)*

sexuality: she must choose between her past world and her future one. She must decide whether she thinks the Opera Ghost really is "Angel" or "Phantom." And she can't decide this because to her the Opera Ghost is both. At this moment of crisis she sings:

> Twisted every way what answer can I give?
> Am I to risk my life, to win the chance to live?
> Can I betray the man, who once inspired my voice?
> Do I become his prey? Do I have any choice?

This is sung to a melody in even quavers that seems quite new.[8] It comes out of Christine's dilemma as the first expression of her own voice: it is her dilemma, her decision, and it is her melody, uncertainly oscillating up and down the scale, unsure of its direction and lacking the confidence of assertive rhythm or cadence.[9] But at this point it is her music.

With its symbolism extended further, Christine's awakening ends less as an assertion of individuality than as a recognition of dependence and a retreat to conformity. By choosing to help trap the Phantom she also rejects the unique creativity as a singer which the Phantom facilitates in favor of domesticity with Raoul; she rejects the struggle and ultimate spiritual freedom that the Phantom can give through music for a life of wifely dependence and comfort. Ultimately, she knows her place and so rejects the overturning of society's rules that the Phantom personifies, turning instead to the societal conventions offered through romance and Raoul. It's the old dilemma of having your man or your career; the options in this nineteenth-century romance don't allow for a more modern solution—that of trying for both. The result is inevitable, for can the assertion of romance ever be socially subversive unless the lovers are to be "doomed"?[10] Romantic happy endings conventionally require the restoration of the status quo. And musically, the

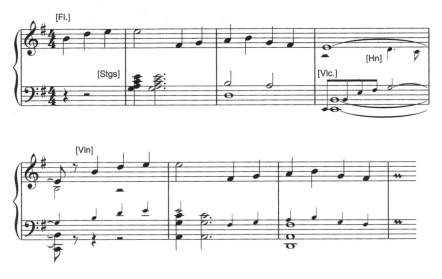

Example 4.4. "Sympathy" theme *(The Phantom of the Opera)*

lovers sing of sharing "one love, one lifetime . . . each day . . . each night";
but it is to the refrain of Raoul's "All I Ask of You." It is Raoul who ultimately,
almost literally a few bars before the end of act II, calls the tune.

Christine is not a strong character and in general reacts rather than acts.
But her strength to the drama is as an emotional lens for others around
her, and again one theme uniquely hers demonstrates this. In act I, when
Christine first awakens in the underground lair, she snatches away the Phantom's mask and reveals his disfigured face for the first time; he angrily rounds
on her, comparing her to Pandora, whose box of evil she has unwittingly
opened, and to the traitorous Delilah. The snatching of the mask is an un-
usually independent move for Christine, and the frightening reaction that it
generates goes some way toward accounting for her later inability to be deci-
sive or proactive for fear of the potential consequences. Next, the Phantom
attempts to explain something of the dichotomy caused by the aspirations
of his soul set against the constrictions of his body. As his words and music
fall apart under the weight of his anguish, she returns the mask to him, accompanied by a beautifully plaintive melody on the flute, then violin and
cello in octaves. The melody, marked *andante con affetuoso*, hovers between
E minor and G major, rejection and support, with an unsettled poignancy.
Later in act I, as Christine describes her experiences with the Phantom

to Raoul, just before his love song, she uses this melody—the "Sympathy" theme—for the lines: "Yet in his eyes all the sadness of the world . . . / Those pleading eyes that both threaten and adore." Christine articulates that moment of discovery, not just from her own reactions but from an empathy with the Phantom's position. It is a simple musical phrase but a powerful dramatic moment.

It is Christine who unwittingly reveals in music the first hints of the Phantom's threatening character and destabilizing influence; as the student of her teacher she cannot help but assimilate elements of his voice. The first time the audience encounters the Phantom, as a disembodied voice praising Christine's singing at the gala concert, it is accompanied by a phrase whose repetitions descend in whole-tone steps. This becomes the coda of the following song, "Angel of Music," to Christine's words (punctuated with interjections from Meg Giry): "He's with me even now . . . All around me . . . It frightens me." The whole-tone descent of these phrases from Db major, through B major and A major, to end on G minor, and marked by single chimes on the glockenspiel, is musically unsettling. Her preceding paean to her Angel of Music has been resolutely diatonic, with minor (verse) and major (refrain) tonalities used to portray, respectively, the past incorporating her dead father and the present incorporating her "unseen genius" of a teacher.[11] The whole-tone characterization of her teacher is thus otherworldly, at this point for her the other world of heaven whence the Angel of Music has been sent by her father; but to the audience it is the darker/other side of human nature. Christine has heard the notes but does not yet recognize the tune.[12] This "Regression" theme suggests something vague and receding in its avoidance through the whole-tone pattern of a harmonic goal, while its open-ended hypnotic quality is well-suited to portraying the allure of the Angel of Music.[13]

Shortly after the scene with Meg Giry, Christine and Raoul meet each other for the first time in many years, prompting memories of their youth. They reminisce, intoning over a high string accompaniment whose distinctive four-note phrase finally becomes the vocal melody as well, for Christine's words "No—what I love best, Lotte said, is when I'm asleep in my bed and the Angel of Music sings songs in my head!" It is music for the Angel, and so for the audience at this stage—but not yet Christine—it is also music for the Phantom. A set of mainly minor triads in parallel motion support a melody which is once more based on a whole-tone scale (and again, principally a descending one). This also incorporates melodically in its opening

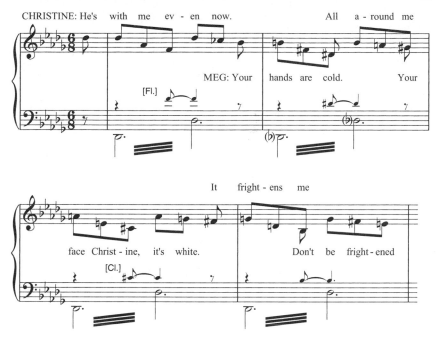

Example 4.5. "He's with me even now . . ." (*The Phantom of the Opera*)

motif (E-F♯-D-C) the interval of a tritone, at the heart of the whole-tone scale, and the antithesis of secure, conventional diatonic scales. It has also been known in Western culture for centuries as "the devil's interval" and has figured in much diabolic music, probably the most familiar of which is the opening solo violin of Saint-Saëns's *Danse macabre*, whose *scordatura* is so distinctive.[14] As Christine sings this melody we are aware of its harmonic strangeness, but the combination of slow movement, triad accompaniment, and high string texture make it seductive, relegating the whole-tone and tritone elements to a subtle shading rather than a blatant statement. It is easy to see how Christine, desperate for a link to her late father (represented most directly through a high solo violin phrase at the line "Father playing the violin"), latches onto the seductive surface rather than the subversive undercurrent in this music. Although the first appearance of the theme suggests something of a clouded memory, later occurrences are more direct. It is the location for the memory that is represented, the physical world of the Phantom, his lair beneath the opera. At the beginning of Christine's first visit to the underground lair the Phantom declares to this theme:

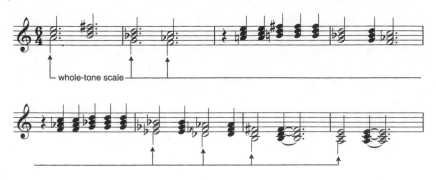

Example 4.6. "Phantom's Lair" theme *(The Phantom of the Opera)*

> I have brought you
> to the seat of sweet music's throne . . .
> to this kingdom
> where all must pay
> homage to music . . .
> music . . .[15]

The Music of the Night

Everything in the story revolves around the Phantom; he drives the action and colors the responses of the characters and, indeed, the audience. He is a figure of nightmare, and his scenes take place in the dark. He can take many forms, and is represented physically in the design in obvious disguises (Red Death, Don Juan), in the clothes of concealment (cloaks, masks, and the impersonality of evening wear), but also as shadows on the wall and disembodied voices. He stands for the disfigured human, Erik, and the aspirational Angel of Music, but first and foremost as the show begins, he is the embodiment of threat and fear.

Not surprisingly the musical world of the Phantom is the broadest and most detailed of any character's in the show. Everyone else is perceived in relation to him, and their music responds to his promptings. His first obvious characterization in music is also the most melodramatic and corny. The auctioneer announces, "Perhaps we may frighten away the ghost of so many years ago with a little illumination, gentlemen?" and the chandelier rises up high into the auditorium to the sounds of a cathedral organ playing big minor chords which descend in semitones. The music and the staging under-

Example 4.7. Phantom opening overture theme *(The Phantom of the Opera)*

He's here...   the Phan - tom of   the Op - era

Example 4.8. "He's here . . . the Phantom of the Opera" *(The Phantom of the Opera)*

score the Grand Guignol of the story. It is melodramatic, with its shades of silent movies and crazed composers, villains in swishing opera capes, and shadows in vaults.[16] Yet before this big moment, there is one little musical motif that is hardly audible, placed in outline only in the underscoring to the auctioneer's final sentence. The major 2nd and rising 5th that make up the "Name" motif of the Phantom (shortly to be articulated by the corps de ballet: "He's here . . . the Phantom of the Opera!") provide the musical background for the "ghost of so many years ago."[17] The Name motif and the chromatic Descent motif most immediately capture the mythic character of the Phantom. Not as seductive as the Angel, not as blatantly honest as other music yet to be discussed, these two themes deliberately portray the Phantom as a caricature, the embodiment of human fears, yet for all that not real, not the true image. By starting the show with a familiar sound-cartoon of the horror villain, Lloyd Webber has ensured that development can only move away from that caricature toward a more rounded portrayal; he begins with the musical version of our prejudices that the myth invokes, but ends with an entirely different view of the (anti)hero.

The silent-movie Name and Descent themes are how others perceive the Phantom. He portrays himself rather differently. First, he is the seductive Angel, best shown in the inspirational song (for Christine) "The Music of the Night." It is a broad, romantic melody in Db major, with a wide vocal range, beginning low in the register. If that sounds a familiar description, then Raoul's "All I Ask of You" is not so far away in key, sentiment, or characteristics; in fact the opening phrase of one is pretty much a musical anagram of the other, for both encompass the same pitches, Ab-Db-Eb-F, and both are bounded by their dominant at lower and upper octaves. Both men are trying to lure their prey, initially one ostensibly for art and one for human love, but ultimately both for emotional and physical love; both are investing Christine with their own desires and aspirations; each represents a different potential within Christine. Raoul sings to Christine of a controlling future in "All I Ask of You": "Let me be your freedom, . . . / I'm here with you, beside you, to guard you and to guide you"; in the introductory section to "Music of the Night" the Phantom informs her that he needs her "to serve me, to sing, for my music." Raoul and the Phantom are two sides of the same coin. Where one lives in isolation below ground, the other lives in society above, where one is linked to night and darkness, the other exists in daylight. The Phantom wants to keep Christine in his subterranean lair beneath the opera house, Raoul wants to summon his carriage to drive them both away from the opera house. Where the Phantom is the ugly antihero, deformed in body and spirit, Raoul is one of the "beautiful people" of his day. In fact, neither Raoul nor Phantom is intent on keeping Christine performing on stage for the public, for each wants to provide her with a private audience of one. Can Christine have an operatic career after she chooses to be Raoul's wife? After all, Trilby lost her voice when Svengali died. The question has been addressed in many of the dramatic incarnations of Leroux's novel. In the 1925 film the Phantom warns Christine that she "must forget all worldly things and think only of your career—and your master!" In the 1943 version Christine is first told by the Musical Director of the Opéra, "You must choose between an operatic career and what is usually called a normal life. . . . You can't do justice to both. The artist has a special temperament and he must live his life exclusively with those who understand it." Her singing teacher then tells her, "Music is first, music is everything. . . . You don't understand; women never understand." So the choice of Raoul is that of Christine as woman rather than Christine as supreme musician, and the last words of the musical are from the Phantom: "It's over now, the music of the night." The statement seems as much for her as for him.

The Phantom and Raoul are reflections of each other—each defining himself through his opposite number—yet they share a common purpose in the seduction of Christine; and so it is appropriate that their two big vocal gestures should have common features. The costume design stresses their similarity, for both are most commonly seen dressed in immaculate evening dress; only their faces point the difference. Just as the flawed characters of Judas and Eva Perón provided earlier inspiration, so here it is the Phantom

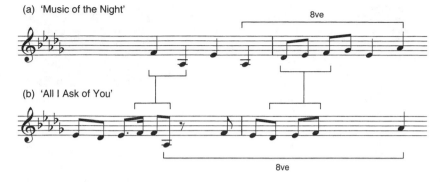

Example 4.9. (a) "Music of the Night": opening (b) "All I Ask of You": opening *(The Phantom of the Opera)*

and not Raoul who is more fully drawn, dramatically and musically. The putative villain is always much more intriguing, and maybe a little thrill of the dangerous is inevitably behind the responses of the naive, innocent Christine to her teacher and erstwhile suitor—which would at least explain why she takes so long to acknowledge what everyone else has known about him for some time!

The romantic, caressing "Music of the Night" provides one important musical summary of the Phantom's character. The final bars include a set of "mystic chords": F♯ major-D♯ minor-D minor-C major-C♯ major [enharmonic of D♭ major]. Both the upward moving melody and the descending bass describe tritones (respectively C♯-G♮ and F♯-C♮), and both are resolved by a final upward slide of a minor 2nd. This motif also ends act II, and thus the whole work, providing a final aural image of the Phantom not as the silent-movie villain but as something more enigmatic and otherworldly, yet ultimately finding its resolution, reconciled in some way to the "real" world. It is mystery, not horror, that prevails. The resolution is also musical, for the mystic chords contain within them the opposing forces of whole-tone and diatonic scale, the tritone and the perfect 5th—dark and light, Raoul and Phantom.

Curiously, the title song, one of the best-known of the show, seems the least convincing, and it is partly because of Christine's presence in it. Why does someone enamored of an Angel of Music sing that "the Phantom of the Opera is there—inside my mind"? Surely it was the Angel of Music that she referred to a few lines earlier when relating,

(a) The Phantom and Christine; (b) Raoul and Christine. © 1999 The Really Useful Group Ltd.

Example 4.10. "Music of the Night": closing chords *(The Phantom of the Opera)*

> In sleep
> he sang to me,
> In dreams he came . . .
> that voice
> which calls to me
> and speaks
> my name.

There is no denying that it is a great scene: the moving platform shifts slowly downward and the becloaked Phantom and Christine rush across it at ever-lower levels as they descend into the depths of the opera house; then the gondola carrying them both glides through an eerie mist, illuminated by a weird blue light (described in Leroux's original text), dodging the candelabras which rise from below.[18] The shift into prerecorded tape is an irritating if practical necessity for the staging, though it does facilitate a nice aural moment shortly after as the live orchestra kicks in again a few verses into the song. But for all the indulgent staging it remains the number least integrated into the score, where takeout pop(ular) song jars with dramatic integration, and as such marks one of the work's boundaries between megamusical and operatic ideals.

The least attractive side of the Phantom (and remember, he has more than one, for it is a half-mask, as only half of his face is too hideous to be revealed) is best portrayed through his opera *Don Juan Triumphant*, where the full force of his creative mind is given rein. Hints of this musical world permeate act I, but only hints. In act II they gradually dominate the melodies, harmonies, and especially the orchestral textures, as the most distorted part of the Phantom gains increasing hold over both him and the opera house. When Christine is awakened from sleep in the underground lair in act I, it is by an extract of the Phantom's own opera played on the organ. The work is

Example 4.11. "Don Juan Triumphant," act I *(The Phantom of the Opera)*

reflexive, for the Phantom is Don Juan in optimistic mood, and he has been temporarily triumphant: he has Christine in his lair. Indeed, it is the presence of Christine that has sparked this bout of composition in which, as the script describes the moment, he is "playing with furious concentration. He breaks off occasionally to write the music down." Christine is the object of his professional and personal desire; she is his muse, the Madonna-like mannequin in a wedding dress of his shrine now incarnate. She roused him to the outpouring of "Music of the Night" and now spurs on the composition of his opera. Handfuls of clusterlike chords are matched by a rising whole-tone bass scale; these opening two phrases are optimistic in their jaunty rhythm and simple scale melody, whose whole-tone inflections and diatonic chord clusters prove later to be some of the least modernistic of his opera. The effect is rounded off by a discordant version of the chords of the Lair theme to which Christine sang earlier with Raoul in "Little Lotte." Next she hears the little monkey music box, with its attractive A major melody of "Masquerade" (so we are later to find out), a song about the illusion of image, the deceptiveness of appearances. The contrast between the two sound worlds is striking.

This scene continues with a succession of motifs. First, Christine recalls what has happened (the Impressions theme as she struggles to inter-

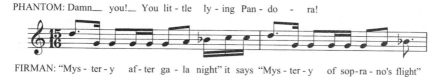

Example 4.12. "Damn you! You little lying Pandora!"/"Mystery after gala night" *(The Phantom of the Opera)*

pret something not quite clear), with little orchestrational touches to depict the "mist" (harp) and the "glassy lake" (synthesizer). As she approaches the Phantom (who is absorbed at the organ with the composition of his opera), the sound of the solo violin, now associated with Christine's dead father, plays the major-key section of "Angel of Music," for the Phantom is still just that to her—her Angel. To the minor-key section she sings "Who was that shape in the shadows? Whose is the face in the mask?" and moves to take the mask away. He is taken by surprise and she sees his full face, recoiling in horror. His musical response to her actions is not a Gothic horror restatement of the Descent motif or the Name motif, but something much more human. It is anger, through a new musical idea, an "Interruption" theme, later used to mark the start of each of a succession of interruptions in the managers' office in this act and also in act II. Marked *allegro con fuore*, it is explosive as he curses her, with staccato horns accompanying an assertive theme that employs a strong descending interval of a perfect 5th as a headmotif to its first two phrases. The second stanza of this outburst is decorated in the orchestra with a fast, flurrying whole-tone scale high on violins and piccolo, which emphasize the true nature of the Phantom. As his anger is spent he cries "Damn you! Curse you!" (a whole-tone descent from C♯ major to B major); after a pause, he moves into a strange piece of music in G minor which conveys his uncertainty and his own fear as he attempts to explain his situation to Christine, that of the "repulsive carcass, who seems a beast, but secretly dreams of beauty." This is one of the most overt references in the libretto to the *Beauty and the Beast* fairy tale that is woven in with elements of the Faust legend in the tale of the Phantom. Something of the poise that lurks behind this music, portraying the attempt to be controlled while talking of something so personal and painful (and talking to others is not one of the solitary Phantom's strengths), is indicated through its distinctive marking *come gavotte* and the shifting meter, between 5/4,

4/4, and 3/4. And at the end we hear for the first time the Sympathy theme described above, after which the return of Christine to the world aboveground is marked with a quasi-fugal passage, using the Impressions theme as its subject and the whole-tone scales in flute and trumpet as decorative countersubjects, musically a mix of the man and the myth.

The idea that the Phantom should find creative expression through an opera, *Don Juan Triumphant*, is from Leroux's novel, and Christine's description of the first sounds of it are a clear inspiration for Lloyd Webber's stage work, even suggesting the contrast between "Music of the Night" (the charm of the Phantom) and *Don Juan Triumphant* (the horror of the Phantom): "And then I began to understand Erik's contemptuous phrase when he spoke about operatic music. What I now heard was utterly different from what had charmed me up to then. His *Don Juan Triumphant* (for I had no doubt that he had rushed to his masterpiece to forget the horror of the moment) seemed to me at first one awful, long magnificent sob. But, little by little, it expressed every emotion, every suffering of which mankind is capable. It intoxicated me."[19]

There is a major problem in creating music for the Phantom. How does one express this anguish and anger in a musical which itself contains a variety of musical styles, from the techno-pop influences of the title song to the pastiche of grand opera, taking in on its way the theatrical music of the opera house characters and the romantic intimacy of Raoul and Christine? The show already has a broad musical palette with which to deal. Equally, if the Phantom writes truly good music for his opera, then would not the world aboveground appreciate it, and where would be the problem in the Opéra staging it? Blackmail or traps would be unnecessary. The story requires that the music of the Phantom's opera is to be that of the outsider, off-putting and jarring, a strong contrast with the other musical worlds. Through the adoption of whole-tone and dissonant styles, the Phantom's music presents a new, modern musical world that foreshadows the techniques of Debussy and Schönberg to parallel his belief in the new vocal sound of Christine. This musical modernism is not just a threat to the operatic stage—Piangi cannot cope with this new musical world, failing to sing a whole-tone phrase—but the symbol of the Phantom's more general threat to a wider status quo; fear of him represents fear of another unknown: the future. At his most stark, stripped of any seductive veneer, it is the modern that portrays musically the most visceral and violent urges of the Phantom. One motif expresses this in combining the whole-tone scale with semitonal decoration

Example 4.13. (a) "Your chains are still mine. You will sing for me!"
(b) Phantom-related theme of seconds (*The Phantom of the Opera*)

when the Phantom is at his most threatening. After the Phantom (as the Red
Death) has presented the manuscript of his new opera to André, he addresses
Christine with the words "Your chains are still mine—you still sing for me!"
His vocal phrase contains the elements of what is to be a "Threat" motif,
heard especially in orchestral passages and with increasing frequency as the
Phantom's diabolic nature increasingly dominates act II. This is the theme
that Christine throws back at the Phantom in their final confrontation, acknowledging his darkest side with the lines "Have you gorged yourself at last,
in your lust for blood?"

Alongside its rawness of character and modernistic vision, the Phantom's
music also must lack any sense of discrimination between good and bad.
Through this it marks the supreme belief in one's own abilities, despite the
evidence, that is, the mark of the megalomaniac, a quality of which there is
more than a little in the controlling Phantom. To show just how disturbing
Don Juan Triumphant is to the world of opera and how it portrays the more
fundamental threats and flaws that the Phantom presents, some consideration is needed of the opera singers and operatic music of the show.

The Opera of "The Phantom"

Lloyd Webber has clearly found more than a little fun in creating his operatic language for the show. He has had to create a pastiche repertory for the
opera house, an everyday musical language for the opera managers Firmin
and André along with their prima donna Carlotta and tenor sidekick Piangi,
and also the new sounds of the Phantom's *Don Juan Triumphant*.

Leroux provides a detailed description of the first of these categories in the second chapter of his novel, many of which seem to foreshadow elements of the story to come in amusing ways, just as the auction does in the musical. A gala performance includes Gounod conducting his own *Funeral March for a Marionette* (perhaps a premature piece in honor of Christine?), Saint-Saëns conducting his *Danse macabre* and *Rêverie orientale* (maybe a reference to the Middle Eastern history shared by Erik and the Persian, a guiding figure who also appears in the 1925 film), and Delibes conducting extracts from his *Coppélia* (the doll created by the controlling inventor). Christine Daaé sings a few passages from Gounod's *Roméo et Juliette* (the story of doomed love), along with the trio from *Faust* (the luring of innocent womanhood by the demon who is finally thwarted by goodness and beauty), in which Christine has replaced an indisposed Carlotta.[20] This last work has figured most strongly in various earlier adaptations of the story, with analogues between the Devil and Erik and between Christine and the saintly but doomed Marguerite, while both Faust and Raoul are saved through the intercessions of their lovers.[21] In the novel and the 1925 film, the chandelier crashes to the stalls during a performance of *Faust*.

Lloyd Webber's original concept for *The Phantom of the Opera* was to create a score using existing pieces of operatic repertory appropriate to the story's time and place, but this idea was abandoned, and in the process he moved toward re-creating something of the character of such operatic works through pastiche of the repertory of the Paris Opéra at that time. But such pieces had to be primarily amusing, as their point was to throw into relief other elements of the score and particularly to expose the opera singers Carlotta and Piangi to ridicule, along with the opera managers, very much in line with Leroux's characterizations in his novel.[22] The world of nineteenth-century opera is not to be taken too seriously; it provides the lighthearted counterpoint to the more serious "genuine" music of the show, and so it must appear artificial as befits this stage-within-a-stage. The opera on stage is not the main drama but a subplot in musical style to what is primarily a backstage (and belowstage) story of Christine, Raoul, and the Phantom. It is a musical equivalent of Ado Annie and Will Parker, rather than Laurey and Curly.

"Opera" is defined the moment act I begins. The blackness of the auction prologue is replaced by a rehearsal of a scene for Chalumeau's opera *Hannibal*, replete with a painted backcloth of palm trees and an exotically dressed chorus of slaves. The first image of the operatic diva Carlotta Giudi-

Carlotta, the operatic diva. © 1999 The Really Useful Group Ltd.

celli (the Spanish La Carlotta in Leroux's novel) is that of a screeching
woman holding a bloody, severed head. She is playing Elissa, Queen of Car-
thage, displaying a gift from Hannibal, who has just returned with his army
to save the city from Roman invasion under Scipio. It is a symbol (aural
and visual) of extremes; it is a cartoon world. The following choral music
"with feasting and dancing and song" is a lumbering *andante moderato* in
F major, scored with a period orchestration that marks a clear shift from the
tonal palette of either the auction or "chandelier" sections preceding it. The
classic image of opera is reinforced by the appearance of the large Italian
tenor Piangi as the heroic Hannibal. He begins a recitative, but is interrupted
through his problem in having to say "Rome" rather than "Roma"; clear and
intelligible diction is not to be found at the opera, at least not in a cartoon
world. The use of a familiar recitative style also marks the artificiality of the
opera world; as the characters in the musical converse primarily through
sung phrases, the use of operatic recitative with its accompanying chords to
mark cadences makes the fluid speech-in-music of the offstage world a more
easily accepted mode of "naturalistic" delivery. The contrast here is not principally between sung and spoken dialogue, but between different registers of
musicalized speech. The formulas and conventions of the opera recitative in

the onstage world make the rest of the sung dialogue more easily accepted as a more natural form of communication in the offstage world. When characters do resort to ordinary speech, it is for plot exposition; for example, the opening scenes at the rehearsal introducing the managers, singers, and dancers. But as the show progresses and the emotions of Christine, Raoul, and the Phantom become its pivot, factual exposition gives way to emotional development, and thus speech gives way to music. In act II Madame Giry narrates the history of the Phantom through speech, for it is fact, not attitude, that has to be conveyed.

The rehearsal of *Hannibal* continues, introducing the audience in quick succession to a top C for Piangi, then the opera ballet, whose music in the minor key and based on minor 2nds and tritones possibly hints at the connection between the ballet mistress Madame Giry and the Phantom, for whom she acts as messenger. Christine Daaé in the corps de ballet is picked out when she falls out of step; then the final chorus begins and an elephant arrives, marked musically by bass drum strokes, a melody played low and loud in trombone (reinforced by the synthesizer on a similar sound), double bass, and cello. Removed for a couple of bars from their role as harmonic and rhythmic filler, the horns swoop up an octave to emulate the trumpeting of the beast. Piangi—fatter and older than any heroic Hannibal should be—lumbers onto its back.

As for the style of this music, it is very much in the mold of French Romantic grand opera of the 1830s and 1840s, and the usual model identified by commentators has been Meyerbeer.[23] The scale of the imaginary *Hannibal* with its exotic setting and historical source material are indeed appropriate to Meyerbeer, but also to other composers of the period.[24] The operatic pastiche is not sufficiently sharp to be pinned down to one specific composer; nor is the later pastiche of classical opera, *Il muto*. The point of the onstage opera in *Phantom* is that it is generic, playing to a present-day, musical-theater audience's prejudices of opera, playing upon stereotypes. The onstage opera of *Phantom* is there for laughs.

At the end of the rehearsal the elephant is turned around to be led off, and so revealed to be a model whose head movements are worked by stagehands sitting inside. Indeed, all through this first section, the audience is presented with a variety of methods in which appearance and reality are shown to be far divergent; even the scenery has been assembled in view of the audience, which thus knows it is fake. By such means, the opera sets up the most important undercurrent in the whole show, that "things are seldom what they seem." In one sense, *The Phantom of the Opera* is reflexive, its story reflecting on the very nature of its delivery: what is real and what is illusion.

The next piece of opera in the show is more problematic. Carlotta sings her act III aria from *Hannibal*, "Think of Me," for the two new managers of the opera house, Firmin and André. In the full score the opening has the performance indication *moderato e poco rubato*, qualified with the interesting addition "(like Schubert!)"; the second verse is marked "even more like Schubert." There is a simplicity and directness to this melody, with its basic accompaniment that articulates the straightforward harmonization.[25] Carlotta's rendition is interrupted by a backdrop crashing down, after which we get for the first time the explicit statement of the Name theme by the ballet girls. Why the act III aria has to be so understated in terms of the expected Romantic opera style becomes apparent at its next presentation, when Christine sings it first in rehearsal and then transformed into her performance of it at the gala concert. In her rendition the song conveys the freshness of her young voice, the almost folklike opening statement now a long way from Carlotta's opening cadenza.[26] Christine's cadenza, when it comes at the end of this number, is much lighter and simpler than was Carlotta's at the start of the *Hannibal* scene, for Christine has to begin in the musical with operatic potential rather than as a full-fledged operatic star in the manner of Carlotta. As Sarah Brightman explained: "It is essential that Christine, a ballet girl suddenly plucked from the chorus to sing a leading role, develops her voice as the plot moves on if Andrew's idea of the character is to work. I had to control my voice and develop it as Christine would have done, so I couldn't start off too strong."[27] The music does some of the work in its lighter and melodically direct style, but the voice must also represent something new, different from Carlotta. As Lloyd Webber said, "The Phantom believes in her voice because it represents a new sound in music, purer than a conventional soprano."[28]

Alongside its musical subtext—new singer and new sound—the aria from *Hannibal* provides a dramatic subtext, one that first links Christine to Raoul. After Raoul recognizes his childhood friend as the singer and cheers her from his opera box, the aria "Think of Me" becomes an implicit commentary on their preexisting relationship in these lines at the conclusion of the aria:

RAOUL: What a change! You're really not a bit
   The gawkish girl that once you were[.]
   She may not remember me, but I remember her[.]
CHRISTINE: We never said our love was evergreen,
   or as unchanging as the sea[29]
   But please promise me, that sometimes you will think of me!

For this to work the music must straddle that gap between the show's onstage operatic world and the offstage "real" world. In this light, it would be difficult to sustain an aria that was strongly a period pastiche and one in which the singer was too obviously an archetypal opera diva.

After the straightforward, onstage opera pastiche and the qualified pastiche of Christine's introductory number, there is another level of pastiche to consider, one that links the backstage opera management with the onstage opera. In a finely constructed ensemble the interruptions of the various interested parties in "Notes"—in which the managers, Raoul, Carlotta, and Madame Giry exchange messages from the Opera Ghost and argue about their significance—leads directly into the number "Prima Donna," in which Carlotta is persuaded that she must appear on stage: "Prima donna, first lady of the stage!/Your devotees are on their knees to implore you!" It is a waltz of increasing vocal complexity as the characters break into ever-more separate, contrapuntal lines to voice their own individual concerns. Placed after the "Notes" scene, "Prima donna" has something of the poise found in those slow lyrical sections in opera finales, when time seems to be suspended as everyone reflects on the consequences of the dramas around them. But it also has that lyrical appeal of operetta, brought home most clearly in the recording by the Hamburg cast, in which the introductory phrase is subjected to that distinctive *Luftpausen* (hesitation) at the top of the melodic line and subsequent return to tempo which puts it firmly in the tradition of the Viennese waltz.[30] This is theater people talking to each other in theater language, and the false flattery of Carlotta is heightened by the adoption of such a "false" and "stagey" form for its delivery. The use of a set-piece number also represents the choice within the work itself to play on operatic conventions whose structures often halt the dramatic flow, and more continuous musical styles which allow for greater dramatic impetus.

But there is a little more going on here than the entertainment provided by a wonderfully indulgent and diverting ensemble. The waltz begins resolutely in C major. It is announced by major 2nds in the brass (F-G as the skeleton notes of a dominant 7th) that resolve into the "um-cha-cha" accompaniment on the tonic major, and so clash with the C♯/D♭ world of the Phantom. In this way, the oscillating semitones that underpin the Impressions theme represent the clash between the two worlds: "real" and "Phantom." To push the idea slightly further, it is worth considering whether, in the second refrain of "Prima Donna" (now modulated to F major) it is no mere accident that Madame Giry sings the word *Angel* in reference to Christine (and thus the Phantom, Christine's Angel) at the same time as André and Firmin sing the word in respect to Carlotta.[31] Madame Giry's "Angel" is sung to D♭, the theater managers' to D♮. In the "Notes" section before the "Prima Donna" ensemble, Madame Giry has been the earthly messenger and consequently the voice of the Phantom, adopting whole-tone descents for her warnings, "Who scorn his [the Phantom's] word, beware to those./The Angel sees, the angel knows," and then shortly afterward, "This hour shall see your darkest fears./The Angel knows, the angel hears." And Madame Giry continues this role as the mouthpiece of the Phantom in "Prima Donna" itself. Buried away in the middle of the contrapuntal texture of the second refrain (in F major) is her phrase "Heaven help you those who doubt./This miscasting will invite damnation"; these words are sung to a slightly altered form of the Impressions theme, so the Phantom, however hidden, is still present, still watching.[32] More overtly, the number concludes with an orchestral blast of chromatic scales derived from the Descent motif (see example 4.7), a defiant announcement that the Phantom is most definitely here.

Almost immediately on the tail of this late-nineteenth-century operetta ensemble comes a piece of classical opera pastiche, *Il muto* by Albrizzio. Again, critics have identified a variety of sources for this—Handel (surprisingly, given his writing of *opera seria*) and Salieri, for example—but it seems more to represent a fairly rough and ready generic pastiche of classical opera centered on Mozartian-style motifs of arpeggios and scales. The characters of the Countess and the breeches role (a woman playing a young man) Serafimo would tend to suggest the shade of *Le nozze di Figaro*, although cross-class liaisons and infidelity abound in late-eighteenth-century *opera buffa*. But the use of a rising five-note scale for the laugh in the main aria verse, its subsequent echo on the flute, and the following staccato coloratura arpeggios suggest *Die Zauberflöte* as a specific operatic influence. Beyond this, there is another possible source for *Il muto* more specific to French opera. André and Firmin have revived an old favorite at the Opéra; as it begins they comment:

"Il muto." © 1999 The Really Useful Group Ltd.

> ANDRÉ: Nothing like the old operas!
> FIRMIN: Or the old scenery
> ANDRÉ: The old singers
> FIRMIN: The old audience
> ANDRÉ: And every seat sold![33]

In the mid-eighteenth century, the Paris Opéra changed its repertory in an attempt to raise money and gain greater public support after losing the financial backing of Louis XV. Consequently, in 1752 the Opéra introduced not retrospective works of its own repertory but the novelty of Italian *intermezzi*, short comic works to be played between acts of the main theatrical presentation. They tended to have small casts who enacted dramas often involving the tricking of a man by a cunning woman in the cause of matrimony, or the cuckolding of a husband. Musically, they concentrated on direct, simple melody and harmony for the arias, but a good deal of linking recitative, similar to *Il muto*. The appropriateness of the reference for *The Phantom of the Opera* is that the 1752 performance at the Opéra of Pergolesi's 1733 intermezzo *La serva padrona* acted as a rallying point for those opposed to revivifying French opera through Italian influence; by extension, the debate called into question the political goals of France itself.[34]

The fierce dispute that resulted ran for two years and was named the Que-relle des Bouffons (War of the Buffoons) after the troupe of performers—the Bouffons—who had been employed to present the intermezzi. The idea of questioning the repertory, setting one style against another to provoke comparison and judgment, is a major theme underlying the shifting musical worlds of Lloyd Webber's show.

However, an exact source for *Il muto* is not that important for it to make its effect: the audience just needs to know that it is an old opera, older than *Hannibal.* The harpsichord accompaniment of the recitatives creates a gen-eral sense of period in a single chord or two, and the orchestration follows period conventions by centering on strings and harpsichord, with prominent oboe, immediately creating a distinction with the Romantic opera brass of *Hannibal* and the operetta woodwind in the refrain of "Notes."

Il muto serves a more fundamental structural purpose than that of being the vehicle in which Carlotta falls foul of the Phantom. It provides a classical model whose distortion becomes the opera written by the Phantom him-self, *Don Juan Triumphant,* part of which we see in act II. The characters in these two onstage operas are related but also reflect on the central story of Phantom, Christine, and Raoul: seduction provides the driving force of their plots, while deception and disguise are methods employed for achiev-ing it. Yet musically we are at an extreme in *Don Juan Triumphant,* with the classical certainties of tonic-dominant polarization replaced by atonal and whole-tone systems, and the regularity of classical periodicity now mutated to irregular phrase lengths and 5/4 or 7/8 meters. Virtually all of the musical material in the Phantom's new opera has already been introduced and so brings with it resonances from elsewhere in the show. For example, the open-ing chorus phrase is sung to a dissonant harmonization of the Impressions theme, which is appropriate enough, for the words of the chorus serve both Don Juan in the opera and the Phantom's announcement through others of his intentions toward Christine. The chorus (with the addition of Carlotta in the second stanza) sings:

Here the sire may serve the dam,
here the master takes his meat!
Here the sacrificial lamb
utters one despairing bleat!

Poor young maiden! For the thrill
on your tongue of stolen sweets

you will have to pay the bill—
tangled in the winding sheets!

There is a second meaning beneath the surface of the opera text, through which the Phantom presents on the public stage his private fantasy of Christine's submission to him as payment for his gift of song to her.

Just as Don Giovanni changes places with his manservant Leporello to effect his seduction of Donna Elvira's maid, so Don Juan has changed places with his manservant Passarino. But the world of the onstage opera has spilled over into the real world of the Opéra: the Phantom has murdered Piangi and taken his place as Don Juan. With this substitution, the *Don Juan Triumphant* scene becomes the real attempted seduction of Christine by the Phantom as the characters of Aminta and Don Juan, respectively. Moreover, with the choice of a banquet table as the setting for this scene, it is impossible to escape further associations with *Don Giovanni*. It is at the end of the banquet scene in Mozart's opera that Don Giovanni is finally dragged down to hell in retribution for his life lived so flagrantly outside the rules of society. At the end of the scene in *Phantom*, Christine is dragged down to a version of hell, the Phantom's lair; but her abduction in full view of the opera house staff, singers, audience, and armed gendarmes prompts the formation of the mob that ultimately hunts him down.[35]

The music for *Don Juan Triumphant* is labored. Its juxtaposition of existing thematic material is obvious and its effect fragmented. The structural blocks of this short extract are clumsy, and its attempts through tonality, meter, and orchestration to seem different sound forced. This is entirely appropriate, for the Phantom is the outsider whose view ultimately we must fail to share; he is also a sterile character, his urge for artistic creation consequently subject to his own self-aggrandizement, the promotion of his own ego.[36] He is the character of Christine's present—not future or past—and thus his modernist musical vision is dramatically fixed, unable to evolve. The ultimate sign of his musical failure comes, paradoxically, in the most effective part of the opera and indeed one of the best sections of the whole show. In "The Point of No Return" tonality is reestablished—G minor for the verse (using the Memories melody [see example 4.6], by this point so familiar), and F minor (a depressing effect on the tonality, amplified by the funeral march effect of the *andante deliberato* pacing) for the refrain. Or, to look at it from the opposite direction, the deliberate fragmentation of tonality and meter in the introductory sections of *Don Juan Triumphant* makes "The Point of No Return" suddenly sound focused and direct.

Throughout the scene, as each sings of an impending choice, of no way back, the audience in the theater is drawn in by the duality of Christine/Aminta and Phantom/Don Juan and the consequent ambiguity of the lyrics. Christine's words as Aminta fight with the thoughts of Christine herself; the Phantom has given Christine his scenario and the audience knows it is not hers:

> I have come here,
> hardly knowing the reason why. . . .
> In my mind
> I've already imagined our
> bodies entwining,
> defenceless and silent.[37]

But when Christine continues, "And now I am here with you: no second thoughts, / I've decided, decided," is she reasserting herself or voicing the Phantom's fundamental understanding of what the true outcome must be? The declaration of her own death sentence seems clear in the following refrain, as an on-the-beat snare drum conjures a march to the scaffold. Eventually the Phantom's Don Juan mask drops and he becomes himself for his declaration of love, again using Raoul's love song from the end of act I, "All I Ask of You."

The Point of No Return

The final section of the show is a rapid rerun of dramatic and musical material already established. To the stark contrast of now-familiar musical themes, the positioning of Christine between her two opposing suitors is re-rehearsed, a précis before the decision required for the dénouement. Having been swept back down to the underground lair, Christine confronts the Phantom directly by adopting the whole-tone phrase decorated with minor 2nds, punctuated by the insistent repeating clashing 2nds, all from *Don Juan Triumphant*: thus she speaks to him in his own language. It is here that the full force of the modernist drive in the Phantom's musical language is made clear, as Christine utters vocal phrases in a manner far from her lyric style in the rest of the show:

Have you gorged yourself
at last, in your
lust for blood?

There is an ugliness and angularity in both the words and the music of this, and the contrast between the more lyrical vocal expectations of her and the raw reality of the sound gives the phrases an added sense of shock and power. Set to the Threat motif (see example 4.13), the words take on a defiant tone, especially with the upward leap that accents the final word, *blood*. It is the shock of new, made more apparent through the vehicle of its delivery. She, however, can cope with it better than Piangi, whose inability to come to terms with new musical ideas, as exemplified by his repeated inability to sing a whole-tone phrase, results in his murder as the ultimate gesture of artistic criticism.

There is a challenge in the music of the Phantom to which the young Christine is able to rise; she comprehends his intentions dramatically and musically, but does not wish to adopt them for her own. The resolution of the story which joins her to Raoul is a vote not just for social convention but for artistic conservatism. The adoption of the Don Juan story for his opera has a further level, in that the Phantom is interpreting a familiar tale in a new way; he acknowledges the old form but wants to sweep it away with his own new version. His musical language is in direct competition with that of *Il muto* and *Hannibal*, and even the lyrical music of the offstage Opéra world. And that musical language owes much to Stravinsky in its contrasting sections and textures, dissonant harmonies, and aggressive style, anticipating, within the drama's chronology, some of those elements that shocked audiences when *Le Sacre du printemps* was first performed in Paris in May 1913. As related through the Regression (see example 4.5) and Lair (see example 4.6) themes, the Phantom's musical language in the earlier parts of the show seem to belong to the whole-tone, impressionistic world of Debussy. But as act II progresses, his musical tone becomes something more visceral and brutal, with a Fauvist vision decades ahead of itself, forming yet another part of the commentary that Lloyd Webber's stylistic pastiche creates through the whole show.

After Christine has rounded on the Phantom in so unexpected a way, the Phantom attempts melodramatically to subdue her through a self-pitying description that plays on his deformity, corrupting the seductive associations of "The Music of the Night," to which the lyrics are set. But he receives an unexpected rebuff when, to a version of her earlier Sympathy theme (example 4.4), she declares that his disfigured face is not the root of his corruption, but "It's in your soul that the true distortion lies." She has rejected him not for his looks but for his malign soul and wicked actions, a distinction that distinguishes this version of the story from most of the previous dramatic adaptations. The arrival of Raoul, however, prevents the Phantom from responding to Christine's insight, which has been long in coming; having failed in his initial tactics, he now uses Raoul for his bargaining power. Raoul pleads for him to free Christine (the Interruption theme [see example 4.12] to reflect his intrusion), but to no effect; indeed, the Phantom entices him further into the lair and traps him in a noose. Christine can now save him only if she gives in to the Phantom. But again, Christine is having none of this bullying; she ripostes with the Sympathy theme variant again to the lines:

> The tears I might have shed
> for your dark fate
> grow cold, and turn to tears
> of hate.

The Phantom is emotionally foiled again.

The following trio weaves together the three principals' voices: the Phantom sings of Christine's need to choose, to the music "The Point of No Return"; Christine interpolates her disillusionment; Raoul, still the lover, in phrases from "All I Ask of You," declares his life finished without her. Finally, Christine gets to do something positive, empowered by her realization of the truth about her erstwhile tutor. She plays on his vanity by appealing to him as the Angel of Music, the one worthy element of him that she knows, and the persona of the Phantom that she was formerly prepared to trust unquestioningly.[38] The Phantom does not give in but demands that she choose at once. Still to the "Angel of Music" song, Christine's pity overcomes her fear and she kisses him. The Phantom releases Raoul. For a third time the resolution of the emotional triangle is prevented, for the mob is heard approaching to hunt down "this animal," "this monster," "this murdering beast," "this creature"; back with the myth of the Phantom, their music is not surprisingly that of the title song, the Phantom of the horror caricature. Over these chorus cries the Phantom tells Christine and Raoul to take the boat and leave, a scenario that evokes the climax of Benjamin Britten's opera *Peter Grimes*.

The final section pulls together in fast succession all of the most sympathetic ideas of the Phantom in one sequence. The deformed imagery is touchingly portrayed as the Phantom sings along to the little music box words which by now have a literal/physical and metaphorical/emotional meaning:

> Masquerade
> Paper faces on parade
> Masquerade
> hide your face
> so the world will
> never find you

Christine reappears, to music marked *con molto passione*, and hands back the ring the Phantom gave her. This breaks the final link between them as she asserts herself apart from him: she will never be his. The Phantom makes one last declaration of love to her, one whose cadence is resolved only when we hear Christine singing of her love in the distance to Raoul. The verbal and musical reply to the Phantom's "Christine, I love you" is sung to the other man, and in that central key of Db major, Lloyd Webber's key of "resonance." The Phantom's final outburst, to the closing phrases of "Music of the Night," emphatically marks the end: "It's over now, the music of the night." There is neither a Descent motif or a Name theme at the very end, nor any reference to the main "Phantom of the Opera" song: that Phantom has been vanquished, losing his power to terrify. Thus the last bars we hear are of that sequence of Mystic chords (see example 4.10), a representation not of the horror myth but of the Phantom's highest aspirations, both musical and romantic, the ones that make him most identifiably human.

A Piece of Hokum?

There is no doubt that *The Phantom of the Opera* has been one of the most successful pieces of musical theater ever in terms of its sustained popularity and global dissemination. At the time of writing, the London production has been running at Her Majesty's since October 9, 1986; the New York production at the Majestic has been running since January 26, 1988: more than seventeen and sixteen years, respectively. It has toured extensively in the United States and Canada, and productions have been mounted around the world: in Europe (Austria, Belgium, Denmark, Germany, the Netherlands, Sweden, and Spain in 2002), Australia, Latin America (Mexico), the

Far East (Japan and Korea, with China also in future sights). Cast recordings have sold in vast numbers. What accounts for the show's longevity? What has made it so consistently attractive to audiences? Is it the quality of the work itself or the manner of its presentation? Has the "hokum" of Gaston Leroux's tale been translated into something more substantial in the stage adaptation? For Michael Walsh, the show "was Lloyd Webber's most daring and sophisticated score, and it perceptibly changed his reputation. Musicians who had remained resistant to the charms of his melodies suddenly began to take notice, and those for whom opera was not by definition a dead art form quickly realized that here, indeed, was serious new work."[39] Frank Rich took a different line when reviewing the New York opening, finding the show "long on pop professionalism and melody, impoverished of artistic personality and passion. . . . *The Phantom of the Opera* is as much a victory of dynamic stagecraft over musical kitsch as it is a triumph of merchandising über alles. . . . Mr. Lloyd Webber's esthetic has never been more baldly stated than in this show, which favors the decorative trappings of art over the troublesome substance of culture and finds more eroticism in rococo opulence and conspicuous consumption than in love or sex."[40]

Certainly it is a triumph of stagecraft, with Hal Prince's direction very much that of the broad image and the large-scale gesture. The focus on romance rather than realism and the sheer indulgence of the direction in that whole concept strengthen the sense that the show is about more than just three characters, for its sentimentality can find some point of resonance in everyone in the audience. Perhaps the sheer scale of it all begins to tire in act II, which is principally focused on just three people, but spectacle is a crucial part of the original story, and the continued reflection of this in the stage musical is more than apt. Maria Björnson's design amplifies this with the indulgence and artifice of the opera costuming in brilliant colors, contrasting with the elegant and dark restraint of the evening dress. Beyond this, the bright opera sets themselves, with their detailed naturalism—albeit painted on and one-dimensional—have a different quality of reality from the more sparse and dark settings of underground lair or rooftop. Moreover, a formal backdrop is used only in the onstage opera scenes, creating a further contrast as the consciously restricted space of the opera house stage in performance—a world of control and limitation—is juxtaposed with scenes that extend into the unknown of the surrounding darkness, a realm of possibility and surprise.

Authenticity in design is evident (the chandelier is a copy of the one

The Phantom as the Red Death. © 1999 The Really Useful Group Ltd.

at the Palais Garnier, for example), and this lends authenticity to the story: the historical accuracy of the imagery spills over into the plot itself. Again, the real and unreal blur at the edges. In London there is even greater resonance, for the theater that launched the show is closely linked to the story's atmosphere. A theater has been on this plot in the Haymarket since 1705, when the Queen's Theatre opened on April 9 with an opera by Giacomo Greber, *The Loves of Ergasto*. It became the King's Theatre in 1714 after the death of Queen Anne; Handel's first opera for London, *Rinaldo*, premiered in 1711 at this theater, which became considered the city's home for Italian opera. After a fire in 1789 the theater was rebuilt, opening on March 10, 1791; reconstructed again in 1818, it was generally known as the Italian Opera House, but was officially renamed Her Majesty's Theatre in 1837, the year of the accession of Queen Victoria. A third theater with the same name was constructed in 1868–69 after yet another fire and opened as an opera house in 1877 with a production of Bellini's *Norma*. In 1891 its contents were auctioned off—as in the *Phantom* prologue—prior to demolition in preparation for a new building. A fourth theater, with the same name, was built on the site in 1896–97, and this is the present building: an opera house with decoration and design from about the era of the *Phantom* story.[41]

There is reputedly a ghost in Her Majesty's (but then most theaters in the West End seem to have one), and on the first level below the stage are pieces of original Victorian stage-machinery winches. Contrary to the usual tale—and to Hal Prince's wish expressed on the first day of rehearsals to return to such mechanical authenticity—these are not used in the performances; they stand idly by as tributes to an earlier age, while more modern equipment fulfills their roles. The old star trap is still used for the disappearance of the Phantom as the Red Death, but most of the technology of the show is a modern reworking of an earlier idea. Although the old device of Pepper's Ghost could create the effect of the Phantom's appearance in the mirror of Christine's dressing room, it is in fact achieved with a mirrored gauze.[42] Mid- rather than hi-tech—there is no fancy tracking for the gondola: it is a motorized go-kart steered by remote control from the wings— the mechanics do retain some nod to tradition, with more manual operation than would perhaps be expected nowadays in a complex staging such as this. But sitting in the theater now one still has a sense of rightness: a late Victorian opera house hosting so apt a show. And below the stage today are three cellars; from the first the other two can be vaguely seen in the receding gloom. In Leroux's novel, it was through the third cellar below the stage of the Palais Garnier that the Phantom entered his underground lair.

Credit for the show's phenomenal staying power must also go to the adoption of a strong and familiar storyline. The symbolism inherent in the central characters and their relationships is accessible on many levels, and it is impossible not to sense at least some part of this underlying web of interpretational possibilities. With its referencing of such fables as Beauty and the Beast, Trilby and Svengali, and Faust, alongside a long list of related films and direct film adaptations, any member of the audience is likely to have at least one point of ready recognition before the prologue starts. And the issues in the drama are portrayed clearly, made all the more tangible by the self-evident nature of much of the thematic structure of the music. For some, the often blunt moves from one theme to another lack subtlety, but then the show's fundamental construction aims to reveal character through the clashes of these musical worlds rather than through progressive motivic evolution—a technique in Lloyd Webber that was first seen in *Jesus Christ Superstar* and further explored in *Evita*. But where *The Phantom of the Opera* differs from those two predecessors is in its more coherent use of theme and motif around the still-present, more full Lloyd Webber melodies. This focusing on smaller portions of musical material, each to be identified with an emotional area within the drama and thus used to invite reflection or commentary upon them, bridges the gap between the aggressive and larger melodic juxtapositions of *Evita* and the greater thematic fluidity of *Aspects of Love*. The dovetailing or jarring of these juxtapositions has its own drama that contributes to the effectiveness of the score; there is musical conflict to match the emotional conflict. This blatant presentation of the musical material is disarming: it is very clearly exactly what it purports to be. From such a stance, it adds its own coherent structure and emotional coloring to the show beyond some kitsch level that requires obfuscation through the visual drama of the production itself. In other words, the musical material is handled in as "up-front" a way as the rest of the production. Equally, while the big numbers with changed lyrics are portable from show to show (many of Lloyd Webber's melodies have begun in one project and finished up in another, a practice common to most show composers), they are nonetheless integrated within this particular score.

Old and new are also set against each other throughout the show, in a cross-genre, cross-temporal hybrid. In his biography of Lloyd Webber, *Cats on a Chandelier*, Michael Coveney sees "the balancing of operatic pastiche with his own idiosyncratic rock romanticism [as] a distinctive feature of Lloyd Webber's score."[43] Such a score and such a production as this questions the boundaries of musical and opera. Is this a popular opera or an operatic musical? The answer is that it is neither; the cross-fertilization between the various forms of lyric theater and between classical and pop music have given the work its own identity.

The Phantom of the Opera is Lloyd Webber's very own "piece of hokum," but it knows it and he knows it. For in the theater, this is not a show of wry reflection and overt self-analysis but one of quite deliberate indulgence. As Lloyd Webber put it, "I wanted to write from my heart rather than with my head."[44] It presents Leroux's story sentimentally by concentrating on the emotional lives of the three central characters and elevating mystery above explanation. It is melodramatic in the heightened dramatic and musical responses of the characters. It is a show of broad gestures and demonstrative passion. It is indulgent of the audience in its sensual appeal in sound and look. It is wrapped in both romance and Romanticism.

 CHAPTER 5

"I'm Ready for My Close-Up": Lloyd Webber on Screen

Although he had periodically denied he was a movie lover, Lloyd Webber had long been obsessed with cinema. Ever since he was a boy watching *The Sound of Music* for the twentieth time in one of the Leicester Square theaters, he had dreamed of getting his musicals up there on the big screen as well.
—MICHAEL WALSH

T RANSLATION TO CINEMA IS NOT A SURPRISING AMBITION FOR A fan of musical theater, for the life of a stage musical is complemented by a screen life. In the 1950s, the decade during which Lloyd Webber became aware of both stage and film, big-screen versions of many major Broadway shows were made, many of them quite faithful to their Broadway originals. There had always been a relationship between the Broadway musical stage show and the Hollywood musical. For example, in the 1930s several operettas were put on screen (Herbert's *Naughty Marietta*, 1935; Romberg's *Rose-Marie*, 1936, and *Maytime*, 1937; Kern's *Show Boat*, 1936), and Broadway's song composers and lyricists—George and Ira Gershwin, Cole Porter, Irving Berlin, Jerome Kern, and Richard Rodgers, for example—were also those of Hollywood. Many film musicals were made in the 1940s, especially with the gradual ascendancy of the Freed unit at MGM, but not until the 1950s did faithful Hollywood transfers of Broadway shows really take off. Until the early 1970s most of the major hit Broadway shows became films, including such works as *Kiss Me, Kate* (1953), *Oklahoma!* and *Guys and Dolls* (1955), *Carousel* and *The King and I* (1956), *The Pajama Game* (1957), *South Pacific* (1958), *West Side Story* (1961), *Gypsy* and *The Music Man* (1962), *Bye Bye Birdie* (1963), *My Fair Lady* (1964), *The Sound of Music* (1965), *How to Succeed in Business* and *Camelot* (1967), *Sweet Charity* and

Hello, Dolly! (1969), and *Fiddler on the Roof* (1971). Economics increasingly played a part in the decline of what was inevitably an expensive branch of the film industry, and beginning in the 1970s film versions of stage shows became exceptions, although sometimes notable ones: *Cabaret* (1972, with a substantially changed storyline), *Annie* (1982), *A Chorus Line* (1985). *Chicago* (2002) seems to have prompted a new interest in the genre.

For anyone wanting to get to know the core repertory of musical theater, film versions of stage shows are an ideal place to start, easier than finding locally a live, professional performance: films are frequently screened on television, and many are on video and DVD. A widely distributed new film can reach many more people in a day than a successful stage show can in a year of Broadway or West End sellouts, and that in turn allows for the musical numbers to be disseminated ever more widely. Think of the Disney musical cartoons and the way in which the songs from their scores have become part of a certain cultural consciousness, whether it be "Whistle While You Work," "Supercalifragilisticexpialidocious," or "The Circle of Life." Film musicals present a clear advantage to any composer or lyricist.

The stage musical canon has also been informed in a large part by what has been accessible on film. A score and libretto may serve the more experienced and trained enthusiast, while a cast recording may allow for a familiarity of the music numbers; but for most people it is the clear presentation of the music and characters within the structure of the whole drama that is satisfying, and in the absence of a live performance only film can do this. In turn, the existence of a musical on film can affect the stage repertory, as producers of professional stage shows or local amateur societies, eager to attract their audiences, choose works with a "name." Plots and scores may have been altered en route to the big screen, but this does not matter—the title alone is enough to generate a familiarity and commercial appeal. How many audience members escape the image of Julie Andrews as Maria or Liza Minelli as Sally Bowles when they watch a live performance, even though Mary Martin or Jill Haworth created on stage those iconic musical theater characters? And how many amateur performers on stage imagine themselves similarly transformed? The canon of stage musicals has undoubtedly been influenced by the film repertory, essentially American and strongly weighted toward a period from post–World War II to the mid-1960s.

Not every stage show has been filmed, and those that have not find it harder to retain their place in the active stage repertory: availability and exposure are essential to longevity. British musical theater has particularly suffered. There was never as strong a link between the British film industry and the West End as there was between Broadway and Hollywood, so very little of the West End repertory, no matter how successful in the theater, was filmed. Vivian Ellis, Ivor Novello, and Noël Coward are all thinly represented, and the few films there are of their works are poor; extensive rewriting for the film of *Expresso Bongo* (1959) did a fine and innovative show no favors; *Half a Sixpence* (1967) and *Oliver!* (1968) were later exceptions. Equally, shows considered today as worthy of revival but not immediately successful when first produced do not exist on film. Composers who have benefited through the rarer more recent film adaptations (although to varying degrees of success) have included Jerry Herman (*Hello, Dolly!* and *Mame*), Charles Strouse (*Bye Bye Birdie* and *Annie*), and Stephen Sondheim (*A Funny Thing Happened on the Way to the Forum* and *A Little Night Music*). With two feature-film adaptations of his works — *Jesus Christ Superstar* and *Evita* — Lloyd Webber has joined a select group of his contemporaries. Video, with its lower costs, has in part filled some of the gaps, with versions available in that format (often of live performances) of most of the Sondheim repertory and others, such as Broadway's *Victor/Victoria* and the West End's more recent *Oklahoma!* Home video is increasingly a way to tap into the potential circulation that a screen version allows, and Lloyd Webber has taken full advantage of this with his own repertory in recent years.

Film also brings with it the chance of greater financial returns: for example, the film of *Evita* grossed some $45 million in the United States in its first four months, while the video, DVD, and album sales (along with a new Oscar-winning single of the interpolated "You Must Love Me") extended the commercial life and public profile of the show. Such opportunities were clear to the business empire of the Really Useful Group, and in the early 1990s, under the management of the new chief executive, Patrick McKenna, plans included a new film production company based in Los Angeles. The intention was to make seven major films over a few years, beginning with *Whistle Down the Wind*, already completed as a film score.[1] At various points, film plans have intersected with the lives of most of the Lloyd Webber shows, often with unrealized ambitions. Between 1990 and 1995 there were various announcements for imminent film versions of *The Phantom of the Opera*, *Evita*, *Cats*, *Starlight Express* (as cartoon and television series), and *Aspects of Love*.[2] In 1995 Lloyd Webber said: "I'm taking on Hollywood. . . . We don't need a studio to make the pictures. There's nothing we need apart from distribution. And our partners over at Polygram are thinking about a distribution arm."[3] These plans have not come to fruition, at least not in their original form; home video and DVD, rather than cinema, have come to be of increasing significance to the Lloyd Webber repertory. However, the film of *The Phantom of the Opera* is still very much an active project. A screen adaptation announced in 1990, with Sarah Brightman and Michael Crawford as Christine and Phantom and Joel Schumacher as the director, failed to materialize. After many years of expectation, casting rumors, and changing scripts and scriptwriters (at one point a script by Ben Elton, author of *The Beautiful Game*, was under consideration), the filming of *Phantom* finally began at England's Pinewood Studios on 15 September 2003. With a screenplay by Lloyd Webber and Schumacher, the eventual casting includes Gerard Butler in the title role, Emmy Rossum as Christine, and Patrick Wilson as Raoul. Almost twenty years after the stage premiere, *Phantom* is currently scheduled to reach the cinema in time for Christmas 2004.

But the traffic has not been all one way. While stage musicals have been filmed, film musicals have increasingly been staged. Hugh Martin and Ralph Blane took the classic MGM Judy Garland musical *Meet Me in St. Louis* (1944) onto the stage in 1960 (in St. Louis) and in a revised version on Broadway in 1989. *42nd Street*, the Broadway adaptation of a film about putting on a Broadway show, ran in New York for 3,500 performances beginning in August 1980 and has been revived there subsequently. The rights to another Judy Garland classic, *A Star Is Born*, were acquired by Lloyd Webber in 1995, and a version using its Harold Arlen score was announced for the West End stage, scheduled for some two years later, to be produced but not written by Lloyd Webber. However, the production never materialized. More recently on Broadway there has been the stage version of Mel Brooks's film *The Producers*; in the West End, there have been stage versions of *Doctor Dolittle*, *Fame*, *Saturday Night Fever*, and *Chitty Chitty Bang Bang*. With preexisting songs, these works are obvious contenders for musical stage adaptation, provided that the appropriate visual effects can be found to match the expectations raised by the films. But film has also provided a source of straight drama for adaptation to musical form: Coleman's *Sweet Charity* was developed from Fellini's *Nights of Cabiria*, Sondheim's *A Little Night Music* from Bergman's *Smiles of a Summer Night*, and Yeston's *Nine* from another Fellini film, 8½. Two Lloyd Webber musicals have arisen through this route of nonmusical film to musical stage.

From Film to Musical: A Change of Focus

Sunset Boulevard (1993) was the first of two stage musicals from Lloyd Webber based primarily on existing films; *Whistle Down the Wind* (Washington, 1996; London, 1998) was the second. The first show kept close to its source, while the second combined elements of a film and its source novel, then relocated it to a different continent and a different time. While these seem to be substantially different approaches to adapting a film for the stage, in practice both methods yielded similar techniques and concerns to those running through the Lloyd Webber repertory. In essence, the methods of change of each from film to stage reveal fundamental aspects of Lloyd Webber's approach to music drama.

Sunset Boulevard

The level of adaptation for the stage of *Sunset Boulevard* was neatly summarized by Billy Wilder, director of the original, now-classic film: "I congratulate Don Black and Christopher Hampton on something ingenious—they left the story alone, that's already a very ingenious idea. . . . I was very much astonished when I heard the words, many of them retained and some of them to music."[4] Of course, the film story was altered in many ways by Lloyd Webber, his writers Hampton and Black, and his director Trevor Nunn. But Wilder's point is that so much of both the essence and the detail is still there that the impression is of a very faithful adaptation, one that kept so close at points that the car chase, for example, used projections of the scene from the original film.[5] In any case, it would be unwise for anyone to remove such now-classic exchanges as:

> JOE GILLIS: You used to be big.
> NORMA DESMOND: I *am* big. It's the pictures that got small.[6]

The basic structure of the film remains, although with a few transpositions of location. For example, the opening sequence takes place as in the film, with the dead body in the swimming pool and narration from the character who eventually turns out to be the dead man himself. But the film next places Joe in his flat, then on the road visiting the movie man Sheldrake, and then at the golf course which his agent frequents; the musical immediately puts Joe into the world of Hollywood through a scene on the Paramount lot. As in the film, Joe is being pursued by the finance men who

Sunset Boulevard, the American version on CD (photo: Joan Marcus). © 1994 The Really Useful Group Ltd.

intend to repossess his car; Joe's strategies to avoid them cause his accidental meeting with Norma Desmond, and hence spark into action the drama that follows. But the finance men are introduced in the musical after the film studio context is established, not before it. Later, in the film, a shopping trip is set in a gentleman's outfitters; for the musical, the store has been closed and the shop comes to Norma Desmond's mansion. These are not just practical solutions to reduce the number of different locations that have to be presented on stage; the changes fulfill other functions as well: the shift of the shopping spree, for example, helps emphasize the wealth of Norma— although no longer a working film star she owns property and oil—and it brings another scene within the claustrophobic mansion.[7] Where the film could range freely around many locations, it was to the constant advantage of a stage show, essentially built on a chamber scale around only four characters, to use a stronger polarity of film world and Norma's world. So scenes reallocated to Norma's mansion contribute to the growing sense in the musical of a world that Joe increasingly cannot escape.

The major challenge was to find a way of introducing the music, and some of the clues for how to approach this were already present in Franz Waxman's score. For example, the music of Joe Gillis began in a contemporary, film noir style: aggressive and punchy phrases, discordant, something representing the uncertainty and hardness of his life. But with Joe's arrival at the house on Sunset Boulevard a new tone enters the underscoring as he describes what he has discovered.[8] The mood changes further when he meets Norma, and the richer sounds of an exotic theme on strings convey how apart from his world is that of the former film star, while also building on her silent-screen persona through its heightened expressiveness. Joe's wisecracks ("Next time I'll bring my autograph book or maybe a hunk of cement and ask for your footprint") and naturalistic presentation provide the perfect foil to Norma's grand style of speech and movement.

Like the relocation of scenes, the music creates a more polarized mansion-studio opposition on stage. The first sounds in the theater are those of low rich strings in a hypnotic melody of unfulfilled longing, represented in the opening rising phrase that initially shies away from achieving its potential melodic heights. Norma and her romantic era of silent film are introduced before anything else, so the atmosphere surrounding Norma is established — unlike in the film — before we meet her. By contrast, Joe's music is much more restless and anxious, heard immediately in his opening narration: "I guess it was five a.m./A homicide had been reported/From one of those crazy mansions up on Sunset."[9] This aspect of Joe is portrayed most notably in the title song that opens act II, described by Lloyd Webber in a television interview as being specifically "about that restlessness." In the same program, the lyricist Don Black explained that Lloyd Webber

kept on writing this strange, jagged, splintered music, and how do we get words on these notes, because nothing seemed to have a rhyming pattern? And it worked, funnily enough, because we [Black and Hampton] wrote something that didn't really rhyme, but was an emotional outpouring. He [Joe Gillis] says in the middle — and he's singing this to the world really as a general statement—

> You think I've sold out?
> Dead right I've sold out.
>
> . . . .
>
> And if I'm honest
> I like the lady
> I can't help being
> Touched by her folly.
> I'm treading water,
> Taking the money,
> Watching her sunset . . .
> Well, I'm a writer.[10]

The words are a more direct expression of Joe's feelings than anything he says in the film. His understated mood of cynicism needs to be stronger, even aggressive, to carry it over the footlights. It becomes a direct speech "to the world" (the theater audience), musically led by the cumulative effect of the stressed first beat of each bar in the 5/8 melody and the repetition of single-bar sequences, rising, then falling.[11] The song concentrates a slowly growing atmosphere achieved in the film through subtle vocal tone or glance into a clearer, bigger statement. Joe needs to wear his heart on his sleeve, for the musical theater audience at least.

The difference between the tense rhythms and insistent repetitions of Joe and the languorous melodies of Norma becomes increasingly apparent, but Joe's music in its turn sets him apart from the rest of the show's char-acters who inhabit the world on the edges of the drama: Artie, Betty, the film folk, and the shop assistants and beauticians. Youth and the contempo-rary (film) world are portrayed in bright dance rhythms, the short phrases of lively American popular song, animated further with brassy swing band orchestration, as in "Every Movie's a Circus" and "This Time Next Year." When Joe talks to Betty as an equal in this young world, he adopts a con-temporary style, albeit taken from the more romantic end of the popular musical spectrum, first in "Girl Meets Boy," then in its more serious paral-lel—the opening phrases of their refrains are linked—in "Too Much in Love to Care," whose period overtones are those of the Broadway ballad, espe-cially Rodgers and Hammerstein. In this way, Joe's self-obsession to survive in a contemporary hostile world is musically portrayed to counter Norma's romantic self-obsession with faded glory and times past. Both their sound worlds contrast with the rousing, if more impersonal, popular musical styles of the various character groups that decorate but seldom interact signifi-cantly with the plot.

While this opposition of musical styles is presented immediately in the theater, it is a much more insidious force in the film. Musical underscor-ing is limited for the first half of the film to transitional moments as the action moves from one place to another, or to Joe's voice-overs, which de-scribe events from his perspective; the dialogue is not underscored. Thus the music begins as representing Joe's emotional state, and Norma only gradu-ally gains a musical identity as Joe gets to know her more and more. The very long underscoring for the two concurrent New Year's Eve parties, at Norma's guestless mansion and Artie's guest-filled flat, marks a shift in the film's use of music, which now emphasizes the emotions behind the dialogue rather than underscoring transitional passages. Low in the audience consciousness but working away under the surface, the effect is that Norma's heightened reality gradually comes to dominate Norma and Joe's uncomfortably shared world as her emotional undercurrents are progressively voiced in the score in place of his. The uneasy match of Joe's character with Norma's music becomes increasingly noticeable—for example, with the orchestral buildup as Norma becomes more agitated while waiting for Joe to return on what will prove to be his last night alive. After Norma's mischievous telephone call to Betty is thrown into relief through its absence of underscoring, Joe seems unmoved and keeps his distance, at which point Franz Waxman's music parallels Norma's crying and histrionic speech, echoing her emotions, not his. The total subsumption of the film atmosphere within the dominating figure of Norma is marked in the final music, as the sounds of Norma the silent film star match the closing shot of her self-engrossed face.

This is what the stage musical cannot do: you cannot have a close-up in a theater of two thousand seats—at least not literally, as you can on screen. An equivalent effect can be found in the solo song, a musical soliloquy in which a character can express in detail his or her thoughts and emotions, in which "real" time is suspended and music marks the emotionally raised stakes. In the musical of *Sunset Boulevard,* distinctive lines from the film provide the spur for song lyrics in such moments of musical emphasis. The expansion of these crucial ideas or moments into "arias" focuses attention on them in the show just as the film uses the close-up. For example, "With One Look" arises from the first appearance of Norma Desmond as she tackles Joe over the impact of sound on the film industry. Gloria Swanson's overemphatic face and arms in the film provide a hypnotic contrast to the understated performance of William Holden as Joe Gillis and to his world, from which Norma has been insulated in the reclusion of her mansion-cocoon. This change of presentational style in the film—from that of Joe to that of Norma—is reflected in the musical through a solo song for Norma. Now the music and poetic verse structure become a lens to match the film's use of the heightened visual style of Swanson's performance. Music and lyrics in the show reflect the evocation of character by physical gesture in the film. Norma's dominance at this moment, culminating in the commanding spoken words "Now get out," puts her clearly center stage, the place "where I was born to be," as she so evidently believes.

Another example of the creation of a stage analogue to a film effect is found in the sequence where Norma and Joe view one of her silent films. In

Wilder's film it is a strong moment for its silence: no musical underscore, only the faint sound of the running projector as the young Norma in character is seen praying. This silent concentration on the film is broken by Norma: "Still wonderful isn't it. And no dialogue. We didn't need dialogue, we had faces. There just aren't any faces like that anymore. Maybe one, Garbo. Oh, those idiot producers, those imbeciles. Haven't they got eyes? Have they forgotten what a star looks like? I'll show them. I'll be up there again, so help me!" And with the last phrases she stands up in the projector beam, slowly turning to reveal her profile, emphasized by the sudden interjection of a high woodwind trill in the film score. The sequence is all about the image of a face and the power of its unvoiced expression; yet neither the silence nor the use of profile can be as effective in a live musical. On stage, this moment finds its expression in its technical opposite, the song "New Ways to Dream." It is a ritualistic number through its verse structure, prominent reiterations of the word *dream*, and hymnlike melody; indeed, both film and musical make it explicit that the rerunning of Norma's old films, eloquent in portraying her inability to move beyond her past, is a weekly rite.[12]

And to return to that most famous of screen close-ups, the one at the end of *Sunset Boulevard*, in which Norma's undulating and twisting arms are at once repellent and seductive. The idea of the close-up—the intense concentration on a single character—is achieved on stage through three methods. First, the lines of the reprise of the coda to "With One Look" express Norma's total self-belief and self-deception, and the audience is fascinated by its glorious madness:

> This time I'm staying
> I'm staying for good
> I'll be back
> Where I was born to be
> With one look
> I'll be me.

Second the big, solo, vocal finish is impossible to ignore, with a powerful and assured musical sound at odds with the truth of the situation portrayed; in addition, the coda has the flourish of a fanfare, evoking the musical identification of MGM or Paramount, so Norma is announcing the end of her own drama. Third, Norma is physically center stage, spotlit in her grotesquely excessive costume and makeup. Combined, these devices put the focus of the audience totally on her: "And now Mr. De Mille, I'm ready for my close-up."[13]

Other aspects of the film needed adapting to suit the demands of a large theater, particularly an understated quality which, if left unchanged, would not register. Eric von Stroheim's portrayal of Max in the film leaves no doubt as to his possessive attachment to Norma and his deep resentment of Joe, but it is shown in the slightest of gestures, the smallest of inflections beneath an otherwise stern reserve: for example, the way he carries Joe's suitcases out when Joe is finally leaving is just that bit too quick. The stage show needs to signal this more clearly, hence Max's number "The Greatest Star of All," sung as Joe is established in the guestroom over the garage. The increasing passion of the verses gives Max a level of self-expression he would not deign to expose so soon to a stranger in his film portrayal, and the lyrics in fact use imagery from dialogue much later on in the film (such as the Maharajah's stocking). But the musical has to begin characterizing him earlier and giving bigger clues of his idolization of Norma, and so set up the motivation for his complicity in her self-delusions. The Max of the film emerges silently from shadows, he hints but never quite states, he is an ever-critical presence at Joe's shoulder. This portentous, slowly evolving side of the character does not sit so well with a musical that needs more overt emotional material to bring its characters to life.[14]

Although much of the detail remained the same in this adaptation from screen to stage, the way that music and song are employed has altered substantially the pacing of the drama and shifted its emotional center of gravity. It strengthens the faded romanticism of Norma's world at the expense of Joe's cynical and contemporary one, so the whole mood of the work develops into something more rich, lugubrious, and egocentric. In the film the audience observes Gloria Swanson at the end with fascinated horror, adopting the perspective of those transfixed journalists and cameramen on the stairs; in the musical, the final image, visual and aural, seems to swamp the audience, and the musical theater star dominates completely. To put it another way, where the film's final image is of a mad murderess performing to a nonexistent audience of fans (her real audience is that of the newsreel), in live theater it is difficult to escape the reality of the musical theater star performing to a real audience. The passing of the era of the silent film incarnated in one becomes the triumphant reassertion of the stage musical genre itself in the other.

Whistle Down the Wind

Unlike the transition of *Sunset Boulevard* from screen direct to stage, a double heritage is claimed for *Whistle Down the Wind*, arising both from the children's novel by Mary Hayley Bell (written in 1957 and published in the following year) and from the film of the book (1961), directed by Bryan Forbes.[15] The film and musical versions are not separate, parallel adaptations from a common single source, and in a brief foreword to the 1997 edition of the novel, Lloyd Webber acknowledges both novel and film as his inspiration. In fact, the novel has been so strongly mediated by the film on its way to the musical stage that the film seems the primary source of the stage show. The relationship between novel, film, and musical is further complicated in that Lloyd Webber's original idea was not for a stage version but a rock-musical adaptation for film; as such it formed Lloyd Webber's intended moves on Hollywood in the mid-1990s as part of the expansion and diversification of the Really Useful Group, by that point back in his control for some five years after the period of its public flotation. That the screen was the intended destination of the work was reaffirmed in August 1995, when Lloyd Webber reportedly described as "completely untrue" rumors that *Whistle Down the Wind* was to open on stage.[16]

In the event the first of two principal stage versions opened in Washington, D.C., at the National Theatre on December 12, 1996, and ran there until February 8, 1997, but its mixed notices preempted a Broadway opening. The creative team had included Lloyd Webber as composer, with Jim Steinman ("the Wagner of rock") as lyricist; Patricia Knop wrote the book, while Hal Prince was drawn in to oversee the overall development for stage. The show's failure was attributed to the lack of reworking for stage of what had been originally intended for film. After extensive rewriting, a second version played in London, opening at the Aldwych Theatre on July 1, 1998, and closing two and a half years later, on January 6, 2001. The book credit by this point was given to Knop, Lloyd Webber himself, and Gale Edwards, who, in place of Hal Prince, directed. I shall discuss this second version, the one available on disk, the one authorized for staging, and the one that represents a "settled" version—insofar as any Lloyd Webber musical is ever settled.[17] Understandably, given that the primary home of Lloyd Webber's project was in the United States, Michael Walsh could not see the appeal of the work: "Just why a relatively obscure British film, in which a group of Yorkshire children mistake an escaped convict for Jesus Christ, warranted re-

The Man is discovered by the children in the barn in the 1961 film of *Whistle Down the Wind.* © 2004. Reproduced courtesy of Carlton International Media Ltd./LFI.

making, and as a musical at that, was never quite clear."[18] There are answers to this from the British perspective that explain the source as a good choice.

First, the film was far from obscure in Britain, having successfully tapped into a postwar zeitgeist of the need for new moral direction alongside a re-examination of British identity. It gained some success in the United States, was influential in European cinema, and remains a distinguished, time-less, and captivating portrayal of regional British life and community. As the careers of the film's personnel have grown, so has the status of the film by association: it is an early work by someone who was to become one of Brit-ain's leading film directors, Bryan Forbes; it features in the central child role Hayley Mills, the daughter of the author and at the start of a notable act-ing career; the man found in the barn is played by Alan Bates, again early in what proved to be a distinguished and successful acting career; the pro-ducer of the film, Richard (now Lord) Attenborough, is as much a theatrical fixture of Britain (and indeed international film) as is the author's own husband, Sir John Mills.[19] The film thus is part of the dynastic history of Britain's national cinema.

Second, and possibly more significant, given the role played by Ken Hill's dramatization of *The Phantom of the Opera* in demonstrating to Lloyd Webber the potential of that novel, *Whistle Down the Wind* had already been presented as a stage musical by the National Youth Music Theatre in Britain, an organization that Lloyd Webber has sponsored over a number of years. This earlier and well-received musicalization was adapted from the novel and the screenplay by Russell Labey and Richard Taylor, with music and lyrics by Taylor. After workshopping it in April 1992, the NYMT first presented the developed work as part of the Edinburgh Festival in August 1993.[20] London performances, at the Lilian Bayliss Theatre of Sadler's Wells and the Riverside Theatre, followed later in the year. As Russell Labey acknowledged in his notes on the work, this adaptation stayed very close to the pattern of events and the structure of the film, although it reverted, as did Lloyd Webber's subsequent version, to the ambiguous and potentially optimistic ending of the novel rather than adopting the unambiguously bleak conclusion of the film.

So in Britain the story already had a strong identity. Such national considerations were an issue, as Lloyd Webber has explained: "My problem with the material was its credibility today for an international audience. It was so very English. This was shared by some of the producers who saw the NYMT version, even though, like me, they had enjoyed it hugely."[21] The relocation of the drama to Louisiana in 1959 for the musical became a way of broadening its audience appeal through the provision of a more familiar American context. For a recent comparison, the British hit film *The Full Monty* was relocated in its Broadway musicalization from the city of Sheffield in the English Midlands—a setting crucial to its cultural resonance in Britain—to a more American-friendly environment, Buffalo, New York, a town with a similar industrial and employment history to Sheffield. In general, the history of interaction between West End and Broadway musicals has been one in which the works seen by Americans as reflecting on their own country are enjoyed as escapist in Britain, while British musicals whose concerns are domestic have been resisted by an American audience generally unfamiliar with the culture from which the British shows have arisen. Accordingly, the Americanization of *Whistle Down the Wind* might be expected to play to both the American and the home audience. *Sunset Boulevard* had worked the other way: its origination in American film immediately placed it not just in an American but a world repertory of English-speaking film. Through its rightful canonization, and the security of a known title and a familiar storyline, it had a ready-made audience.

None of this, of course, answers Walsh's main question: why did a reworking of this tale seem to hold such dramatic appeal to Lloyd Webber? Primarily, it was the strength of the broad underlying theme. Lloyd Webber described the central message of the story as "universal," one that "transcends time and place"; the stage show as much as the original novel presented for him "a lesson in the enduring power of faith and the great capacity of the human heart to trust and to forgive."[22] The selection for the stage adaptation of some material for the musical from the novel and some from the film strengthened and refined this universal theme. Also, those things newly introduced for the musical reflect the changing times in the forty years or so since novel and film.

The story of Mary Hayley Bell's novel is simple. Three children living on a farm in Sussex find a sick man hiding in a barn and want to know who he is. Surprised when they disturb him, he exclaims "Jesus!" The combination of a childlike literal understanding of the world, his exclamation, the location in a barn—complete with manger—and two holes in his feet lead them to think of him as the Christ of the Second Coming rather than the escaped murderer he is gradually revealed to be. Looking after him in a conspiracy that draws in other children of the region, increasingly determined not to let the adults do to Jesus what they did last time, the children continue in their belief in him (or "Him," as the novel refers to the interloper), despite his amused attempts to disabuse them of their faith. As the police close in and the adults are alerted to the man's presence, the children mobilize their forces until, in the final confrontation, hundreds of them prevent the police from reaching the farm building in which the man is now trapped. The building is suddenly set alight, the fire brigade arrives, but there is no trace of the man in the smoldering remains of the building. Only the sign of a cross on the wall shows that he was ever there.

"I'll take Jesus some comics, and when He's finished reading them Bette Davis can have them," says Poor Baby to Brat early in the novel.[23] This surrealism, typical of Mary Hayley Bell's novel, illustrates the difference in style between the book and the brooding melancholy which characterized the film adaptation and which Lloyd Webber provided with a large dose of extra angst in the musical. Told in the first person by Brat, the middle child of three siblings (Swallow is the oldest and Poor Baby the youngest), the novel contains almost no description of place beyond the strictly necessary and purely literal geography of the farm, a site from which the story never moves. The period is contemporary with the novel's creation, 1957, and espouses a style that mixes the most extraordinary adult-child juxtapositions in its central characters: for example, Brat is hooked on Alka-Seltzer, while Poor Baby carries around a little box containing the ingredients for his favored roll-ups. All three children are independent spirits, reveling in the freedom of country life, unaware of adult concerns. They think adults very strange, not threatening but amusing. And brought up in a farmhouse with father, grandmother, a cook, and other adult visitors, they have plenty of opportunity to observe their elders. There is much interaction between adults and children; neither ignored nor neglected, the children simply live in their own self-contained world. The shadow of a dead mother provides an undercurrent in the film and a main psychological thread in the musical, but in the novel the children's mother has run off with another man. When asked directly by their father whether they miss her, the children say that they do not because they still have him. As for the stranger in the barn, he views the children and their assumptions of his holy origins with amusement, often laughing with them during relaxed discussion. He presents no threat to them; indeed, he sometimes seems as childlike in his pleasure as do they. He is never compared physically with images of Jesus Christ except for the two holes in his feet. He relates to the children as a group, not individually.[24] At the end, the father accepts his children's belief in the returned Jesus—his own act of faith in the children, who are convinced that adults have no faith. Privileging his children's need to regain belief in the adult world over his own adult logic, he plays a neutral role in the final confrontation between adults (principally police) and children.

In the transformation from page to screen, the drama gained a darker and more brooding quality. It became a knowing film of the adult world rather than a naive one of the child world. There is no room in the film to believe that the man is anything other than the very human Arthur Alan Blaket, wanted for a murder; at the end of the story he is arrested, then frisked with his arms held out in a poignant cruciform silhouetted against the sky. (This image was used prominently in the poster design for Bill Kenwright's 2001 U.K. touring version of the stage show; it is a clear case of annexing the film's reputation, given that no such image or event occurs on stage.)[25] A crowd of children look on, seeing what they wish to believe. Even at the end, when the adult world has triumphed, the children's faith remains, with the last lines addressed to two very young latecomers: "Yes, you missed him this time. But he'll be coming again." Those lines were spoken by Kathy Bostock, the oldest of the three children, whose perspective was the dominant one of the film.[26] As part of the film's darker realism the names of the novel were changed: the older Swallow became Kathy, Brat (the female narrator of the novel) became Nan, and their younger brother was changed from Poor Baby to Charles (often called Charlie), the character who expresses the black-and-white pragmatism allotted to Brat in the novel. The musical's reinstatement of the names of the novel—one of the few significant reversions to the novel from the film version—helped to poeticize the tale.

There is no wider community in the book beyond that of the farmhouse and its inhabitants, yet the film clearly defines a close community in Lancashire, taking the events from the open moors to the center of the town, from the barn to the church, from a tearoom to a railway tunnel. The film adopts a specific geographical and social landscape, paralleled in the musical's transposition to the Bible-belt Louisiana township. And that religious dimension is important. Even though faith in "Jesus" is at the heart of the storyline, the novel avoids any sense of a community rooted in religion, while the film makes the religious dimension omnipresent. The screenplay introduces Kathy, Nan, and Charlie as they secretly follow an unpleasant farmhand, then rescue a sack of unwanted kittens that he has thrown into a lake. Soon after, when they come across a Salvation Army band and preacher in the village, Charlie wants the preacher to explain why Jesus allows kittens to be born only to allow them to be killed. The Salvation Army is the more zealous religious organization here—in the musical, this function is fulfilled by the snake preacher—and set as a contrast to the local Anglican vicar. Referred to only in passing in the novel, the vicar is presented in the film as preoccupied and unhelpful. We also see the children at Sunday School with a well-meaning but ineffective teacher; they ask her what would happen if Jesus came back, and how he should be treated, and her answers unintentionally provoke the children's later actions in protecting the Man.[27]

The rescue of the drowning kittens was not in the novel but was introduced into the screenplay, then incorporated into the stage show.[28] The film story rather than the novel also provided the musical with the formal presentation of gifts to the supposed Jesus; the man telling the children a story at their request (in the film he chooses one in a comic over one from the

Bible); the name of Poor Baby's rescued kitten, Spider, its subsequent death, and the questioning it provokes; the hurried journey by Swallow to a railway tunnel to retrieve a hidden package containing a gun; and the rebellious Amos, developed from the local bully of the film, Raymond.[29]

Most significant in their adaptation from the film are the character of the Man, both physical and psychological, his developing relationship with Kathy (Swallow), and the context of a motherless and dysfunctional family. As in the novel, the Man remains nameless, a device which strengthens the ambiguity of his identity by allowing both sacred and secular readings of him. He is the returned Jesus and also a male Everyman figure on a journey of emotional self-discovery. In *The Phantom of the Opera*, the Phantom is the male outsider whose developing yet ultimately doomed emotional attraction to a young woman propels the events of the plot; but he is also given a mystic dimension through his unclear origins and an apotheosis of sorts in his final, unexplained disappearance. As with *Whistle Down the Wind*, the end of *Phantom* provides a question mark rather than a period. In *Jesus Christ Superstar*, the process is reversed: Christ is placed in a context that stresses the secular and avoids the conclusively religious by ending with death rather than resurrection; the emotional attraction is not from him but toward him, in the guise of Mary Magdalene and Judas. All three of these central characters—the Man, the Phantom, Jesus—are presented in a way that encourages both mythic and sexual-psychological interpretation, and all are men with emotional dilemmas at their core. In *Whistle Down the Wind* the brooding, tormented nature of the Man in the musical is an extension of Alan Bates's portrayal in the film of an introverted and taciturn stranger with dark facial hair, whose physical similarity to a standard picture of Jesus is a contributory factor in the children's belief in him as the returned Messiah.[30]

In the film, the Man's developing concern for Kathy remains innocent, although the final scene hints at muted eroticism when she throws him a cigarette from outside the rear of the barn while the police are waiting at the front. In the musical the eroticism is not muted: this developing emotional and sexual attraction provokes the moral self-questioning of the Man as he, in effect, encourages Swallow to prostitute herself for him. The duet that is really a trio in the musical, "A Kiss Is a Terrible Thing to Waste," in which Swallow feigns a physical attraction to Amos in order to gain the necessary motorbike ride to reach the train tunnel in time, is a powerful number. Youthful desire and adult regret, teenage physical attraction and an adult

emotional attraction grippingly collide in the song. The musical goes far beyond the film in this respect, but then the film was already far beyond the
novel, and its example was crucial. As we have seen, the family of the novel
is odd but happy; in the film, however, the absence of the mother is felt, with
the father's sister pushed into unwilling service as housekeeper, while the
father, although not remote, is taciturn. For the musical, this idea has been
moved significantly to the foreground, so that the uncompleted grieving of
the family—reenacted in miniature when the kitten Spider dies, leading to
a restatement of an angry incomprehension of death—is sublimated in the
belief in the Man as the Saviour. The resolution of the crisis engendered
by this quasi-religious stranger ultimately provides a means of reuniting the
family when the father (Boone)—in this case as in the novel but not the
film—takes the beliefs of his children seriously, especially those of the older
Swallow. In other words, Boone begins again to listen to his children, and
the disrupted family unit begins to function once more.[31]

The musical version amplifies significantly the more adult themes of
emotion, trust, control, and morality; these themes go mostly unexplored in
the novel but are just beneath the surface in the film, as in the moments
of innocent intimacy between Kathy and Blaket (the Man) that suggest an
unfulfilled erotic potential. The result is that the musical seems hysterical
in tone when compared with the novel, with its matter-of-fact descriptions
and its relentlessly deflating observations. Furthermore, where the film portrays its undercurrents as just that—it allows the audience to infer much
from an extraordinarily concise use of dialogue, imagery, and metaphor—
the musical makes bold emotional statements. Lloyd Webber needs those
moments of explicit high emotion to hold center stage, and neither novel
nor film works like that. In different ways both use a very English approach
of understatement, which does not generate an emotional intensity that requires musicalization. Indeed, the use of music in the film is very restrained,
principally covering scenes of transition, as when the three children happily
rush off after discovering Jesus: framed against the landscape the three of
them skip around to the strains of the carol "We Three Kings." The bleakness of the landscape generates a bleak soundtrack, principally of the voices
of young children against the expansive geographical setting. Lloyd Webber's landscape is just as forbidding, but it is one of heat—parodied in a song
of lust called "Cold"—rather than of chilling wind and rain. There is obvious sexual intent in the ambiguity of the song "Cold," with such a couplet
as "The barometer is falling / Only she can make it rise." Adult sexuality has

Whistle Down the Wind (photo: Ivan Kyncl and Eric Richmond). © 1997 The Really Useful Group Ltd.

no part in the novel and occupies only the most subtle of undercurrents in the film, but it is responsible for one of the most significant additions to the musical.

The expression of physical desire in the stage show finds its greatest potential in the characters of Amos and Candy, two adolescents on the cusp of adulthood, with the raging hormones to prove it. They represent an uncontrolled element in the moral order of the townsfolk: they are not religious, they aspire to something better than their lot, they respond physically rather than spiritually, and, most immediately apparent, their relationship goes across the color bar—Candy is black, Amos is white—breaking social and even legal restraints. All is summed up in "Tire Tracks and Broken Hearts":

CANDY: I need a man who knows
    What I am really worth
AMOS: Well, I don't give a damn
    About life after death
BOTH: But I gotta get some proof
    That there's some life after birth

With the introduction of these new figures (though Amos has distant forebears in both novel and film), the society of the Louisiana town is broadened into a generational one that neither novel nor film could address. Simply put, the concept of the rebellious adolescent was not sufficiently established at the time of either novel or film. While metropolitan society was freeing itself to some degree, the more remote communities of Britain did not have such a thing as a teenager: children turned into adults without formal acknowledgment of the transitional period. The rebellious portrayals of Elvis Presley and James Dean were not yet established realities in Britain in 1961; for an audience some forty years later teenage angst is commonplace. A pattern of changes now begins to emerge in which Candy and Amos represent the amoral, the rebellious, and the instinctive; the townspeople represent the moral and conformist, unthinking in their regular rituals and later in their violent mob instincts; the snake preacher and his entourage represent the dangers to the community of the outsider extremist who challenges their innate conservatism. It is the recurring structural device of Lloyd Webber's shows, one that creates strongly opposing factions (often unsubtly so) and then allows the drama to result from their juxtapositions. Think of the oppositions of *Starlight Express* (electric vs. diesel vs. steam), the political and social factions of *Evita* (military vs. aristocracy vs. lower class), the different worlds of *The Phantom of the Opera* (high society vs. the opera house vs. the recluse), and most recently the overt politics of *The Beautiful Game* (the independent vs. the indoctrinated). And, of course, the cynical awareness of Joe is set against the self-deception of Norma in *Sunset Boulevard*; more generally, this is a confrontation of the new world (contemporary movies) with the old (silent film). Emotional eruptions are generated in all these shows as the tectonic plates of such clearly defined blocks inexorably clash. In *Whistle Down the Wind*, with the ambiguity of the Man, the postpubescent potential of Swallow, and (though only to a minor degree) the impotence of the father-figure Boone, these characters become the symbols of the fault lines, exposing in their dilemmas the opposing forces at work. The children themselves present the idealism of youth uncorrupted by the compromise of adulthood. That Swallow can survive her dilemmas in coming to terms with an adult world and retain something of her child-like belief suggests that the loss of youthful faith is not inevitable; she says at the end of the musical, "He'll be back. I just know He will."[32]

The defining of the social groups also allows for their musical character-ization, something not so easily done within the more restrictive groupings of the film. Religious devotion provokes the gospel hymn ("The Vaults of Heaven") and is contrasted with the secular anthem of the Everly Brothers' pop song ("Cold"); the impatience of youth is shown in rock ("Tire Tracks and Broken Hearts" and "A Kiss Is a Terrible Thing to Waste"), then thrown into relief by the tuneful preadolescent naïveté of "I Never Get What I Pray For," "When Children Rule the World," and "No Matter What."[33] The im-passioned ballads are primarily reserved for the Man ("Unsettled Scores," and "Nature of the Beast," with its hymnlike refrain), but they also belong to Swallow as she is drawn into the adult world. First and most innocently, she appropriates her mother's song "Whistle Down the Wind," in effect a ver-sion of "You'll Never Walk Alone." Second, through the Man's "love song" of "Try Not to Be Afraid," the shared feelings of the Man and Swallow are signified by shared music and lyrics. Third, climactically in "A Kiss Is a Ter-rible Thing to Waste," the music of Amos is also the music of the Man as a youth, symbolizing what Amos could become.

Strong contrasts of character were present in *Sunset Boulevard*, a cham-ber piece played out on a large canvas, before Lloyd Webber took up the story. The story's leads were already well delineated and located in a dis-tinctive landscape, and the task of musicalization required amplification of already existing tendencies and features. Thus the piece could be musical-ized in the Lloyd Webber vein essentially as it was, with virtually no signifi-cant changes to the dramaturgy. By contrast, *Whistle Down the Wind* was too simplistic in the number and quality of its dramatic oppositions in both novel and film to suit the Lloyd Webber style. It was the creation of a wider society and a concomitant set of more strongly contrasted symbolic forces that formed the backbone of this adaptation, primarily from the film.

From Concept Album to Film: Visualizing Rock

The filming of stage musicals, however, is a much more potent force than the adaption to musical from film. The film version of *The Sound of Music* makes the point well; it is the film rather than the stage version that has been primarily responsible for the extraordinarily widespread and long-lived dissemination of the show. The film of *Cabaret* has also given a new and wider life to Kander and Ebb's stage show, one that has become so prominent that stage directors commonly feel obliged to incorporate elements of the radically altered film score in place of the original stage score: "Mein Herr" instead of "Don't Tell Mama," "Money, Money" rather than "Sitting Pretty." Even the plot of that stage show has surprises for a viewer who has seen only the film, highlighting a potential danger for filmed stage works: the ability to see a film over and over again in exactly the same form—impossible in live performance—can canonize not only the work but also its specific interpretation.

As this book goes to press, two of Lloyd Webber's musicals have made it to the big screen—a third, *Phantom*, is soon to follow—and both, *Jesus Christ Superstar* and *Evita*, were first developed not for the stage but as concept albums. In the case of *Jesus Christ Superstar*, the album of 1970 had been presented in concert versions before a fully staged version on Broadway in 1971, then followed by a different production for its West End premiere in 1972. The film was released in the summer of 1973 as the final stage of a creative, transformatory rush to exploit a hot property. As I explained in Chapter 2, the film had virtually no creative input from Lloyd Webber and Rice in its adaptation from recording or stage, and we will shortly find that an insensitivity to the music in particular undermined the effectiveness of the end result. With *Evita*, however, nearly two decades elapsed between its first stage production in the West End in 1978 and the film's release in 1996.[34] Lloyd Webber's own power—and the education that his exclusion from the *Superstar* film had provided—was such that his involvement in the film of *Evita*, including agreement as to its casting, was a prerequisite of the project. Although he compromised on casting, not necessarily to the film's benefit, overall the music was much better coordinated with the film's imagery and pacing than in the *Superstar* film. A video version of *Superstar* adapted from a late-1990s U.K. tour also improved on its big-screen predecessor. Time benefited the transfer of *Evita* to the big screen and *Superstar* to the small one, and an exploration of just how will illuminate not just the films but also changes in the film medium itself.

As concept albums, *Jesus Christ Superstar* and *Evita* both used an episodic form with limited dramatic linking of scenes. *Evita* made much greater use of multisectional structures and narrative in the lyrics than had *Jesus Christ Superstar*, but many scene-setting directions and character identifications still had to be printed in the libretto accompanying the recording. For example, "On This Night of a Thousand Stars" (track 3) is prefaced: "A nightclub in Junin, Eva's home town. It is 1934 and Eva Duarte is fifteen. The cabaret is nearly over. Magaldi sings the final song of his performance with great gusto." Only the "great gusto" of Tony Christie's performance could be picked up from the recording alone. The printed libretto of the original recording of *Jesus Christ Superstar* did not need such directions, relying as it did on the reasonable assumption that its audience would know the plot and characters, and the same assumption applied to the stage adaptation. The film also had little additional explanatory narrative apart from an early scene between Caiaphas and Annas; in "Then We Are Decided" the priests outline the delicate balance of political power under the occupying Roman force, and its potential destabilization through the political teachings of a Christ perceived as a "craze." The song "Could We Start Again Please" from the stage show was also added.

The stage productions had confirmed to some degree what needed additional dramatization and what did not. *Evita* also benefited from the initial changes made from album to stage, less from wholesale reorganization than through the substitution of clearer narrative lyrics in strategic places. Most noticeable was the portrayal of Che Guevara, who began on the concept album as a historical figure with elements of his own biography woven into the story. By the time he reached the stage, Che had appropriated material allocated to other characters on the album, including "And the Money Kept Rolling In," formerly sung by the manager of Eva's charitable foundation, and lines in "The Rainbow Tour" sung by Juan Perón's political advisers. These shifts strengthened Che's function as an omnipresent devil's advocate. He was still the historical Che Guevara in his initial appearance, but other guises adopted later on stage blurred his identity. The demands of the film, with an essentially naturalistic and historically accurate design, made this "floating" Che trickier to present. Listed in the film credits as Che, with no surname, the Antonio Banderas character is in fact a dissenting Everyman, never identified clearly with the real Guevara: he appears as a barman, a reporter, a caretaker, a union worker, an aristocrat. Without the specific agenda of Che's political activism, he becomes the voice of morality and fairness, experiencing the reality of the regime so that, by the time of the "Waltz for Eva and Che," he has become the voice of Eva's conscience.

Where *Sunset Boulevard* and *Whistle Down the Wind* had required the development of ways to musicalize a screenplay, *Jesus Christ Superstar* and *Evita* required ways of visualizing an existing soundtrack. The completely musicalized film drama is still unusual, the reverse of the more typical use of a soundtrack to amplify from the background the intensity of the drama. Indeed, it is possible to see the best music for most films as that which works on the edge of an audience's perception to shade and color without being noticed for itself. In the filming of a rock opera, though, the music by definition is central to the work. And this seems to be the principle area in which Norman Jewison's direction of *Jesus Christ Superstar* failed but Alan Parker's direction of *Evita* succeeded.

Jesus Christ Superstar

There is a mismatch of sound and energy in *Jesus Christ Superstar*, a failure to key together consistently image and sound. The instrumental music has often been placed too far behind the voices in the mix, as if it were underscoring dialogue, and this undercuts the louder rock numbers. In "What's the Buzz?," "Hosanna," or the first confrontation between Pilate and Jesus, this is especially noticeable, with the rock riffs and orchestral flurries unnaturally suppressed. When this shortcoming is combined with the bland portrayal of Jesus by Ted Neeley and a failure to allow the chorus effects to impress with their power, several key moments seem to have had the musical stuffing knocked out of them. Throughout, the sheer physical presence of the musical gesture is missing, as if a major character had been removed from the story, and this undermines the whole notion of a sung-through screen musical. As Lloyd Webber's musical construction so often requires the direct opposition of big blocks of sound, it fails to make its mark when those big blocks are scaled down, as it often is in the crowd scenes and in the moments of dramatic conflict in the film. Consequently, the film works best in the solo numbers, such as "I Don't Know How to Love Him," the camera following Yvonne Elliman as Mary Magdalene through an atmospherically lit nighttime soliloquy, or in "Herod's Song," in which the use of water for amusement in a forbiddingly arid environment—being casual with what is vital—makes a nice point about the privileges of power and wealth.

The film was shot on location in Israel, and it works well on those occasions when Jewison focuses on the bare and expansive scenery to illuminate the metaphorical isolation of the characters. There are many panoramic shots of the red mountainous landscape, most strikingly for the opening of

Judas's "Heaven on Their Minds," which gradually zooms in through progressive steps on a solitary figure sitting in thought on the top of a rocky ridge.[35] Singing directly to camera, Judas begins to move down the hillside for his second stanza after the introductory verse ("I remember when this whole thing began"); next he appears in a long shot, walking in isolation along a ridge. The instrumental break in 7/8 ("Nazareth your famous son . . .") is illustrated by the image of Jesus in the center of a crowd; the crowd in turn is contrasted with the isolation of Judas in the final image of the number, as, from his position high on the mountain, he becomes a distant observer of Jesus's group walking in the valley. The filming captures well the way in which Judas is already apart in thought from others in the group; at the same time it evokes some sense of the physicality within the music: the tempo, meter, and repeating riffs fit well with Judas's anxious walking as he tries to clear his head of unwanted, preoccupying thoughts. But the effectiveness of such a scene is undermined by others that impose on the music, as with Simon Zealotes's number, in which the rhythmic element has been visually reflected in the manic movements of the choreography. An overanimated Simon sings from the middle of the dancing crowd set in a square of desert, enclosed by ruined pillars. The wrong element of the music has been captured: the gospel-style insistence of the number (marked by the feeling for a handclap on the second and fourth beats of each bar) has been transformed into the double-time, overhyped nervousness of a form of St. Vitus's Dance. It is one of the numbers that betrays the hippie origins of the film's character, in part influenced from the outrageous Broadway staging by Tom O'Horgan.

It is difficult to reconcile the panoramic Israeli landscape with the activity and energy in so much of the music: the grand exteriors need time to be absorbed, while the music needs animated and fast-paced cutting. Nice matches of visual ideas to aural details include the tanks rolling down the hill toward Judas to the sound of a two-flute cadenza and the sudden cutting in of the sound of fighter planes, seen first in total silence. Elsewhere the score has to work hard to grab the appropriate attention for an all-music film. It is finally effective, even if through the use of well-worn imagery, at the end, when the long, slow strings of "John 19:41" cover the return to the bus of the traveling performers who have acted through the drama, each silently reflecting upon what has happened, while a large deep orange sun slowly sets behind the empty cross on the top of the hill. There is no body on the cross, but the actor who played Jesus has not returned with the others to

Simon Zealotes in the 1973 film of *Jesus Christ Superstar*. Reproduced courtesy of Universal Studios Licensing LLLP.

the bus: a subtle and open-ended finish. The emotional space of the music is reflected in the slow-moving nature of the whole scene, and made more poignant by the lack of any diegetic sound—just the music is heard, with the rest of the world silenced.

To damn the whole film—as critics did when it came out—seems harsh today. The framing device of a group of hippie performers reenacting the story on an archaeological site, using a mixture of historical and contemporary imagery, has merit, but the contemporary fashions of clothing and hairstyles dated very quickly between the time of the film's conception in 1971 and its release in 1973. Today, that is not a problem; time has diluted the anachronisms that were close enough to rankle when the film was first released, making it appear simply of its time, some thirty years ago. But as that aspect has diminished in importance, the pairing of music and imagery has become more problematic, for now we are used to the visualizing of rock and pop through the rise of MTV and the ubiquity of the rock video.

In 1973 the examples for music on screen came primarily from musicals; indeed, the choice of Jewison as director for *Jesus Christ Superstar* was influenced by his previous successful transfer to screen of Bock and Harnick's stage hit *Fiddler on the Roof*. But the demands of rock are not those of the popular musical stage, and the film of *Jesus Christ Superstar* suffers from its necessary experimentation.

Two years after Jewison's film of the Rice–Lloyd Webber musical another rock musical was transferred to the big screen. Its history is similar to that of *Jesus Christ Superstar*, having been first released as a concept album in 1969, then presented in concert, before being released as a film in 1975. The original concept album was episodic, with no attempt to be dramatically explicit or complete, and the central theme was one of redemption. The work in question is, of course, the Who's *Tommy*, and the film was directed by Ken Russell. Although by no means totally successful, the film was much better than *Superstar* in transferring the essence of rock music to image. Russell used a wider vocabulary of camera angles and cutting techniques to create a faster-paced and more varied visual diet, more appropriately energetic (particularly in "Pinball Wizard"). In a different way, "Eyesight to the Blind" does the same by reflecting visually the hypnotic rock riff that turns into the "Marilyn" chant as an inexorable, ritualistic procession of organized religion. Such activity in the sensually aware world enables the deaf, dumb, and blind Tommy in his isolated world to provide moments of visual stasis in contrast to those around him—compare the frenetic Cousin Kevin or Uncle Ernie with the passive Tommy in "Cousin Kevin" and "Fiddle About," respectively—matching at times his musical stasis (as in the recurring refrain "See me, feel me, touch me, heal me!"). Russell also drew on the developing world of commercial television, with his references to the techniques of advertising in the slowed-down, romantically blurred glance between Tommy's mother and the doctor (played by Ann-Margret and Jack Nicholson).

The camera itself is much more mobile in *Tommy* than *Jesus Christ Superstar*. Jewison tended to work from relatively static camera positions, often using the angle of the image to reflect the power dynamics: for example, Jesus is often viewed from slightly below in scenes with the disciples but is viewed from above in his address to God in "Gethsemane"; the priests are presented high on a scaffold that gives them a commanding view over others, and the audience often has to look up to them, yet the disciples are based in caves below ground and the camera descends to them. The camera in *Tommy* moves much more freely, with every possible view—extreme close-up, panorama, long tracking shots, and circling images, for example; the effect is less of viewing a scene from outside than of exploring within it. Tommy's final resurrection, following the water all the way from the sea inland to its source at the top of the mountain, leads to his silhouetted figure viewed against a deep-orange setting sun, remarkably similar to that in *Jesus Christ Superstar*. In this case, the sunset imagery reflects the circular form of the refrain "Listening to you I get the music" (occasioned by its ending on the dominant rather than tonic), echoing the film's opening image of Tommy's father. Russell's vision was more dynamic and portrayed the qualities of its rock score better than Jewison's had his.[36]

Evita

With *Evita* in 1996, the central issue was still one of matching image to music, but with the need also to ensure that the narrative was clear. Millions had seen the show on stage or bought the recording, but knowledge of the life story of Eva Perón still could not be taken for granted as easily as could that of Jesus Christ. Some changes had already been made between concept album and stage production that addressed this very issue, and most of them were incorporated into the film. Those that weren't are revealing. For example, the explosive rock number "The Lady's Got Potential" of the album was dropped completely for the stage show. Director Hal Prince explained, "What I had to do was take the 'Top of the Pops' feeling out of the material. I had to get rid of the sentimentality and give it a harder edge. The story takes place in Argentina, not in mid-Atlantic, and it has to look and sound ethnic as hell. What we are doing is a kind of political rally—that's the force of it. Another word for it is documentary theatre."[37] The rock 'n' roll riffs and blues-derived chord structure of the number were distinctly mid-Atlantic, akin to those of such 1970s Anglophonic rock groups as Status Quo.

Prince's remarks also explain the addition of "The Art of the Possible" to the stage show, a number that introduced the expedient rather than the ideological as the military perspective of politics; it survives in the film only as a single stanza, and reallocated to Che at that. But the restoration of "The Lady's Got Potential," though with substantially rewritten lyrics, works well in the film, and its new form provides important historical-narrative background on the developing situation between political and military factions in Argentina.[38] Furthermore, the repeating verse-and-refrain form is ideal for reflecting the series of military takeovers. Most important, the energy of the music is harnessed by the visual. The whole number begins with an electric guitar riff that culminates in an explosion: the running, screaming figures mimic the musical energy, and the coup of the narrative is kicked off both musically and physically with arresting gestures. The ritual of repetition inherent in the structure of the song is picked up with recurrent visual themes, notably the soldiers' marching is synchronized to the soundtrack, never for more than a few beats, just long enough to tie music and dramatic action together. The firing cannons provide a similar recurrent image, both as instruments of aggression and destruction and as instruments of ritual celebration. They fit perfectly with action that is big and busy, conveying a sense of excitement through fast cutting and changes of perspective. And in a crucial difference from *Jesus Christ Superstar*, Antonio Banderas's solo voice has been included in the mix with the instruments—within the action, not distant from it.

From the start, the film depends on visual analogues for sound. For example, the lamentations of the common people after the cinema manager's announcement of the death of Eva Perón are a visual equivalent for the wailing, solo electric guitar which begins the first musical number. The small-scale funeral of Eva's father, with an appropriately small-scale village band sound, is replaced simultaneously with the vast parade of national mourning that is Eva's funeral and with the monumental thematic statement by full orchestra. Further contrast is achieved as the camera moves to the solitary figure of Che sitting in a bar, alone rather than in the crowd, indoors rather than outside. For Che, the music itself is Latinized, more informal and demotic, and the light tango rhythm conveys a sense of movement that is picked up in his wanderings among the mourners. Che breaks the funeral mood when he begins the heavier rock section, "Sing you fools! But you got it wrong," a musical change of direction that matches a lyrical change of direction, as Che turns from cynical observer to vitriolic commentator. This shift is marked in the film by Che's throwing a stone to smash a picture of Eva, which in turn prompts a succession of fast cuts and changing camera angles, and so re-creates in the violence of the dramatic action the inherent energy of the music. If the device sometimes seems to become a bit forced, as in the societal blocks of "Perón's Latest Flame," then it is in part a result of Lloyd Webber's block shifts in the music, as he opposes the *a cappella* formality of the aristocrats with the marching, gutsy unison of the blues-inflected military. The musical poise of one is reflected in the visual poise of garden party or tearoom; the more visceral style of the other is shown in manly marching, communal showers, and fencing (again with little moments of action in time with the music to key it into the score). But the match between music and image can be more subtle, as in the introduction to "Don't Cry for Me, Argentina": the cheering and chanting of the crowds are suppressed beneath the supreme calm of the strings, representing that moment when Eva has finally achieved her dream. The passage conveys supreme confidence and satisfaction, a sense of rightness that articulates the character of Eva beyond the surface image. The disengagement of the music from the visual image at this moment is striking and also anticipates the calculated poise of the following address (as aria) from the balcony of the Casa Rosada.[39]

The physicality of the score is also conveyed through more stylized movement in quasi-dance sections. These, however—unlike the decorative impositions of the Simon Zealotes number or the disco cavern of the title song in *Jesus Christ Superstar*—emerge from the narrative imagery itself. Dance is used at the opening of the film to convey a sense of communal loss and mutual support as the slow tango becomes a means of mourning Eva. When Eva arrives in Buenos Aires with Magaldi, dance becomes a symbolic prediction of Eva's social climbing in Argentina, as her partners become progressively younger and more virile. The nearest the film comes to a dance routine is with "And the Money Kept Rolling In (and Out)," as the water supply to a village is turned on and the villagers dance in celebration. Their steps are not choreographed as a conventional routine, but the outburst of the music in its frenetic 7/8 meter (an effect that owes something to Bernstein's "America" in *West Side Story*) is perfectly reflected in the physicality of the image. Occasionally, the handclaps of the dancing villagers are matched to the handclaps of the soundtrack for a couple of beats, but never long enough to create the formality of a fixed dance section—as with the marching feet in "The Lady's Got Potential." By contrast, the "Waltz for Eva and Che" is transformed into a direct confrontation between the two: it is a dance of death around a marble hall, a space away from the physical reality of Eva in her hospital operating theater and Che collapsed on the street. It reflects the motion of the music, but through its simple repeated movements within the restricted space allows the concentration to be on the content of the antagonists' argument; the music and dance are the structural framework rather than the content per se. It is such an awareness of the physicality of the sound and the sympathetic and creative responses to it that allowed Alan Parker to succeed in *Evita* where Norman Jewison failed in *Jesus Christ Superstar*.

Any Screen Will Do

The new generation of Andrew Lloyd Webber film musicals has come not to the big screen but to the small one, with the release of video and DVD versions of the stage shows. At the time of writing these include *Cats* (1998), *Joseph and the Amazing Technicolor Dreamcoat* (1999), *Jesus Christ Superstar* (2000), and *By Jeeves* (2001). Each has been based on a stage production, namely the West End productions of *Cats* and *Joseph* (1991 revival), the U.K. tour of *Jesus Christ Superstar* (1998), and the Goodspeed Opera House production (2001, transferred to Broadway) of *By Jeeves*.

The effectiveness of these video and DVD transfers varies considerably, but they are designed for a different audience from that of the feature films. The video recording is the ultimate souvenir of an evening at the theater: along with the souvenir program and the sweatshirt, you can now take the whole show home with you. So the filmed version of a production needs to evoke something already experienced—not through a literal record of the theater staging but through an approximation of its live impact. To that end, various additional effects not possible in the theater have been introduced to generate the level of involvement or excitement that the live event may have created. In the case of *Cats*, a virtual replica of the set of the New London Theatre was built and the soundtrack rerecorded. The casting brought the additional element of "star" attraction, more easily attained for the short duration of a film session than for a run on stage: Elaine Paige re-created her role as Grizabella, singing "Memory," and John Mills played Gus the Theatre Cat. The same impulse to broaden audience appeal guiding the casting of *Joseph and the Amazing Technicolor Dreamcoat*: Donny Osmond (who had scored a success in the part on stage) was joined by Joan Collins as Potiphar's wife, Richard Attenborough as Jacob, and Maria Friedman as the Narrator. Such high-profile performers helped the video tap into different audiences: pop-nostalgia (Osmond), popular television and film (Collins), film (Attenborough), and musical theater (Friedman).

Cats used camera angles that retained the sense of a fixed theatrical space, but this was not necessarily to its advantage. The sheer physical presence and immediacy crucial to the theatrical experience of what is primarily a dance show is severely diluted by the restrictions of the small screen. The choreography tends to be seen as though from audience to stage, producing a lack of variety and a static quality. This is very much the video as aide-mémoire of something already experienced. While it is a useful record of the show, it illustrates the advantage that the once-proposed cartoon version would have had: the visual potential of animation might have brought a new form of energy designed specifically for the screen in place of a pale simulacrum of live theater. *Joseph and the Amazing Technicolor Dreamcoat* went further in presenting images that, although still within the confines of a film studio, kept a stagelike style, employing a framing device that amplified the narrator's role. The schoolteacher telling her class a story became the schoolteacher presenting morning assembly; the other teachers turned up in the various named roles; and the proscenium of the small stage of the school hall acted as a gateway through which the schoolchildren could enter a new world of the imagination. It was a nice effect given added poignancy through its setting in Colet Court, the school for which the work had been written in its original incarnation as a short cantata.

The opening device of the video of *By Jeeves* is more crude, a supposedly audience-eye view of arrivals at a village hall in time for a banjo recital by Bertie Wooster, the British upper-class twit of the P. G. Wodehouse "Jeeves" novels, whose eponymous butler is forever extricating him from various farcical confusions and escapades. The loss of the necessary banjo forces Bertie into time-stalling reminiscences while a new banjo is found, and this recounted narrative is dramatized to form the substance of the show. This is home video as straight theatrical record, for we are in the auditorium, with only the close-up and the change of angle to animate what is a live rather than studio performance. It fails because such an approach does not recognize the differences between a stage performance and a recorded one, and the shots of audience reaction emphasize how the communality of the live theatrical experience is removed from the more socially restricted one of video. *By Jeeves* is again video as souvenir. But it has an additional function, one of proselytizing for a work that is little known in comparison to other Lloyd Webber shows.

With adaptions to and from film, and with the films of the shows reflecting different approaches to the use and purpose of the medium, Lloyd Webber's film-related and filmed shows provide a varied set of relationships between film musical and stage musical within one practitioner's output. What unites the four "big-screen" works—*Jesus Christ Superstar* and *Evita*

transferred to film, *Sunset Boulevard* and *Whistle Down the Wind* transferred from film—is the way in which the adaptations have brought out
themes common to Lloyd Webber's whole repertory, those of social dissent
catalyzed by the ambiguous outsider who illuminates an existing order by
threatening it. Joe throws the questioning spotlight on Norma's world just as
the Man does on the society of a Louisiana town; Jesus challenges the order
established by Rome and by Jerusalem, and is in turn challenged by Judas,
just as Eva challenges the class-driven rule in Argentina and is in turn challenged by Che. What is interesting in the various film and video versions of
the stage shows is their comparative effectiveness in translating their central
concepts to suit the different perspective afforded by the camera and the
screen; where the effect of the stage has been reinterpreted within the language of the screen rather than simply filmed, it has proved strongest and
potentially most durable. What is important is that the screen versions add
to the broadening awareness of Lloyd Webber's repertory as one that exists
dynamically in relation to other genres and media, and not only the lyric
stage.

 CHAPTER 6

"Memory": Musical Reminiscences in Lloyd Webber

PREVIOUS CHAPTERS HAVE REVEALED ELEMENTS OF A COMMON strand in the works of Lloyd Webber: the diversity of influences. In fact, his palette of forms, genres, and themes has been so broad that this repertory as an entirety can be read as a critique on the nature of creative influence. Lloyd Webber's work has been thought to reference other music, inspiring such pejorative descriptions as "derivative" and even "soiled from previous use."[1] But such voicings are a symptom of Lloyd Webber's continual antagonism to some firmly inculcated beliefs about the nature of creativity, especially the importance of certain forms of originality in the assessment of a critical reputation. Western aesthetic criteria since the mid-nineteenth century have tended to value certain qualities over others; the concept of the artist as a unique individual and of his works as original expressions of that uniqueness still prevails in many circles. In one sense, idea has been privileged over technique, a clear shift away from the compositional aesthetics of the Baroque, in which borrowings and reworkings from a composer's own and others' repertories were an everyday part of practical music making.

Today, works which seem to copy ideas from elsewhere are valued less than those which appear to be original. But even though originality and uniqueness are seen as cornerstones of aesthetic judgment, it is difficult—even impossible—for any creative artist to avoid being caught between the past (the canon) and the present (innovation). Even our assumptions about the borrowings of composers who represent the ideals of artistic uniqueness manifested through musical originality are now being brought into question.

J. Peter Burkholder has written that "it increasingly appears that borrowing is much more widespread and significant in the music of the nineteenth and twentieth centuries than we have thought. In such company, [Charles] Ives's more thoroughgoing and diverse uses of existing music make him seem, not an exception, but a paramount case of a common condition."[2]

References by composers to the works of others should not surprise us. In bringing into being a "new" work there is inevitably an influence from what has gone before: the example of the past is part of the learning for the future, and, equally important, provides the primary form of access and evaluation for others. In other words, the creative process and its evaluation are most commonly seen to exist within the framework of their identification with the past. But there is also a need for the creative spirit to separate itself from this influence, to be seen as innovating, adding something of its own unique personality to the equation. Even in doing something different there can be motivation from the past, honoring its power through its rejection. So there is an inherent antagonism between heritage and innovation, acceptance of convention and searching for a new and personal freedom, summarized in Harold Bloom's well-known phrase "the anxiety of influence."[3] The question which each creative work has to deal with is how it reconciles its elements of creative change with those that imbue it with its sense of cultural continuity. Lloyd Webber's referencing of the music of other genres and other times is one way to effect such a reconciliation.

Michael Walsh has suggested that "musical history abounds in uncanny resemblances, some intentional, some not. . . . But every composer soaks up music into his subconscious: a particular series of notes may sound 'right' to him as he doodles at the keyboard, because he has heard them before without remembering quite where."[4] Michael Coveney wrote: "You don't hear Beethoven without also hearing Mozart, Puccini without Verdi, Shostakovich without Glazunov. Music invariably incorporates what happened before. And any composer worth his salt is clearly influenced, consciously or unconsciously, by the music he loves."[5] There is something inherently paradoxical in defining Lloyd Webber's particular identity through his continual referencing of preexisting works, yet his music has inspired more comment than most in this respect, and specific sources have been associated with specific numbers as a type of thematic trainspotting. Musical cognates have been cited across such a broad range of composers as Mendelssohn, Friml, Brahms, Weill, Sondheim, Humperdinck, Ravel, Gershwin, Rodgers, Britten, Fauré, Vaughan Williams, J. S. Bach, Stravinsky, and—most frequently—Prokofiev and Puccini. Clearly Lloyd Webber's relationship with past musical repertory is an important one, and often so self-evident as to make covert borrowing unlikely. Indeed, a covert nature is not characteristic of Lloyd Webber's repertory, which—if anything—has been considered by some direct to the point of unsubtlety. What increasingly emerges in studying his works is a core feature of resynthesizing existing materials to create new musical drama through changed juxtapositions. It is as though he has constantly sought to place himself within a broad creative landscape, establishing, refining, and changing his self-definition as he explores the variety of his surroundings. Lloyd Webber's path to reconciling the creation of a personal musical space with the retention of a sense of cultural continuity has been to reshape the past to his own ends; it is an aesthetic of cultural collage and comment. The use of such musical references, rereadings, and reworkings shows a broader continuum of possibilities than the simple dichotomy of originality vs. plagiarism suggests. The following examples illustrate Lloyd Webber's strategy, as well as the benefits and risks that strategy brings to his musical purposes.

Shades of Gray

There are many ways in which a musical element from an existing piece of repertory can become incorporated into a new work. It may be through sheer coincidence: such things do happen, especially when there are similarities of musical vocabulary and thought. This is even more likely when a style imposes limitations on the range of music: for example, the choice of a strophic, twelve-bar blues as the basis for a pop song immediately draws certain boundaries. David Cullen, virtually an amanuensis to Lloyd Webber through much of the composer's output, is acutely aware of the intricacies of Lloyd Webber's work but defends him strongly on this ground of stylistic limitation. "Andrew has this terrific melodic gift, and I do very much resent people criticizing him for borrowing and stealing. He's in the business, generally, of writing very simple melodies. Not simpler than the average pop song but simpler than most show songs, perhaps. If that's what you are doing, you're going to come closer to other things. There aren't that many notes."[6]

However, the sheer volume of criticism Lloyd Webber's music has provoked in this regard has steadily weakened such a position. Thematic similarity may most directly be the result of pastiche—writing explicitly within a particular style in order to evoke memories of and create a dialogue with the originating genre or work. As we have seen, pastiche has been an important part of Lloyd Webber's earlier works, but also represents his most obvious use of existing musical material. In fact, the musical origins must be obvious to the listener in order for pastiche to work; in Chapter 2 I proposed that this may in part have arisen in response to the need to suggest visual imagery for musical dramas conceived as sound recordings. Allusion is another technique that may be employed to stimulate cross-reference to other works; this strategy provides a background of connections rather than a foreground of them as in pastiche. Allusory references may be general, contributing the shadow of another work or works behind the new piece. They may also be highly localized through a single distinctive chord, texture, or interval, for example, but in the process may thus include direct quotation of some musical element from another work. These two techniques—pastiche and allusion—rely to different degrees on the recognition of their sources by the audience, and in dramatic works they cannot avoid creating a narrative link or commentary from one work to the other. Pastiche and allusion need a particular common cultural context for the implicit dialogue between composer and audience to work. Both techniques also evoke a certain self-satisfaction on the part of an audience flattered by the consequent validation of its own status through the recognition of shared knowledge. Thus pastiche and allusion are principally devices of the conscious for both the composer and the audience.

Similar to pastiche in mechanism, but not in intent, is the modeling of a new piece on a template of another to create a certain style, specific not just to a genre but to a piece or group of pieces. The model provides a set of musical springboards from which the composer can then fashion his or her own piece. While including elements of pastiche, the new work attempts to move beyond it to create something "real" in its own terms, although elements of allusion are necessarily a result of its method. In this respect, the model is principally there for the composer's benefit rather than for the audience's, and it is not part of the explicit composer-audience dialogue; it is a conscious method of composing but may remain a subconscious element or an unnoticed part of the effect for the listener.

Pastiche

In Lloyd Webber's cultural dialogue, pastiche ranges from such surreal combinations as King Herod and Dixieland jazz in *Jesus Christ Superstar* to spe-

cific references such as the country and western of "U.N.C.O.U.P.L.E.D." in
Starlight Express, parodying the original "D.I.V.O.R.C.E." by Boddy Braddock and Curly Putnam. I have already discussed pastiche in Lloyd Webber's earlier works, most notably *Joseph and the Amazing Technicolor Dreamcoat,* in Chapter 3. But the use of direct pastiche—songs clearly located
within an originating style and to be understood as such—is found principally only in those works and at those moments in which the narrative is
less important than the manner of delivery. In *Joseph,* the addition of the
pastiche songs is an effective and colorful way of elaborating upon an existing, complete narrative; the songs do not advance action, they give localized
additional color and in the end change the balance of the show to one with
a much more cartoonlike element of exaggeration and posturing. The impetus of the stories in *Jesus Christ Superstar* and *Evita* generates in each its own
sense of place and purpose, and there is little need for pastiche. "Herod's
Song" in *Superstar* has a witty delivery (verbal and musical) to elongate the
presentation of a very short idea; "On This Night of a Thousand Stars" in
Evita is a diegetic number, an actual performance in the story as well as the
musical, and will soon be explained as the result of modeling.

Although *Jeeves* (1975) and its reworking *By Jeeves* (1996) might be expected to be rife with pastiche numbers to evoke the era of the early 1930s
of the P. G. Wodehouse stories, there is very limited use of clearly defined
period writing in either score. While the romantic numbers "When Love
Arrives" and "Half a Moment" do display period elements—most notably
in the former in an elegance reminiscent of Vivian Ellis, in the latter in the
echoes of Kern's long phrasing—many numbers have distinctly more contemporary origins. "Travel Hopefully" had originally used lyrics by Tim Rice
in its incarnation as "Love Is Here" from *The Likes of Us* (set in Victorian
London), a work from the same time and sharing the same pop predilections
as *Joseph and the Amazing Technicolor Dreamcoat.* The use of suspensions
in the ostinato figures that accompany "The Code of the Woosters" is distinctly from early-1970s pop. Additions for the 1996 version of the show also
had former lives. The "'Hallo' Song" was derived from the refrain of "What
a Line to Go Out On," a pop song by Rice and Lloyd Webber (1972) sung by
Yvonne Elliman after her success as Mary Magdalene in *Jesus Christ Superstar.* "It's a Pig" had been heard previously as the Latin pop song "Magdalena" (1977), written for Tony Christie to capitalize on his success with "On
This Night of a Thousand Stars" from the *Evita* concept album. But then
the origins of the *Jeeves* project were mixed, with the initial idea (then a col-

laboration with Tim Rice) being not a period representation but an updating of Bertie Wooster to an early-1970s man-about-town, with rock as the musical basis. With its eventual 1930s setting, musical lifts from earlier shows, and later reworking for the 1996 version (with Lloyd Webber and Alan Ayckbourn by now some twenty years older and more experienced), it is hardly surprising that the result neither attains the sparkle of a period pastiche as Sandy Wilson had managed in *The Boy Friend* (1920s American stage musical) and its underrated successor *Divorce Me, Darling!* (1930s Hollywood film musical) nor hits a contemporary tone. But by 1996 Lloyd Webber's approach to the use of pastiche had changed significantly, and that change came through working on the two shows *Cats* and *Starlight Express*.

With *Cats* there was no linking story, and the work began as a "song cycle" seen at the Sydmonton Festival in 1978, consisting of discrete musical numbers somewhat in the manner of *Side by Side by Sondheim* (first presented the previous year at London's Mermaid Theatre). The original concept of a set of contrasting numbers, without a dramatic narrative, meant that each song needed to establish some sort of musical characterization independent of the others and develop a quick rapport with the audience. Such a rapid familiarity and identification of purpose can be achieved through pastiche. But it was only a musical starting point, for the songs in *Cats* move beyond the straightforward "Elvis" pastiche of *Joseph and the Amazing Technicolor Dreamcoat*; they are less pointed, more the free workings within a range of chosen styles than direct copies of a specific performer or number. The audience responds to the musical differences, given an initial security provided by the familiarity of recognizable, underlying stylistic generalities.

Starlight Express is a more blatant version of the approach and structure of *Cats*. Where the differentiation of characters through music and dance was the clear focus in *Cats* rather than the tenuous plot, *Starlight Express* purported to have a plot, albeit a thin one. Again, the work began as an idea on a much more limited scale, designed for a small audience (in age as well as size), with a simple train story elaborated by clearly differentiated characters. Pop pastiche was an ideal form for creating such differentiation, exactly as in the added numbers for *Joseph and the Amazing Technicolor Dreamcoat*, also a show primarily aimed at children, and no doubt providing a model of sorts for *Starlight Express*. In the expansion to the spectacle that it finally became (through input from Trevor Nunn), the localized and immediate coloring of pastiche provided a counterbalance to the slight story. In this way, the score becomes a succession of familiar pop tributes, from the opening "dirty beat" rock 'n' roll of "Pumping Iron," through the self-referencing "Poppa's Blues," in which the structure of the blues form itself constitutes the lyrics, through the very specific parody of "U.N.C.O.U.P.L.E.D.," to the final up-tempo gospel of "There's a Light at the End of the Tunnel."[7] Story is not the point of this show; instead, it uses quickly grasped images in music and staging to create something akin to a pop revue with Las Vegas speed and spectacle. Pastiche and its attendant conventions suit the rapid-fire presentation.

Beginning with *The Phantom of the Opera*, however, the integration of music into a central dramatic structure again took precedence. As with *Jesus Christ Superstar* and *Evita*, the show's impetus came from the interaction of the main characters; as we saw in Chapter 4, pastiche retained a place in the score as a contributor of period color and also as a device for ridiculing the onstage opera as a means of throwing into sharper relief the backstage story. There is no pastiche number in *The Phantom of the Opera* that works outside its dramatic context. Such numbers as there are, most notably the onstage opera extracts, have interruptions and disturbances from the development of the plot, so are seldom complete. The songs that can be removed from the show as freestanding numbers are those of the main plot, such as "All I Ask of You" and "Music of the Night." Pastiche has become no longer its own self-satisfying end but part of the wider techniques of musical dramatization. "Stand-and-deliver" pastiche numbers—which take advantage of stylistic shorthand and whose focus is the direct presentation from performer to audience and never mind the plot—do not occur. For example, "Parlez-vous Français?" (*Aspects of Love*) and "Cold" (*Whistle Down the Wind*) are presented as though radio broadcasts to establish the periods of the dramas. The first provides a dramatic counterpoint through its stating of the subtext, as Alex attempts to engage Rose's attention; the second has a "live" reprise that emphasizes the black-white racial divide in the American South.

Pastiche for Lloyd Webber appears to have been at first a symbol of a desire for commercial acceptance, a means of buying into existing genre success, and an acknowledgment of his musical roots. Whereas strong plots have led to a more integrated musical style, less derivative and more mature, pastiche has been associated with the opposite side of the coin. So pastiche has been used as a way of holding attention and imposing a localized coherence, if not a coherence for an entire show, when the dramatic line has been weakest. *The Beautiful Game* (Lloyd Webber's most recent work at the time of writing), though it seems rife with opportunities for pastiche numbers, with its Northern Irish setting, its soccer players, and its 1960s setting, is notably free of pastiche. Hints of Irishness come through in the odd modal cadence and the penny-whistle obbligatos, and soccer is evident in the terrace chant of the title song, but it contains no number that is a clear and deliberate pastiche to be immediately acknowledged by the audience. Lloyd Webber's early approach favored literal presentation, probably as a result of the learning process of composition itself: he wrote songs in the styles of music which interested him. Later, pastiche became an undercurrent, just one part of a range of techniques to be freely mixed and matched in the service of the dramatic portrayal of characters throughout an entire score.

In any event, there is a certain joie de vivre in the best known of Lloyd Webber's pastiche numbers, fine examples of their kind and the objects of popular appreciation. In addition, their wit has provided a useful complement to a composer whose works have been much more "musical" than "comedy." Behind even this, there is a sense of ritual within the adoption of pastiche, in its rehearsing of preexisting patterns of action. Here, the audience is invited to recognize not just the musical-verbal style but also the performing context with which it is generally associated: the "Song of the King" requires Pharaoh to pay homage to the performing style of Elvis, and so the behaviors and conventions of the pop concert enter the musical theater.

Allusion

Allusion is often a more subtle technique than pastiche. It provides additional coloring or meaning, but is not in itself the defining element of a piece, so the element of recognition is not as fundamental to immediate understanding as it is for its close relatives pastiche and especially parody. But allusion still requires the composer to acknowledge the source material somehow with the expectation that at least some of the audience will at some level pick up on the significance of the reference. For this dialogue to work, the composer must be allowed the expression of such knowledge. Allusion is knowing not just of the moment but of its associated connotations. Treating every potential referent (classical or otherwise) as an unsophisticated borrowing—as many critics of Lloyd Webber seem to do—denies space for allusion. Yet creative people establish their own relationship to artistic tradition through their works, through the inclusion, rejection, adaptation, and even quotation of what has gone before. Allusion is a part of this process of self-definition for Lloyd Webber.

Allusion with a clear point of reference appears in *Aspects of Love* in music associated with George. We hear this spiky little tune at the start of act I, scene 18, as George relates to Giulietta (who is sculpting him) his embellished recollections of his encounter with Alex, Rose, and a gun:

> GEORGE: And then with a swift karate chop
>   I removed his gun —
>   You should have been there!
>   Poor chap didn't know what hit him . . .
> GIULIETTA: Still, George!
>   If you can't keep your tongue still,
>   You will have the face of Edith Sitwell!

The music is a clear allusion to the "Gavotte" third movement from Pro-kofiev's Symphony No. 1, the "Classical." Lloyd Webber has kept the open-ing gesture of quarter-note leaps but inverted their direction, retained the four-square phrase structure, and noticeably retained the chromatic rise at the end of the whole melody. More important, the harmonic and melodic gestures have been kept alongside—quite crucially—the same quality of tone and articulation. What makes this an allusion rather than an indiscrimi-nate borrowing? The answer is found in the character of George, with whom the music is associated. He is intelligent and sophisticated, well-read, with refined tastes. He appreciates the finer things in life; he is cultured, and his actions and words—witty, erudite, and sometimes barbed—are moderated by an intellectual gloss. These qualities in themselves suit the observed re-straint and concision of the Prokofiev theme. But beyond this, George has made his money as a forger of other people's paintings; his own work is a reworking of that of others. Through his paintings and literary bons mots he recycles the works of others for his own use. The neoclassicism at the heart of the Prokofiev symphony, so piquantly portrayed in its Gavotte, match this very quality of appropriation and reinterpretation that George displays, and Lloyd Webber's example is well-observed as a result.

More general allusion can be found where the evocation of a specific atmosphere is important but direct pastiche would damage the integrity of the dramatic moments: the creation of a sound world for the whole show is more important than the momentary diversion of pastiche, with its fore-grounding of detail. For example, the increasingly inebriated apostles at the

Example 6.1. "And then with a swift karate chop" (*Aspects of Love*) and Prokofiev's "Classical" Symphony: *Gavotte*

Last Supper in *Jesus Christ Superstar,* a labored chorus of voices struggling to reach the high note, evoke an "all lads together" atmosphere of the pub or football terrace, but not to an extreme that undermines the more important contrasting sections with Jesus and Judas.[8] In *Evita,* the restrained *a cappella* homophonic harmonization of the ruling classes brings with it associations of church choirs and hymns and thus formality, rigidity, and control; it is an allusion that summarizes quickly and effectively both social status and attitude. Norma Desmond's music first heard as Joe discovers her mansion adopts an aspirational theme that is melodramatic when set against the popular songs of Joe's contemporary world; in its broad melody with low string scoring it evokes the epic film score, an apt idea that is developed through the show. "God's Own Country" in *The Beautiful Game* uses modal harmony (VIIb) to evoke the appropriate "traditional" Irish atmosphere without breaking away from the underlying ballad style; it is a coloristic allusion that places the song quickly within its geographical-cultural setting.

Modeling

The idea of modeling a new work on the template of an existing one occupies ground between pastiche and allusion. Elements of pastiche are present in the desire to re-create a specific sound world and access its cultural significance, yet there may be an ambiguity in that the source is not well-known or immediately made clear. To understand pastiche or allusion the audience must know the music being pastiched or the style or work alluded to; in allusion, the placing of the reference must be such that it invites the effect to be noticed and the comparison to be made. But what if the music in question seems to lack the sense of self-knowing playfulness that runs through the most clear examples of Lloyd Webber's pastiche or lacks sufficiently widespread references to be identified? Here there is room for the technique of modeling, in which another work has provided the stimulus for composition and elements of it remain, obscured through alteration so that the original stimulus is sensed rather than overtly stated.

The similarities that exist between the ballad "On This Night of a Thousand Stars" in *Evita* and the Latin standard "Cherry Pink and Apple Blossom White" (1950, music by Louiguy) are self-evident. Their structures are the same (AABBA); the opening phrases of each respective section are identical in gesture and substantially similar in execution, especially in rhythm; their overall melodic and harmonic contours are similar; the prominent pitches which define the main phrases are the same, for example the rise to 5 in the opening motif of the A section, or the falling pitches beginning with 8-7 at the start of the B section. In fact, you can sing much of one tune to the accompaniment of the other.[9] In effect, Lloyd Webber has formulated a new Latin ballad through shadowing the most characteristic structural elements of "Cherry Pink and Apple Blossom White." Dramatically, the style of song is appropriate. Magaldi is a singer of popular Latin ballads, so it is possible to see the link also as one of allusion: "Cherry Pink and Apple Blossom White" is simply the right sort of song for a popular Latin melody of the 1940s, at least if you are from Britain (or indeed America), the cultural background of Lloyd Webber and his prospective audience.[10] The song provides a

Example 6.2. Motivic connections between "On This Night of a Thousand Stars" *(Evita)* and "Cherry Pink and Apple Blossom White"

convenient method for establishing a geographical and temporal placing by latching on to the already familiar: shorthand both for the composer in conveying his ideas and for the listeners in quickly understanding the context of the music.[11] So by fixing on a particular example of a Latin song (albeit from a filtered perspective) and from about the right time, Lloyd Webber has found a template from which to create an appropriately sounding new number. In fact, in the way that it sticks so closely to those features which create the character of the original Louiguy number, the whole piece can even be seen as a vocal extemporization around "Cherry Pink and Apple Blossom White" in the manner of an interpretation-in-performance of the original.

There are other, more shadowy, examples which suggest the use of a harmonic-melodic starting point from another work as a trigger, but which, after receiving that initial kick start, develop in their own way. The song "Go, Go, Go Joseph," added to *Joseph and the Amazing Technicolor Dreamcoat* by the time of its recording by Decca in 1969, begins with an alternation on the half-bar between I and IV at a speed and with a texture that evoke the Manfred Mann hit song "Pretty Flamingo" (1966). The second half of the *Joseph* melody (4-5-4-3-1 [Bb-C-Bb-A-F]) matches the outline of the main descending phrase of the Manfred Mann song (2-3-2-1-lower5 [A-B-A-G-D]), essentially having been shifted downward by a tone; the aural similarity is strengthened by the same rhythms for the specific phrases, a more general match of speed and rhythmic style, and similar vocal and instrumental qualities. There is enough in the *Joseph* number to provoke a recollection beyond a generic contemporary late-1960s pop style, inviting cross-reference to a specific song; as a reworking of such a sound idea it suggests the presence of the Manfred Mann number as a stimulus.

The persistent paralleling throughout the whole of "On This Night of a Thousand Stars" with "Cherry Pink and Apple Blossom White" seems to point toward a clear and consciously identified model work, a piece we can hear as a ghost throughout the number. "Go, Go, Go Joseph," with its more limited correlations, suggests the shadow of a style or an aural image to create a sense of audience identification rather than to evoke a whole piece. In this case the forebear has been reworked and reinterpreted so that it is integrated into the Lloyd Webber piece and now works within it, independent of its source. And if anything suggests conscious modeling rather than an unconscious borrowing, it is the use of the similar musical material overtly within the same genre—here that of 1960s pop—through which the composer buys into a specific musical culture: the audience for the new piece is similar to the audience for the model. The use of the compositional model can then act as an implicit acknowledgment of familiarity with the genre (as for pastiche and allusion), but it additionally becomes a claim for acceptance of the new work as part of the same style grouping. The numbers above and their suggested models do have such relationships, both between them and with their respective genres, and so argue for what can be seen as a rewriting of history. In taking something that has already existed and using it in another way, Lloyd Webber has effectively rewritten the earlier musical history to reshape it in his own preferred image. Such reworking is part of the quest for the artist to deal with the past, to accommodate a sense of heritage. When preexisting material is used in a manner different from its original, it gains a new dimension: it has been treated in such a way as to bring out other latent musical possibilities of the material left unexplored in its original version. This principle will become even more apparent in the most obvious of Lloyd Webber's borrowings.

Returning to *Evita*, there is a resemblance that straddles another border-line, and on first glance may go beyond modeling or allusion toward musical borrowing. It is found in the opening phrases of "I'd Be Surprisingly Good for You," in which Evita introduces herself to Juan Perón, immediately after Magaldi has sung "On This Night of a Thousand Stars" at the charity con-cert for earthquake relief. (Magaldi sings only the last few phrases, a reprise just long enough to trigger the recollection of the whole song and its earlier circumstances.) Looked at in isolation, the melody and harmony of the first four bars are similar to bars 2–5 of the Beatles' standard "Yesterday." Yet the resemblance does not leap out when the number is put in context. Why? First, the opening rhythm of the Beatles' number, based on the word *yester-day*, does not occur at the start; the similarity begins in the second bar and thus wrong-foots the resemblance from the outset, especially in the harmony by changing an establishing tonic major to a minor. Second, the descending scale in the fourth bar of "Yesterday" is matched in Evita's number by a rising one on the last three notes of the bar. These may seem like small changes, but the similarity is further disguised, for rhythm, harmony (as a relative minor variant), and melodic shape of the opening section of "I'd Be Surpris-ingly Good for You" also closely resemble the preceding "On This Night of a Thousand Stars." In particular, that distinctive final rhythm of each line, which in Magaldi's number covers the words *thousand stars* and *heaven's door* and in Evita's number is sung to *must believe* and *nothing planned*, emphasizes the link between the two numbers. There is a resemblance to "Yesterday," but there is also one to Magaldi's song heard immediately be-fore it. And there is a dramatic link as well, as Evita uses on Perón her own intimate reworking of Magaldi's overt concert song of seduction, promising him his own night of a single star—her. It is an effective dramatic reflection, taking the audience from the public to the private, at the same time showing Evita's ability to manipulate what she has to hand (Magaldi's song) in the pursuit of her own ambitious goals. To suggest "Yesterday" as an influence— possibly one of those musical ideas remembered but not recognized—is rea-sonable; but equally there are obvious links that relate to the music already present in *Evita*, which accord with the dramatic placing and its subtext.

Borrowing

In 1969 Ross Hannaman released two songs by Lloyd Webber and Rice on a single. The A side, "1969," is a straightforward presentation in pop form of Beethoven's piano piece *Für Elise*.[12] The B side, "Down Thru' Summer," is clearly indebted for its opening phrases to the famous melody from the Largo of Dvořák's Symphony No. 9, "From the New World."[13] Tim Rice has commented: "I never questioned why Andrew relied so heavily on the classics for quite a few of his tunes at the time. But there had been plenty of original efforts too and it would be a brave popular composer who could put his hand on his royalty statements and claim he had never borrowed from the deceased. In fact it is annoying that it is virtually impossible for lyricists to do the same."[14]

Of course, the appropriation of classical music for popular song and show themes is not new. In American musical theater, the generation of "Hey There" in *The Pajama Game* from Frank Loesser's suggestion of the opening phrase of Mozart's "simple" sonata in C major is a well-known anecdote. Al Jolson famously—and to his cost—appropriated Cavaradossi's act III aria "E lucevan le stelle" from *Tosca* for his song "Avalon." Others have more openly adapted classics, as with the metamorphosis of Chopin's étude in E major (op. 10, no. 3) as the song "So Deep Is the Night" or the lyrical second section of the Fantasie Impromptu in C♯ minor (op. 66) as "I'm Always Chasing Rainbows." More recent pop songs have made similar adaptions: the Prelude in C minor of Chopin's op. 28 was reworked by Barry Manilow as "Could It Be Magic"; Billy Joel's "This Night" is a stylish 1950s version of the second movement "Adagio cantabile" of Beethoven's Piano Sonata no. 8, op. 13 ("Sonata Pathëtique"); and the eighteenth variation from the *Rhapsody on a Theme of Paganini* (op. 43) by Rachmaninoff became "I Could Change the World" for the British group the Korgis, just one of very many reworkings of a famous theme also treated by Lloyd Webber in *Variations*.

Of significance for Lloyd Webber in particular is the trend to create rock versions of art repertory works in the classic rock of the late 1960s and the 1970s. Emerson, Lake, and Palmer in particular combined rock presentation and inflection with a more orthodox tradition as in their uses of Bartók, Janáček, and Mussorgsky, while more suggestive in effect was the Bach-like melody of Procol Harum's "A Whiter Shade of Pale."[15] The influence of classical music was never far from the rock of the 1960s and 1970s, which sought a more serious identity that would distinguish it from the self-consciously ephemeral and transient sounds of pop. The potential symbiosis between the classical music repertory and the worlds of pop and musical theater clearly was evident to Lloyd Webber early on. But a deeper philosophical motive was behind the simple musical appropriation of such borrowed material: the need to pull away from tradition yet also to gain acceptance within it. By reworking signifiers of the past into something different, shifting genre and use, Lloyd Webber opened a new creative space in which the past could be reclaimed as part of the present. The move breaks previous associations by undermining them, then re-creating them through reuse. So the interest in Lloyd Webber's musical borrowings comes less from their actual use than from the repertory from which they have been drawn and the circumstances in which they appear—a dialogue between the past, as represented by established repertory and its canonical values, and the present day, as represented by reworkings that appeal to different values and a different audience.

For example, one of the most well known of Lloyd Webber's classical reworkings uses the slow and lyrical second movement of Mendelssohn's Violin Concerto in E minor (op. 64) as the melody for "Kansas Morning," the pop song to lyrics by Tim Rice which eventually became "I Don't Know How to Love Him," a hit from *Jesus Christ Superstar*.[16] From a musical standpoint, the resemblance between the pop melody and the concerto is so obvious and continues through such an extended passage (some seven bars) that any claim to coincidence is untenable. But the effect of the reworking has provided Lloyd Webber with a significant and effective number for his repertory, and the Mendelssohn source is easily overshadowed by the resulting pop-folk ballad. In particular, the strength of the number, in which Mary Magdalene expresses her confusion over her love for Jesus, lies in the contrast between the placid musical opening which gives way in its middle section ("Should I bring him down") to a feeling of increasing intensity— through rising pitch, short phrases, verbal repetitions—to the unexpected, musical exclamation point on the words "I never thought I'd come to this"; harmonically the exclamation is marked by assertive fourth relationships including the modal flattened VII major chord (I-VII♭-IV-I [D-C♮-G-D]). The return to the opening section thus becomes more than a simple repeat, as it brings the strong emotional undercurrents from the middle section: we hear the more restrained, almost distancing self-observation by Mary Magdalene, yet know it is the smooth surface of something more tempestuous. Rice's lyrics, meanwhile—direct, almost matter-of-fact at times ("I'd be lost/ I'd be frightened/I couldn't cope"), yet also insecure ("I don't know . . ." and "What's it all about?")—effectively reflect this dual character within the music. Furthermore, Mendelssohn's eight-bar theme has been extended to an unusual but natural-sounding ten bars, and the rhythmic emphasis of Mendelssohn's bars 5 and 6 has been displaced to produce a more assertive

Example 6.3. "Memory" *(Cats)*: opening harmonic outline

phrase (through landing on the lower dominant), where it previously had been more questioning (rising away from the lower dominant). The whole number is more than a simple melodic appropriation; it is a reinterpretation of its lyrical nature through another genre and another instrument. The transformation is achieved by the changes of meter (from 6/8 to 4/4), genre (from lyrical berceuselike quality to late-1960s folk ballad), and melodic quality (from pure sustained melody to an expressive and dramatic vocal line), and the direct lyrics and balanced phrases, altered to result in an effortless twenty-one-bar refrain, enhance the effect. Lloyd Webber has refashioned something of the past to create something moving and atmospheric in its own right.

Another of Lloyd Webber's most famous melodies has also been attributed to a classical antecedent. In his biography of Lloyd Webber, Michael Coveney describes how the widow of the composer of the 1940s popular song "Bolero Blue" claimed that "Memory" was from her husband's adaptation of Ravel's *Bolero*—which suggests something of the biter being bitten![17] Both the Ravel and Lloyd Webber melodies are elaborations of a descending scale, but what initially distinguishes the former from the latter is its phrasing: long and seamless in the Ravel, flowing over bar lines, and each note that is temporarily settled on acts as a pivot to the next part of the phrase. In contrast, "Memory" is constructed from two distinct musical ideas: the first repeats a single tone (emphasized by the words "Midnight . . . pavement . . . memory" in the first stanza), while the second is a turnlike figure used to decorate the approach to and strengthen the effect of the repeated notes.

While the Ravel privileges melody over its static harmonic pedal, "Memory" is fundamentally an assertion of the movement of the harmony. That harmony begins with a I-vi-IV-iii pattern [B♭-Gm-E♭-Dm], which is much more akin to the I-vi-IV-V [B♭-Gm-E♭-F] of pop(ular) song, with the final substitution of V by its relative minor (a typical Lloyd Webberist manifestation of a Puccinian influence). In addition, for a composer who is known to write at the keyboard, it seems self-evident that the melody fits as a decoration of the tones present at the top of the chord pattern, shifting down the keyboard in a parallel movement between left and right hands. The use of such a chord pattern in combination with the 12/8 time signature of a slow rock 'n' roll ballad, archetypal since the mid-1950s ("Unchained Melody," for example), suggests an entirely different provenance from French art music. The same stylistic features occur in "Our Kind of Love" in *The Beautiful Game*; its initial chord pattern is the related sequence I-vi-ii-V7 [C-Am-Dm-G7], and its meter is the same four-beat triplet pattern of 12/8. This fits much better Lloyd Webber's interest in pop and rock music, especially when placed alongside his serviceable piano playing and piano extemporization in the process of composition. In one philosophical sense "Memory" can be seen as a reworking of *Bolero*, for there are elements in common. Yet the antithetical treatment of just about every element of the Ravel fails to answer the key question of why that melody should be so distorted as not to betray its origins more convincingly. Rewriting history as a method of staking a personal creative claim still requires that something significant is left to draw attention to the reworking. There has to be a sense (undoubtedly a subconscious one) of "Look what I've done; aren't I subversive?" The subversive element works only when there is still some clear sense of what has been subverted. Such an element is not convincingly present in "Memory."

A double reworking of the past is found in "Don't Cry for Me, Argentina" in *Evita*. Its verse structure and accompaniment not only is based on the Prelude in C major, the first of J. S. Bach's "48," but also owes part of its melodic approach to the Gounod adaptation (as a setting of the Ave Maria) through the superimposition of a sustained melody line over Bach's broken chords. Unlike Gounod's version, Lloyd Webber uses only the first six bars of the Bach chord sequence, completing them as a fifteen-bar unit (another unusual section length, as with the Mendelssohn adaptation). The melodic line, however, shadows the contour of the Gounod version by beginning a 3rd below at the start, then coinciding with it on the 5-2-3 [A♭-E♭-F] for the words "feel . . . That . . . done" and on the expressive 6 [B♭] which follows on the second syllable of "believe." Having established this highly appropriate connection to the Ave Maria—for Evita is "Santa Evita," the Argentine Madonna—the verse takes a new direction with which Lloyd Webber claims the musical idea for himself through the use of the warm but assertive horn chords on the phrase "I had to let it happen, I had to change." This provides an interesting hint of a double meaning: not only does it apply to Evita's life, it refers as well to the music's own shift of attention from Bach-Gounod to Lloyd Webber. The second section of the refrain gains through its reduction from broken chords to homophonic harmonic skeleton, and combines with the new strength (expressed in the lyrics' exposition of taking personal control) to produce a moment of almost hypnotic stasis at the center of the show. All this is in D♭ major, Lloyd Webber's favorite key of "resonance." With the return of the verse "And as for fortune and as for fame" the accompaniment shifts one stage further when a soft-rock bass line is added (with decorated upbeats to each bar), and broken chords are reintroduced in a pattern more typical of the slow pop ballad. What began as a Bach prelude has been reduced to its most basic harmonic outline and then built back up again into the shape of another genre.

But if the introductory verse of "Don't Cry for Me, Argentina" brilliantly sets up a situation, the refrain is something of an anticlimax. Criticism of it has in part centered on the idea that it may be constructed from unrelated fragments culled from other numbers. When *Evita* opened on Broadway, Howard Kissel identified three musical similarities in the song, which "starts with a paraphrase of the opening line of an old Latin standard, 'Yours,' veers off into the first line of 'Rose Marie,' then quotes a few consecutive phrases from Brahms's *Violin Concerto* before going off on its own."[18] This analysis is unconvincing because the melody has its own integrity and needs not stand on external sources; in fact, its internal relationships create a remarkably static and limited melody which seems to explain better its anticlimactic relationship to the verse.

The first two phrases consist of running up the notes of a pentatonic phrase complementary to the tonic harmonic pedal; then, having reached the tonic octave as a high point, the melody runs down the same notes. Given the relationship between the first and second phrases alongside their combined relationship to the tonic pedal, there seems no reason to view the

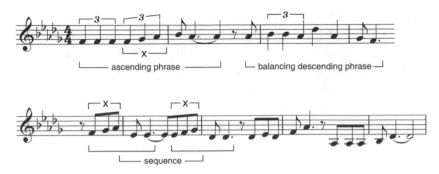

Example 6.4. "Don't Cry for Me, Argentina" *(Evita)*: refrain

second phrase as discrete from the first. They act as a single phrase, and any attribution of the second phrase to a source independent of the first does not make sense. There is an almost exact antecedent for the phrase in Lloyd Webber's own output, the opening phrase of "Stone the Crows" in *Joseph and the Amazing Technicolor Dreamcoat*, itself linked to the opening phrase of "Any Dream Will Do" from the same work. As Lloyd Webber frequently reuses whole numbers and distinctive phrases of his own, why look beyond stylistic similarity within his own repertory? As to the similarity with a passage from the Brahms violin concerto in the following, simple descending sequence, there is a more obvious source in the opening bars. This particular sequence begins with the opening motif of the whole refrain, and so the sequential phrase arises naturally out of the material of the song itself. To look elsewhere for a source of an undistinguished musical motif seems unnecessary. Indeed, if a direct link between the Brahms and Lloyd Webber works is not being made, the comment is meddlesome, merely allowing the commentator an opportunity to claim his own cultural high ground through knowledge of the classical repertory. By implication, this reduces Lloyd Webber's work to a lesser status through its undigested musical recycling, its essential lack of originality.

Rewriting the Repertory

The "mosaic" method of tune construction, as Kissel's description might be called, has also been applied to "Music of the Night" in *The Phantom of the Opera*. The opening four notes are the same as those of "Come to Me, Bend to Me" *(Brigadoon)*, while the climactic central phrase is from Dick

Johnson's act I love song in Puccini's *La fanciulla del West*, "Quello che tacete me l'ha detto il cor." Set against a process of reworking musical material to claim some sort of ownership of it through its reinterpretation—by in some way realizing an unfulfilled potential within the original musical idea—the theorizing of a compositional technique that draws on such disparate sources for such small fragments of melody is unconvincing. A wider view of Lloyd Webber's interaction with Puccini suggests not just *what* may have been used, but, more important, *why*.

There are undoubtedly Puccinian allusions and echoes in *The Phantom of the Opera*. One specific and haunting moment, when Raoul and Christine sing the end of their love duet in unison from a distance, carries the clear resonance of Rodolfo and Mimì at the end of act I of *La bohème*. The vocal quality of the offstage ending to a love duet is similar in both cases, although a mere couple of notes in Puccini become a restatement of the entire theme in Lloyd Webber. There is also a more extended offstage section at the very end of *La fanciulla del West*, for Dick and Minnie, in which a single note is repeated many times by both of them to the word *addio*, fading as they ride away together into the distance. The effect is like that of Christine and Raoul sailing away in the gondola from the Phantom's lair at the end of act II. What has been adopted in *The Phantom of the Opera* is a dramatic gesture, as well as a distinctive tonal quality, and these allude to appropriately operatic, and specifically Puccinian, forbears.[19] As we have noted, the use of opera, its expectations, and conventions, was very much a part of the intergenre dialogue of *The Phantom of the Opera*, and the musical manifestation of this was seen in the ways in which generic impressions of opera were created. Both temperamentally for Lloyd Webber, a lifelong admirer of Puccini's work, and musically in the setting of the story itself, Puccini's musical language provides an accessible point of reference and allows for the reworking or re-presentation of its mannerisms as a form of musical theater-opera reflexivity. Puccini is thus found in *Phantom* in both the general atmosphere of Romantic-*verismo* interaction and in moments of sound which evoke Puccini opera in timbre or theme.

The offstage voices provide a reference in timbre, while the "Mystic Chords" theme, first heard at the end of "Music of the Night" (see Chapter 4), provides a more tangible example. This theme seems to reference one well-known moment, only a few bars before the offstage vocal phrase in *La bohème* already mentioned. It is the "sempre più sostenuto" recitative-like passage in which Mimì and Rodolfo agree to go together to join his

Example 6.5. Evocative chords in *La bohème*, act I, and "Music of the Night"
(*The Phantom of the Opera*)

friends at the café. The sustained chords, framed by the stepwise ascending
top line and descending bass, present a series of chromatic colorations that
move from A major to D major. Although the progression is not identical
to Lloyd Webber's mystic chords, which use a sequence of straightforward
majors and minors, it is nonetheless very close in its IV-I harmonic outline
(F♯ to C♯ majors), bass and treble movement (the Lloyd Webber substitutes
whole-tone for chromatic in the ascent), and orchestral quality. The occurrence of both the offstage voices and evocative chords in *Phantom*, which
are also in such close proximity in the Puccini, reinforces the allusion.[20]

    An even more specific thematic link is found in the opening melodic
ideas of "The Music of the Night," variously attributed to Frederick Loewe
("Come to Me, Bend to Me" in *Brigadoon*) and to the song "School Days."[21]
In fact, the two main motifs of the refrain can be linked to Puccini. To take
the second of these first: this repeated musical motif is first articulated by the
lyrics "Silently the senses abandon their defences." The phrase is the same as
the climactic section of Dick Johnson's declaration to Minnie of his love for
her in act I of *La fanciulla del West*, expressing "a strange joy, a new peace
that I cannot describe."[22] The words provide the emotional link from one

Example 6.6. Motivic connections between *Tosca*, *La fanciulla del West*, and "Music of the Night" *(The Phantom of the Opera)*

musical theater work to the other. The themes are used in such a similar way that it is impossible to believe that as knowledgeable a musician as Lloyd Webber would place his theme so prominently purely by accident; it seems placed to evoke operatic associations of musical style, dramatic moment, and associated emotions. As for the opening motif of "The Music of the Night," another source suggests itself, and establishes more surreptitiously this overt, romantic, Puccini–Lloyd Webber declaration.

A more appropriate source is Cavaradossi's act I aria in *Tosca*, "Recondite armonia," whose climactic phrase is the same as the first phrase of "Music of the Night."[23] Lloyd Webber's song thus has behind it the ghost of an aria which begins with the words *mysterious harmony* and goes on to extol the alluring attraction of La Tosca; the implication is that Cavaradossi is to Tosca as the Phantom wishes to be to Christine. Just as in the developing use of the Bach prelude in "Don't Cry for Me, Argentina," such a reworking of a climactic phrase as an understated, more seductive introductory one brings out a different quality from its original source, presenting it in a new light.

Example 6.7. Motivic connections between *La fanciulla del West* and "All I Ask of You" *(The Phantom of the Opera)*

And the operatic and emotional cross-references continue in "All I Ask of You," Raoul's musical counterpart to the Phantom's "Music of the Night" — but a counterpart in which the object of his affections, Christine, vocally participates. The most demonstrative phrase of the song begins the central refrain when Christine sings, "Say you love me every waking moment"; its distinctive outline runs parallel to Minnie's main motif, symbolic of romantic yearning, in *La fanciulla del West*. Here the symbolism is the same, with Christine's longing for love; but Puccini's motif—presented orchestrally and in a succession of transposed statements—has been transformed into a more extended theme and is delivered vocally.

The nexus that exists between Puccini and Lloyd Webber in this work centered on opera takes the musical references beyond the idea of simple thematic borrowing into a much richer sequence of resonances and reminiscences. In this, of all Lloyd Webber works, it is appropriate that we should be aware of another opera playing alongside the one we watch in the theater. These Puccini links are a tangible and effective way of doing this, allowing both composer and audience to retain their sense of cultural continuity, while also allowing the composer to surprise and entertain in his own way.

Original Sin

Lloyd Webber's musical borrowings of whichever shade are clearly part of a more general aesthetic that reshapes and manipulates what is already in existence. The way that such influences in the music have been woven into the dramatic purpose with increasing subtlety has demonstrated considerable skill. But because originality is considered so important in our widely established aesthetic conventions, any approach that relies so strongly on re-working will invite criticism. It may also invite lawsuits. The title song of *The Phantom of the Opera* became the subject of legal action for plagiarism twice in the early 1990s. First, a British amateur songwriter, John Brett, claimed that it was plagiarized from his own material sent on demonstration tapes to Elaine Paige and Tim Rice. As the subsequent court case established, Lloyd Webber's song had been performed at Sydmonton before the tapes had been posted by Brett. Second, Ray Repp, a writer of hymns, instigated court action in the United States against the same song, claiming that the melody had been taken from his devotional song "Till You," written and copyrighted in 1978. What proved conclusive for the jury, who found in favor of Lloyd Webber in 1998, was that Repp's performances of his song—a version of the Magnificat—and its distribution on a cassette of his works (*Benedicamus*) were on such a limited scale and within such limited religious contexts (at, for example, convention centers, churches, and Catholic universities) as to preclude the likelihood of Lloyd Webber's having heard it. Expert musicological evidence presented for Repp made a convincing case for similarities of melodic motifs, rhythms, and phrase structure; yet "substantial similarity" was not in itself proof of infringement (knowing or otherwise) of copyright.

The question of interest here is not the one decided by the courts but rather a more general aesthetic one. In the light of Lloyd Webber's constant expressions of intertextuality, what advantage to the context of "The Phantom of the Opera" would such an appropriation from Repp have brought? The whole sound world of *The Phantom of the Opera* is built upon intertextual relationships—film-stage, opera-musical, classical-pop, and so on—and as such is probably Lloyd Webber's most closely argued work. There seems to be no advantage in referencing an obscure and musically indifferent song by a relative unknown in a context of Lloyd Webber's previously observed patterns of reworking significant pieces of musical repertory or widely known works of contemporary repertory. Lloyd Webber's technique requires some audience awareness of what has been referenced, and that was clearly not the case with Repp's "Till You." The rewriting of musical history and the working through of the "anxiety of influence" require that the previous repertory in general and in its specific works presents some sort of threat to be overcome, removed of its power through a new and personal appropriation. Reworking Puccini addresses such issues; reworking Repp does not.

In addition, the intended audience itself must not be overlooked. In the case of Lloyd Webber, his work has aimed to be widely accessible in a commercial field. Throughout his output, Lloyd Webber's references to a variety of musical genres, styles, and even specific works have been used as a method of allowing the audience to relate to what is heard by providing a sense of the familiar that can then be shaped in unexpected ways. The desire to appeal to a broad and popular audience—a desire from which, given its origins, musical theater of any type should not recoil—in itself limits to some extent the range of possibilities. Inclusivity rather than exclusivity becomes the guiding force, understood through the audience's own expectations. In this sense, Lloyd Webber could have been a victim both of his own success and of his audiences to a much greater degree than has been the case; contrary to the usual expectations, his repertory has shifted direction and fought against any easy categorization or repetition. The familiar element of the music used— built up through patterns of referencing his own and other known repertories—allows other facets of the shows to be developed more boldly. The music's interest in manipulation more than generation acts as a counterbalance to the shifting challenges of the dramas' themes and presentation. Lloyd Webber has negotiated the musical boundaries between heritage and innovation, between joining the canon and fighting against it, in a demonstrative and persistent way, and so has contributed to his unique status. The claims of unoriginality and familiarity will persist, for a technique of reworking and referencing sidesteps what is widely considered the most important definer of aesthetic quality. This is not what the Lloyd Webber shows are about. Lloyd Webber has created a sense of ongoing musical memory in his works, evoking and changing the familiar to his own ends, reflecting and reshaping what is around and what has gone before. Such an approach is not limited to musical memory and musical reference but, as we shall explore in the final chapter, is just one part of a wider view in which his works address fundamental questions of genre definition.

CHAPTER 7

"Now and Forever": Canons and Challenges

L LOYD WEBBER'S REPERTORY OF DIVERSE AND WIDE-RANGING INFLU-
ences gains a sense of integrity through a web of expanding and shifting intertextual relationships and cross-genre reflections. At the heart
of this web is a question, a constant challenge to the boundaries of the genre
itself: what can a musical be? The work of a "Broadway master" requires
challenge and change to the genre through a specific show that becomes
canonical (held up in the future as a yardstick for other works) or through
a more general approach that affects the course of the genre and brings in
its wake reflection and reevaluation. What Lloyd Webber has done through
his eclecticism and changes of direction is continually to prompt this central question of the musical's self-definition. Response to his questioning has
not always been positive; his detractors have emphatically denied him "master" status. This in turn has led some of his promoters to suggest that sour
grapes, especially on the grounds of nationality, may have produced such
thinking. While there is certainly a need to examine that view in due course,
another more basic reason may be nearer the heart of the cause of such resentment, found in the way that the canon of the musical has been created
and subsequently interpreted.

The Canon

The evolution of the musical-theater canon—the genre's benchmark works
—has principally developed with the aesthetics of European "high art" in
mind. It privileged those shows which represented the establishing of the

Andrew Lloyd Webber during rehearsals for *Starlight Express*, London, 1984 (photo: Nobby Clark). © 1984 The Really Useful Group Ltd.

"integrated musical" (*Oklahoma!*, in 1943, has been commonly taken as the key reference point for this) and then built upon that premise.[1] Canonical works progress toward and uphold the values of originality, thematic unity, and organic development; these are the criteria one would associate with the evaluation of, for example, a symphony, an opera, or a novel. The relationship of a new work to these valued characteristics, exemplified by canonical forebears, is an important part of the way that it will be assessed, for we tend to respond to new works with a sense of retrospective comparison rather than forward-looking prediction. We look for continuity with a commonly valued past. Both journalistic and academic commentators generally look for works to support or develop canonic values, measuring them as successful or unsuccessful in how they match up to those accepted criteria. Even the recognition of innovation can take place only within a context of convention, with the added restriction that where genre development is seen to occur, it is most frequently perceived as a linear and forward-moving continuum. Anything that deviates from the established concepts of the genre exemplified in the canon, or that retraces steps to earlier and superseded variants of the genre, runs the danger of being measured not for what it is but for what it is not.

Lloyd Webber's shows do not sit easily with the concepts of the musical as expressed through its canon. As we saw in Chapter 2, his route through musical-theater territory was one that began with formats and musical styles foreign to established musical theater. We have also explored the areas from outside the musical which Lloyd Webber has brought into its sphere. For this repertory requires more than a single perspective, from within the genre confines of the musical, and this in itself challenges genre identity. Such a broad appreciation of cultural placing and motivation has been increasingly recognized in the growing academic research into musical theater but has not generally filtered back either to the popular critics or, more important, to the audience. Given that the creative forces in the early Lloyd Webber works were extrinsic to the predominantly classic American book musicals of the canon with which he grew up, his works were fundamentally non-canonical. Furthermore, as such pieces were presented within the context of musical theater, they could even be considered anticanonical, a challenge to genre content from the outset.

Lloyd Webber has challenged each of the canonic building blocks from a fundamental base of eclectic interests and inclusive style. As we saw in the previous chapter, he has been consistently attacked for lack of originality, yet his referencing of other music has been coherent and aesthetically guided. Thematic unity lies uneasily with the collage effect of varied musical styles in close combination, especially in those shows up to and including *Starlight Express*. In particular, *Cats* and *Starlight Express* work against the central thrust of the "integrated" book musical and its later developments: it is as if *Cabaret* (1966), *A Little Night Music* (1973), and *A Chorus Line* (1975), for example, had never happened. Yet Lloyd Webber's shows have their own deliberate structure and clear purpose: he has not failed to match the canonic example but has chosen to do something different. Again we see the necessary breaking away from the past or the reshaping of it in order to fashion a personal creative space. Lack of organic development has also been charged because of the sectional approach to the form characteristic of all Lloyd Webber's works. This has been most prominent in the early shows, partitioned through the overtly antagonistic attitudes of the characters as much as through their descriptive musical styles. Musically, organic development sits uneasily with the notion of the take-out hit ("Memory" being Lloyd Webber's most obvious such number) and the stylistic pageant.[2]

So how can those often unwitting upholders of the canon respond to a show such as *Cats?* It defies the thrust of the canon toward integration, toward sustained exploration of character, toward the identifiably human, and even toward the central role of romantic union; and yet it has become the longest-running musical in both of the two generally accepted centers of musical theater, Broadway and the West End. It is along this fault line that so much of the polarized expressions for and against Lloyd Webber have begun: upholding the canon and its assumed directionality, or challenging those values and allowing for reinvention and reappraisal.

A genre is formed out of an accumulation of its works but thus contains an essential paradox in which present and future are in opposition. How can a work be accepted within the continuum of the genre (present), while at the same time being both a challenge to the genre identity and a force for its development (future)? In practice, this may result in a kind of self-selection by commentators on the grounds of their own preferred directions of development. Most prominent in this respect has been the work of Sondheim, whose intricacies and introversions of music, lyrics, and plot match well those established nineteenth-century values of originality, thematic unity, and organic development. He has been the natural heir to the canon. He trained through an apprenticeship in musical theater, becoming its upholder by direct descent through his work with Hammerstein, Bernstein, and Rodgers in particular. His work is musically complex, adopting the gestures of motivic allusion and conscious game playing in both music and lyrics. In this way Sondheim's musicals have resonances with the condition of opera, a form at the root of the established canonic and genre assumptions of the popular lyric stage after the espousal of the "integrated musical." Consequently, it is no coincidence that *Sweeney Todd* now appears in the repertories of major opera companies around the world.[3] More recent shows such as *Ragtime* clearly espouse similar values. Conversely, Jerry Herman has often been held in low critical esteem because his shows have not adopted "operatic" tendencies, and as those tendencies gained prominence through the 1980s so Herman seemed old-fashioned and the "number" musical a form of the past. Yet Herman as much as Sondheim will personify for many a classic image of the musical that includes strophic songs in catchy, popular style interspersed throughout a comic play. Indeed, a return to the form of the musical comedy seems to be a recent trend, expressed through such shows as *Mamma Mia!*, *The Producers*, and *The Full Monty*. With such thoughts in mind, it becomes clear why *Aspects of Love* has been seen as one of Lloyd Webber's most serious works, for it reinforces the thrust of the canon: sung-through, organic development through recurring motifs, a focus on the emotional analysis of human love relationships. In fact, what the show seems to do is reach toward a much more subtle accommodation of "number" show and "through-sung" show, in part masterly if ultimately unsuccessful.

Genres, however, are not necessarily static. They are formed from concatenations of and new negotiations between previous genres—in the case of the musical those of operetta, revue, vaudeville, ballet, and so on—and hence their identities shift through time. The Rodgers and Hammerstein model of the integrated musical has been seen to represent the achievement in the genre of a critical mass, the stage by which the previous forms drawn upon had coalesced sufficiently to be considered as a specific entity with its own readily identifiable integrity. The 1940s and 1950s musicals had in effect provided a new working definition of what a musical could be, and the "musical-comedy" and "musical play" tags became redundant. In *Coming Up Roses*, Ethan Mordden writes, "In the 1950s the Broadway musical was beginning the fourth decade of its golden age." Later he observes: "This is the first decade filled with shows that are revived not just for their music . . . but for articulate, searching storytelling. . . . This was the key to the musical's confidence, the security of its science: once, the great shows were the best of a particular kind. Now the great shows are unique."[4] Such comments reinforce the idea of the genre reaching a point of culmination (the 1950s). The creative challenge is to see that point not as the apogee of a "golden age," with all the potential paralysis for the future that such retrospective glorification can provide, but as the starting point for rich exploration after a "golden beginning."

Once a sense had been established of the new genre identity, questioning and developing that genre became the focus, undertaken from the mid-1960s on as a process of reinforcing or refining its characteristics. But there are dangers in such self-awareness. Canonic values may provide the means for the first judgment upon a new work, but over time that first impression is likely to be subject to modification. After the initial novelty has passed, a broader contextual awareness takes over and places the work alongside others of its day, revealing in the process what was the same and what was different.[5] By this point, however, any influences from the new work will already have begun to make their effect on works by the same or other creators: the analysis of an influence is always retrospective, for the influence must be sufficiently established to be recognizable as such. But the canonic values that these influences subsequently generate can also be seen as prescriptive, and the strength of assumptions and accepted ideas inherent in the concept of the canon can restrict the scope of a future perspective. In other words, it's easy to see what we have been taught to look for and easy to ignore what we have not.[6] Critics have looked for the support of canonic qualities in Lloyd Webber, and therein lies a good part of the reason for the mixed reception his shows have received, despite their considerable popular success. The critics have tried to squeeze Lloyd Webber's square peg into their own round hole of preconceptions. As Michael Walsh put it: "The [American] critics were so inconsistent, so hard to figure out, blasting *Superstar* and hammering *Evita*, then turning around and awarding the latter show a fistful of prizes and praising the *Joseph* revival on Broadway. And *Cats*, what was one to make of its reception? Some called it irresistible, and others were allergic to it."[7]

"The 'Broadway' Musical"?

The term "Broadway master" has been used so far as if it were shorthand for "musical theater master." But is such an assumption valid? There have been differing critical responses in the West End and on Broadway to Lloyd Webber's shows, the former favorable or mixed, the latter mixed or poor. Here, Lloyd Webber's challenge has been to the integrity of Broadway itself. As Clive Barnes wrote in an article on the reception of *Aspects of Love* on Broadway, "The slightly chauvinistic feeling [is] that the Broadway musical is primarily a Broadway concern and the British have no real right to come over here trying to teach us how to suck eggs."[8] In both artistic and commercial senses, Lloyd Webber is the sole British composer of musicals after World War II to warrant a place in a series entitled Broadway Masters. Other British creators of musicals have found some Broadway success: Noël Coward *(Bitter Sweet)*, Sandy Wilson *(The Boy Friend)*, Lionel Bart *(Oliver!)*, David Heneker *(Half a Sixpence)*, and more recently Willy Russell *(Blood Brothers)* and the retro-success of Noel Gay's *Me and My Girl* (first presented in London in 1937; first presented on Broadway in 1986). But all of these represent isolated success with musicals on Broadway, unlike the serial success of Lloyd Webber. The greatest of the British musical theater writers in London post-Edwardian musical comedy, primarily Vivian Ellis and Ivor Novello, have been unrepresented on Broadway in that genre despite their achievements in the West End.[9] A series entitled West End Masters would have a very different roster from this one. Novello is especially of note in relation to Lloyd Webber, presaging his scale of achievement nationally in terms of long runs, multiple simultaneous tours of his works, financial return, popular appeal, and output in both number and style of presentation. There is some similarity with Lloyd Webber in Coward's stylistic ranging — operetta (Bitter Sweet), period comedy of manners (Conversation Piece), ponderous literary adaptation (After the Ball), gangster musical comedy (Ace of Clubs) — if not in his attainment of international success.

But the primary appeal of all the British composers mentioned above has been to a British audience, and the predominant themes of their shows have included the British class system, monarchy, and regional or historical British settings. American success was a welcome bonus, not a principal aim. Lloyd Webber's origins in the growing internationalism of the 1960s prompted a transatlantic or even international focus. There is little specific to Britain in the Old Testament, the New Testament, an Argentine personality, cats, trains, and Gothic horror; and a specifically American focus is clear in the choice of Sunset Boulevard and the transatlantic relocation of Whistle Down the Wind. This is all a long way from the class-based, postwar operettas of Ellis and A. P. Herbert, the Dickensian sing-along of Bart, the twee retrospection of Wilson, or the monarchy-led Ruritania of Novello.[10] That Lloyd Webber should be a major figure on the Broadway stage, not just through the long runs of the works, but through the financial implications of his success for both employment opportunities and the generation of revenue, has represented the most sustained counterargument against the musical as a strictly American art form in favor of one that has a more international status. Thus for "Broadway master" it may be better to read "international master."[11] A musical no longer has to be, or aspire to be, American. In itself, this is a significant redefinition of the "Broadway musical," moving it toward a global art form, with expressions of national identity becoming more a localized coloring than an essential element of the musical's identity. Lloyd Webber's involvement as creative instigator and producer of Bombay Dreams in London in 2002 made this point clear: the show looked to India and Bollywood film for its plot, characters, and musical and dance styles. Will the modern musical in an international age be able to escape the geographical boundaries associated with its own earlier contributory forms (vaudeville, musical comedy, and so on) or related genres (operetta and zarzuela, for example)? With Lloyd Webber's work now well known through performance in the Far East—in September 2001 a concert of his works was presented in The Great Hall of the People, Beijing, and a production of *The Phantom of the Opera* in China has been under consideration—we may be seeing the answer to that question.

The Magpie

And so to some of the ways in which the Lloyd Webber repertory has challenged the identity of the musical and forced reappraisal of the genre or rejection of the challenge in its wake: extrinsic forms and tone, nonlove stories, and religion. Holding disparate influences together in a new unity is the central strand of eclecticism, and it has caused comment from the start of Lloyd Webber's success. Witness Clive Barnes on *Jesus Christ Superstar* in New York (1971): "The music itself is extraordinarily eclectic. It runs so many gamuts it almost becomes a musical cartel."[12] This is a technique of inclusion expressed through magpie gatherings from diverse sources. These have run through, among others: the concision and monothematic approach of the pop song; the atmospheric choral response and comment of oratorio; the homophonic delivery of such choral material, in turn contrasted with the individual expression of the rock singer; and the classical orchestra set both beside and within contemporary pop and rock instrumental resources. These have all been used to musicalize a panoply of dramatic and literary forms, including the epic, the passion play, the documentary, Greek drama (through commentary from a Chorus), and especially the soliloquy for sustained solo emotional exposition (here obviously overlapping with the operatic aria). More specifically, the concept album of *Evita* includes "Eva's Sonnet" ("Those shallow mean pretenders to your throne . . ."), in which her linguistic style notably turns away from the more common demotic and direct speech she has previously employed toward a formal structure of high poetic art that aggrandizes her by association.[13] The sonnet form chosen by Tim Rice symbolizes the extent of the journey Eva has made in the show: from lower-class whore to poetic orator, from insignificance to the embodiment of Argentina. The musical setting by Lloyd Webber stresses the rhymed couplets, while its musical material is drawn from fragments of motifs used throughout the show, but in sufficiently distanced versions to suggest that same journey as symbolized by the sonnet.

There has been a magpie element in the way that these disparate musical and dramatic forms have been pulled together to produce a drama in which their different techniques and emphases have acted as a series of lenses. It is culturally kaleidoscopic in the cumulative effect of the varied focuses. Furthermore, the collisions and comparisons of these various sources produce a drama all their own through such stylistic inclusion, and so form a subtext that reflects on the forms of expression of both vernacular and high culture, as in the description of *Jesus Christ Superstar* as a "rock opera." At the beginning of Lloyd Webber's career, particularly in *Superstar*, such an interplay had its clearest origins in the progressive rock album; but when it was moved into the sphere of musical theater, it seemed strikingly new.[14]

The Lloyd Webber shows have also seen an expansion of tone in the use of the musical as extended question rather than statement; the result has been polarization rather than resolution. This is a pronounced element of *Jesus Christ Superstar*, particularly articulated through Pilate, Caiaphas, the priests, and most prominently Judas, whose title song late on in the work summarizes the questioning of the whole drama:

> Every time I look at you I don't understand
> Why you let the things you did get so out of hand
>
> . . . .
>
> Don't you get me wrong—I only want to know.

The work is not so much narrative as discursive, its libretto constantly voicing questions from the characters' contrasting points of view.[15] Consequently, scenes of action are few and not sustained, for their purpose is to move the characters into new situations to provoke new, quasi-philosophical viewpoints.[16] Judas's introductory number, "Heaven on Their Minds," is set outside of a specific time and place so that his attitude establishes from the start the framework through which the rest of the show is to be viewed. Questioning and removed from time, Judas becomes the skeptical Everyman of each generation. An exact location and time is only introduced for the following number, "What's the Buzz?" (described as "Bethany, Friday Night"). In addition, the attitudes of Jesus, Judas, and Mary toward one another, rather than their actions, are made the focus of numbers from the opening through to the end of "Everything's Alright."

Where there are moments of specific action in the show, they are framed by considerations of the emotional and moral contexts, as in the scene with the money changers ("The Temple") or Judas's visit to the priests ("Damned for all Time / Blood Money"). This aspect has presented the greatest problem to stage presentation of the work, for there are long periods of discursive

Jesus Christ Superstar, London, 1980. © 1980 The Really Useful Group Ltd.

and musical activity which have no natural physical activity to accompany
them. The drama investigates concepts and emotions. "Jesus Christ. Who
are you, what have you sacrificed? . . . Do you think you're who they say you
are?": the questions are the focus and remain unanswered by the work. In its
use of what is effectively a series of musicalized soliloquies—explorations of
attitude rather than action—applied to a known biblical episode, the work
is more oratorio than musical, with operatic aria in the musical style of pop
and rock as its main modes of expression. The same ideas recur in *Evita*,
whose storyline is necessarily given in clearer detail than that of *Jesus Christ
Superstar* as the life of Eva Perón was less well-known than that of Jesus. But
the floating perspectives in which Che becomes a type of Judas figure to
Eva's "Santa Evita" continue to provide a challenge to the narrative form of
the musical. The discursive elements are still there, notably in numbers of

overt philosophizing, three of them constructed on the opposition of views from the contrasting sides of a debate: "High Flying Adored," "Waltz for Eva and Che," and "She Is a Diamond" (with its repeated "But on the other hand . . ." to make the point self-evident). They are all placed near the end of the show as a gradual heightening of the implied philosophical subtext.

"Love Changes Everything"

One of the main foundations of the musical is the course of a love relationship (principally male-female), however dystopian or reinvented its portrayal may have become in the years after *Oklahoma!*, as in the gay pairings of William Finn's *Falsettos* trilogy or the range of relationships in Larson's *Rent*. Most of Lloyd Webber's central characters fail to achieve lasting romantic union; some are not even seeking it. This in itself is a major shift of emphasis for a genre predominantly based on the search for love. Lloyd Webber's perspective has elements of the antigenre, redefining the form through its opposite, deliberately preventing the guy from getting the girl. When Lloyd Webber does enter the territory of love, it is not the romance of Liat and her Lieutenant Cable, who is "Younger Than Springtime," and the consummation of that love is almost always prevented. Instead, there is the pull between sexuality and religiosity of Mary Magdalene or of Swallow and the Man, the idolization of Christine by a figure (the Phantom) who is kept otherworldly and mysteriously vanishes (resurrects?) at the end of the show, and the emotional merry-go-round of *Aspects of Love*. Where consummated romance occurs in *The Beautiful Game* it is portrayed through the saccharine glow of a wedding and the primarily comic aftermath of sexual inexperience. But this is in Lloyd Webber's most conventional musical after the retro musical comedy of *By Jeeves*; and in any case, the relationship is not allowed to survive as politics, violence, and bigotry crush the spirit of love; maybe in this as in other ways, *West Side Story* provides the principal antecedent from the canon for *The Beautiful Game*, but it is still the opposite message to that of an archetypal show.

Love for Lloyd Webber's characters is commonly a matter of some confusion. When Alex states the theme of *Aspects of Love* in his opening anthem, he acknowledges that "Love changes everything" and "brings you glory, brings you shame"; the music has an almost sobbing effect in its descending appogiaturas of the key phrase, that "nothing in the world will ever be the same." The lesson is that love brings with it the danger of change, and change is an unpredictable force that does not necessarily act for the good. Lloyd Webber's characters do not go around exclaiming the name of their adored partners ("Maria" or "Rosemary"), they do not get "Lost in His Arms" during "Some Enchanted Evening." On one of the few occasions of such romantic indulgence, "Too Much in Love to Care" in *Sunset Boulevard*, the mode of expression carries the air of stage falseness as a Rodgers-like theme is used to convey old-fashioned sentiments that contradict the dominant antisentiment of the show. Joe and Betty seem to be performing a number from a contemporary film musical, accompanied by lush orchestration and presented against a film set whose artificiality literally dominates their scene.

As with Sondheim or Finn, for example, Lloyd Webber has dissected the anatomy of unresolved relationships in his works, in his case frequently through triangular forces: Judas–Jesus–Mary Magdalene, Perón-Eva-Che, Phantom-Christine-Raoul, Norma-Joe-Betty, or Alex-Rose-George for example. The central character of each threesome is caught between polarizing forces. The musical comedy archetype is based more on romantic pairings, such as Laurey with Curly or Ado Annie with Will Parker. When a third character arrives to disturb these couples — here, respectively, Jud Fry or Ali Hakim — the purpose of the interloper is to confirm that the original romantic pairing was the right one and create a sense of resolution when that pairing is restored. But the triangular relationships of Lloyd Webber are seldom so straightforward, for there is a genuine dilemma involved that commonly prevents a clear-cut choice, a neat resolution. One figure is ultimately forced to choose, and that choice will exclude the third character. The immortalizing of the excluded third provides an alternative, quasi-spiritual resolution to compensate: the Assumption of Jesus is implicit if not explicit; the last words in *Evita* go to her embalmers ("Eyes, hair, face, image. All must be preserved. Still life displayed forever. No less than she deserved"); and the Phantom and the Man mysteriously vanish.[17] Lloyd Webber's shows have repeatedly challenged a basic element of musical theater storylines by replacing the conventional man-woman love story with unresolved triangular relationships or ones based on a central character and an unseen force, whether God (*Cats* or *Whistle Down the Wind*) or their own imaginings (*Sunset Boulevard*). There are indeed rewards to be found in heaven, but the mainstream commercial musical has not generally been the forum for the expression of such beliefs beyond their use as more localized expressions of individual character. In this regard, Lloyd Webber's has been a unique perspective, both a reflection and a reinforcement of a process of maturation in which the musical need no longer limit itself to songs, dances, and jokes in the course of true love but can justifiably probe and question more serious subjects with more serious implications. Lloyd Webber's example of the nonlove-story show has provided high-profile models whose challenge goes literally to the heart of the musical. That few have pursued his line may be an indication that it is a step too far, and even in that way a useful defining of a boundary.

"Vaults of Heaven"

My third brief example of genre challenge is in part an extension of the replacement of the central love story with something more indeterminately aspirational, expressed through a spiritual-religious awareness. Religious tone in musicals had previously symbolized hope, the will to go on, the belief in the certainty of things eternal: Nettie's "You'll Never Walk Alone" and its climactic reprise at the end of *Carousel*; Tony and Maria's private "wedding ceremony" as they pledge "One Hand, One Heart"; the wedding of Maria to Captain von Trapp in the Nonnberg Abbey; the "tradition" of *Fiddler on the Roof*. (These also run parallel to central love stories: religious optimism is an expression of romantic optimism.) But Lloyd Webber's religiosity is different. It is seldom so ecclesiastically specific, lacking a context to link it to the diegetic context of a real religious service. Its cross-genre use consequently changes the semantic content of itself and its surroundings: *Starlight Express* finishes with a "Light at the End of the Tunnel," part sing-along finale, part gospel statement of hope—the ambiguity is intentional. "Nature of the Beast" (*Whistle Down the Wind*) is another inverted genre as the hymnlike melody of the Man's refrain becomes not a call to the Lord for help but one of resignation at his total isolation, lacking any hope:

> You can say a prayer for everyone
> You've known or you might see
> Say a prayer for all of these and more
> But there's still no prayer for me
>
> Say a prayer for every living thing
> The unborn and deceased

Whistle Down the Wind, London, 1998. © 1998 The Really Useful Group Ltd.

> But I haven't got a prayer—I know—!
> That's the nature of the beast.

The drama is in the song's use of religious construction: the intoning lists of the verses, the repeated phrases of intercession, the four-square melody and rhythm, the Victorian hymn harmony (especially in the third line), and the sense of ritual which these all combine to create. All this is put to the service of an antireligious message, which thus comments on its mode of delivery at each moment of its delivery, all set within the secular world of a musical-theater entertainment. It is at the same time anthemic show ballad and hymn tune, secular drama and sacred text, all in the form of a soliloquy.

It is bold, even perverse, to tackle so directly some of the most firmly held assumptions about the nature of a musical. It is as though Lloyd Webber has sought a space for *his* musical theater on the other side of the road from everyone else's, an understandable impulse arising from the nature of artistic creation and recognition: everyone wants to be identified as unique. But we recognize difference only when we can compare it to sameness, and the validation of the search for self-identity and self-knowledge comes through the recognition of that difference by others. Norma doesn't desire just to be a star again but to be treated like a star, for that's the only way she can know she is one. And so Lloyd Webber has demanded that his shows are treated as musicals, even though they have defied many of the cherished features that have so fundamentally characterized the genre.

The Cuckoo

After magpie gatherings comes the more aggressive territorialism of the musical-theater cuckoo. Lloyd Webber has refuted the need to acknowledge some accepted boundaries, stating, for example, that he "never saw why composing songs to be pop hits should be different to writing successful numbers in musicals."[18] More recently: "I never thought there was any difference between opera and musicals that are through-written. Music theatre is music theatre. It either works for an audience or it doesn't."[19]

The Phantom of the Opera constantly acknowledges opera: the pastiche operas of *Hannibal*, *Il muto*, and *Don Juan Triumphant*; the use of "operatic language" for the characters in "Prima Donna" (complete with coloratura singing for the eponymous victim); the use of wide vocal ranges, near-continuous music, musicalized dialogue, and so on. Through these, Lloyd Webber has taken over the operatic nest. At the same time as he acknowledges opera, he sends it up, asserting as the "serious" musical language, the one of the show's most immediate and "real" world, his own contemporary musical theater. After growing up in the first half of the century, the musical—the new kid on the block of the lyric stage—has muscled in on one of its elders. In addition, it is precisely this feature of writing not opera but something that runs parallel to it that gives *The Phantom of the Opera* its interest: the interplay of conventions adopted, developed, or ignored from both sides creates a drama of genre. *Aspects of Love* fell down when Lloyd Webber tried to converge these separate developmental lines into one and so blurred the sense of simultaneous and cross-referencing genres into a muddy mix of both.

Genres external to musical theater have found themselves internalized throughout the Lloyd Webber repertory, as with the gospel music of *Starlight Express* and *Whistle Down the Wind* or the film music and film narrative of *Sunset Boulevard*. Of course, this is not the preserve only of Lloyd Webber; he can be seen throughout as catching the spirit of change rather than creating the change itself, and similar developments can be seen in Broadway and West End works contemporary with Lloyd Webber. For example, Sondheim had reflected on similar operatic territory in *Sweeney Todd* (1979), while the use of history, epic scale, and opera is as much a part of *Les Misérables* (London, 1985) as it is of *The Phantom of the Opera*, especially when one takes into account the appearance of the "Humming

Chorus" from *Madama Butterfly* in "Bring Him Home" as a further example
of the use of operatic musical rhetoric subsumed by musical theater. The
trend continued more recently with the historically based *Ragtime*, along
with many other unsuccessful attempts at "quasi-operatic history" (the West
End's *La Cava* and *Napoleon*, for example). But through its subject matter and presentational style *The Phantom of the Opera* was the work that
set itself specifically as a mirror on the operatic world, and in this respect it
differs both from its near contemporaries and from such earlier operatically
influenced shows as *Candide* or *The Most Happy Fella* (both 1956).[20] Indeed, by its very reflexivity, it validated the "operatic" approach of the many
subsequent works by others in the style.

"Show Song or Pop Song?"

In the opposite direction, Lloyd Webber's work has been subject to reinterpretation to allow it to move into territories outside of the lyric stage. One of
the most prominent legacies of Lloyd Webber must be that of his big show
tunes: "Any Dream Will Do," "I Don't Know How to Love Him," "Don't
Cry for Me, Argentina," "Memory," "All I Ask of You," and "Love Changes
Everything" have become modern standards. Although not exclusively so,
these have been the songs typically released as pop singles ahead of the shows
themselves in order to create advance interest and familiarity. The success of
this strategy has varied—commensurate with chart success in a fickle market—and has increasingly relied upon the additional credibility of a particular performer or group. In 1976 "Don't Cry for Me, Argentina" appeared
from out of nowhere to become a major British hit in the same form as the
Evita concept recording; in 1998 "No Matter What" from *Whistle Down the
Wind* required major changes to achieve its extended British chart success.
The song was removed from its dramatic context, sung by a group of four
young men, Boyzone, rather than by children, as in the stage show, and the
lyrics were significantly altered to reflect a teenage angle on romantic love
rather than the naive and literally childish adoration of the supposed Jesus
in the show.[21] The musical delivery was also altered to match the style of its
pop performers: two principal solo singers were backed with group harmony,
accompanied by a lightweight instrumental led by guitars with a discrete
synthesizer pad, and later with a high sustained string line. The number was
reinvented to allow the show song once more into the pop song nest.

The song score of *Whistle Down the Wind* was subjected to an even further level of transmutation. Most of the songs were recorded on an album of cover versions by a variety of prominent performers, and so the material was explicitly positioned across the boundaries of stage and pop record.[22] The choice of performers for these tracks reveals the desire to attract a broad audience on both sides of the Atlantic. Those familiar with the Lloyd Webber stage shows can note the names and theater-singing styles of Elaine Paige ("If Only"), Michael Ball ("Unsettled Scores"), and Donny Osmond ("When Children Rule the World"), all of whom have led productions of the Lloyd Webber repertory. The rock brigade is included through Meat Loaf ("A Kiss Is a Terrible Thing to Waste") and Bonnie Tyler ("Tire Tracks and Broken Hearts"), while the appeal of an earlier pop age is supplied by the Everly Brothers ("Cold") and Tom Jones with Sounds of Blackness ("Vaults of Heaven"). This last track also broke into a more recent pop audience through the longevity and reinvention of Jones as a chart-topping performer across some four decades, combined with the gospel appeal of the backing choral group, which also has its own track with the textually appropriate "Wrestle with the Devil." Alongside Tom Jones was also set the vocally lightweight but equally middle-of-the-road personality pop of Boy George ("Try Not to Be Afraid"). Teen-pop was appealed to nostalgically with Donny Osmond, and in a more contemporary vein through Boyzone ("No Matter What") and the Australian pop singer Tina Arena ("Whistle Down the Wind"). The stage show itself was acknowledged through Lottie Mayor, from the original London stage cast, reprising the title song, with ownership of the project claimed through Lloyd Webber's own piano playing for this final track.

Such steps possibly reflect concern for a narrowing audience base, partly engendered through the increasing limitations of pop music itself. The big show ballad at the top of the hit parade and in the sets of dance bands has become the mutated song rearranged to suit the contemporary charts.[23] Show songs no longer find their way easily into a pop music culture increasingly based on continuous rhythms for dance rather than the melodic periodicity and lyric content of the typical show ballad. Additionally, while the rule is for singers to record their own material—the heritage of the singer-songwriters of the 1960s—there are few to take up show songs for their own cover versions. Barbra Streisand's recording of "As If We Never Said Goodbye" in advance of the opening of *Sunset Boulevard* was an exception. When "Our Kind of Love" from *The Beautiful Game* was released as a British pop single by Hannah Waddington (from the original cast of the London show),

even its drippy video—literally, given the lingering shots round the swimming pool—could not propel it to a position of any significance in the charts.
Such changes in the pop music scene have not served the show ballad well;
the show ballad today can no longer easily become part of everyday culture.

Yet the *Whistle Down the Wind* cover album did yield some gems. The
opening track, "Vaults of Heaven," begins with a hint of the tongue-in-cheek
from Tom Jones but works its way up to a glorious gospel sound, replete
with rich backing choir and wonderful playing from the horn section. The
freshness of Donny Osmond's voice and sincere, smiling tone brings a new
accessibility to "When Children Rule the World," and the knowing sexuality
of Bonnie Tyler's "Tire Tracks and Broken Hearts" is suitably provocative. In
short, the album brings out that very eclecticism at the heart of Lloyd Webber. Of all contemporary musical theater composers, he is the one whose
works have suited such transgenre shifts. Just as he has annexed styles and
approaches from a variety of popular styles in service of the musical, so many
of his best songs can be metamorphosed to muscle in on their related territories. This flexibility may prove one of the strongest factors in establishing
the longevity of the Lloyd Webber repertory in pop(ular) song.

Bridging the Divide

Much of the breaking away from the more usual confines of musical theater in Lloyd Webber's shows is balanced by features that keep them locked
into the genre's conventions. He has experimented with the boundaries, not
broken away from them completely, and this pull from convention and the
canon has increased as his repertory has developed. Such conservatism has
been seen as the use of the show-stopping ballads, and the concerted set
pieces have increasingly come to the fore, especially with the gradual move
toward the book musical.

In *Aspects of Love*, Lloyd Webber is seen at his most skillful in bridg-
ing the divide between the need to innovate and challenge and the desire
to reflect the established and familiar. Through its first substantive dramatic
section, from the meeting of Alex and Rose, through their mutual acknowledgment of attraction, the use of recurring motives is artfully combined with
strophic show songs. The thematic repertory is drawn predominantly from
some six major motives, several of them linked by a prominent phrase of
an ascending or descending scale, usually over a perfect 5th. Alongside this
organic and developmental material are set the conventions of the strophic,

"Love Changes Everything," *Aspects of Love.* © 1988 The Really Useful Group Ltd.

musical-theater ballad, a form which has three opportunities to makes its presence felt, two of which are frustrated in the interests of dramatic propulsion. The architecture of act I, scenes 1–6, is that of an arc, anchored by show ballads, with its midpoint marked by another light ballad that functions as a commentary on the beginning of the romantic negotiation between Rose and Alex. The effect is that of a self-contained section all its own, a mini-musical within a full-length show.

The three strophic show songs are:

1. Scene 1. "Love Changes Everything": a show ballad, establishing the general emotional theme of the work. As with *The Phantom of the Opera,* the first sounds are not those of a big musical introduction: a solo piano accompanies a solo voice singing "Love, love changes everything," the repetition of the first word making sure that audience gets the point immediately.[24] The song reflects both the soldier on stage and the intensity of his feelings. It is a bold move to place the "big" song of the show at the opening, which raises the problem of where can the show go next: if the audience has heard the high point at the outset, why bother with the rest? But an instrumental phrase ends the rendition before the final tonic is reached—unlike the ringing top Bb of the single release of the song or in its performances outside the context of the show—and the action moves to an onstage performance of Ibsen's *The Master Builder.*

2. Scene 3. "Parlez-vous Français?": a period popular song, commenting on Alex's situation with respect to Rose. During the scene Alex tries, with difficulty, to engage Rose in conversation.[25] The number finishes on the

radio to coincide with a hiatus in the stunted conversation. Reprised on the radio, the song is not allowed to finish, for Rose calls out, "Oh, turn the thing off!" The popular song is presented in full, but the effect is deflated and seems incomplete when the standard reprise is abruptly curtailed.

3. Scene 5. "Seeing Is Believing": a big, broad-themed love song with a classic ending device. The voices of Rose and Alex combine to mark their shared emotions, and the orchestration (timpani rolls and horn countermelody, for example) heads toward the climax on the high tonic of the word *love*.[26] There are similarities between "Love Changes Everything" and "Seeing Is Believing," but the latter is allowed an unambiguous end to mark clearly the first dramatic section, which concludes with the establishment of Rose and Alex as a couple.[27]

4. Scene 6. "Seeing Is Believing": show reprise as dramatic coda.[28]

These structural pillars describe the emotional exposition of the central characters; they are in essence soliloquies aimed directly at the audience. So it is appropriate that each is presented in the heightened emotional style of the ballad, whose poetic use of the strophe and rhyming scheme is matched by an equal musical formality of meter and cadence. It is all familiar territory for musical theater. Tying these numbers together is a strategy taken from opera or symphonic writing, in which fragmentary ideas are assembled to more volatile effect, for the linking scenes of dialogue need to capture the flow of conversation and require something less formalized, more fluid. This is achieved through a patchwork of motives, whose thematic recurrences create an emotional atmosphere rather than a specific meaning. In other words, the motives have usually been combined to convey the flow of the emotional subtext rather than a particular moment of significance.

Motif 1 (a). "The toast of the town": Rose expresses her frustration with the poor reception of the play in a jagged melodic figure.

Motif 2 (b). "Rose, I thought of everything": the producer Marcel tries to calm Rose, set to a longer-phrased figure accompanied by brittle woodwind and harpsichord (synthesizer).

Motif 3 (c). "Why did I agree to accept this bloody tour?" Rose ripostes; the phrase begins with a scale rising through a fifth.[29]

Motif 4 (d). "Three nuns and your mother": Rose complains to Marcel about the poor audience for their play.

Motif 5 (e). "Show him a smile": Marcel tries to reach some sort of accommodation with Rose. The musical phrase drops by a perfect 4th [D-A], and she replies to him in almost the same musical vein, but fills in the degrees of the scale of his 4th [D-C♯-B-A]. The

         defusing of Rose's anger brings out her better side, so she tends
         toward the descending scale and thus becomes more receptive
         to the music of Alex and love.

Motif 6 (f). "I don't need some crooner crooning / Or a stage-door Johnny
         swooning": Rose's frustration, with a sideswipe at Alex, uses a
         distorted version of the scale in 5/8, sequentially descending by
         whole-tone drops.[30]

The effect of these running motives is to put the action into a time frame,
active and forward-moving; the two enclosing ballads, "Love Changes Everything" and "Seeing Is Believing," take the action out of a time frame and into
emotional exposition of the moment; "Parlez-vous Français?" is a mixture
of both. All these opposing elements are linked through a simple scale, first
heard in the key phrase of "Love Changes Everything" to the line "Nothing in the world will ever be the same." This phrase is the most expansive in
pitch in the song—beginning on the tune's highest note (as unaltered for a
big ending on the tonic high octave)—and the most consistently flowing of
a melody notable for its feeling of constraint. The phrase recurs as summary
at the end of each of the three stanzas.[31]

    When Alex introduces himself to Rose, the first love of his life and of the
show, he ends with the phrase "Seeing you on stage has changed my life,"
set to the prominent, descending scale phrase from the opening song of the
show. Thus Alex reinforces the initial idea associated with him, that "love
changes everything." The introduction of the word *seeing* at the top of the
phrase is also important, as the combination of the descending scale led by
that word in the lyrics provides the transition for the musical phrase from
"Love Changes Everything" to the later "Seeing Is Believing." "Parlez-vous
Français?" provides further linking of this musical idea with Alex's romantic
designs on Rose, for its principal motif is a descending scale to the title words
of the number. The development of the descending scale as a motive reflects
the emotional flow of the whole passage: it is Alex and love, inverted when
we first hear Rose singing it as a rising scale in anger and frustration ("Why
did I agree . . . ?").

    The underlying use of musical themes is not that of a crossword, with a
constant series of exact and cryptic clues passed from one lyric to another.
There are links. We hear them in motif 3, used by both Rose ("Why did
I agree . . . ?") and Alex ("That girl can really act!") to express frustration.
Also, Alex is tied to Rose through his characteristic downward scale—in act I,
scene 13, the "Chanson d'enfance" of Rose begins with such a scale—and

Example 7.1. Motivic connections in *Aspects of Love*, act I scene ii:

(a) "The toast of the town . . ."

(b) "Rose I thought of ev'rything . . ."

(c) "Why did I agree . . ."

(d) "Three nuns and your mother . . ."

George also has a few musical motifs that directly relate to him. But beyond
these, the use of themes seems more to do with setting limits for the musical
language within scenes to create a more general sense of musical characterization; it is the equivalent of a painter restricting his palette to only certain
colors in order to bring out a particular mood. In another sense of stylistic
parallel motion, it is an equivalent to recitative, but it is not recitative. The
dramatic propulsion of recitative in opera is evident, yet the emotional story
of the ballads is also allowed to run concurrently, related both thematically

(e) "Come on, show me a smile!"

(f) "I don't need some crooner crooning . . ."

and stylistically through its sympathetic basis in melodic fragments. For example, the brittle themes of the theater company of act I, scene 2, retreat as the actors leave and the attention focuses on Rose and Alex; as Rose becomes more interested in Alex and she begins to return his attentions, so his musical language of the broad lyric phrase, dominated by the downward scale, gradually suffuses the music around both of them.[32] This pertains more to the allocation of sound worlds within dramatic blocks than to carrying exact references from one phrase to another. Support for this approach is found both elsewhere in the show and in its development. First, there is the musical characterization of George, the sophisticated older man, whose music is much less broad; as Alex becomes older and socially more accomplished, he too begins to address George in this musical style, rather than in the sweeping scales and big tunes of his youthful heart. Second, when presented at the Sydmonton Festival in 1988, the musical construction of the show was pretty much identical to the version subsequently played in the West End the following April, although the lyrics had by then been noticeably changed in many sections, especially in the opening scenes. Individual lines of lyrics were changed materially in content, but not the lines of music; the new lyrics had to fit in with the retained emotional flow of the existing music. As Lloyd Webber said just before the opening of *Aspects of Love:* "I do . . . like to control what's done with my scores. The composer must dictate the evening because you are, in the end, the dramatist. It's marvelous if you've got a director like Trevor Nunn to argue with at a later stage, but Trevor has changed practically nothing; he's accepted completely the idea of a musical structure you don't tamper with."[33]

The values of the canon are clearly at work: the long-established ones of the discrete, take-out show ballads, alongside more recent, dominant ones of organic, motivic construction. The first act demonstrates this pursuit of organic unity to a greater degree than any of Lloyd Webber's other works. But the technique is not without significant exceptions in the individual moment. By act II the sheer weight of fragmentary motifs thrown around becomes wearisome: for example, something of the joie de vivre (literally) that accompanies "The Wine and the Dice" is lost because its central musical theme has become too familiar by the point the number is heard in full, and also because the phrase is repeated so often in the number itself. The dropping of a quaver beat to create a subsequent 7/8 dance section along with some impressive orchestration that introduces the suggestion of earthy regional color cannot disguise the thinness of the material by this point. Yet the buildup to "Seeing Is Believing" in act I is truly effective, the novelty of the musical ideas not yet having worn off. *Aspects of Love* is not among Lloyd Webber's most successful shows, dramatically or commercially, but the framing of the whole opening section by two big ballads—after all, one of the areas in which Lloyd Webber has consistently displayed a fine talent and one where his heart especially leads him—is dramatically and structurally effective. It represents that amalgam of past and present, convention and reinvention, that has marked so much of his output.

Journey of a Lifetime

Whether in the detail of his musico-dramatic thought or in his expansive
use of popular melody, Lloyd Webber remains a remarkable and complex
definer of musical theater. What most immediately unites his work is its free-
ranging quest for the potentials that can arise from new combinations and
accretions of styles and approaches. It is a paradoxical repertory which brings
an extraordinary effectiveness to the conventionality—even unoriginality—
of many of its essential building blocks through the resonances created by
unusual juxtapositions and surprising combinations. So often it is through
opposites brought together in a single-minded, musical-dramatic thrust that
tensions are generated. More widely, the sheer eclecticism of Lloyd Webber's approach brings a sense of vibrancy to his output: listening across the
decades, from early works to late, is to appreciate an inventive, mercurial,
and restless mind at work. One just needs to compare an early song such as
"Any Dream Will Do" with the more narrative passages of *The Phantom of
the Opera* (such as the "Notes" ensemble) to see the shift from supremely
accomplished, infectious pop to the more fluid expression of dramatic characterization. The orchestral rock palette of *Jesus Christ Superstar* contrasts
with the distinctly populist synthesizer sounds of *Starlight Express*, which
later give way to the acoustic chamber orchestra timbres of *Aspects of Love*.
The fundamental relationships of music to narrative run from the most conventional of book musical effects in *By Jeeves* and *The Beautiful Game* to the
continuous musicalization of *Aspects of Love*, taking in various intermediate
stages in *Starlight Express* and *Sunset Boulevard*.

What Lloyd Webber has done so successfully is to see musical theater not
as an isolated genre but as part of a much larger web of cultural connections.
Through this, he has opened up diverse new ways into the form for a wide
range of people. His extraordinary ability to communicate so directly with
so broad an audience is not rooted in the perception of an internal world of
musical theater to be refined and self-referenced to challenge its own preexisting audience and concerns. Instead, it is just one particular doorway
into a vast cultural space whose features can be highlighted, melded, and
contrasted in ever-new combinations. He has inverted the usual order of
things. Rather than first formulating his ideas within the restrictive box of
the genre, dutifully observing a set of prescriptive canonical ideals, he has
from the start worked from outside the box, using a very personal instinct.
Increasingly, more established canonic ideals have become prominent, yet

frequently they have been employed with some personal spin that under-mines or usurps them. In effect, they have been assumed when the need of them has been felt, not just because they provided the security of prece-dent. Such an autonomous nature is ever present in the repertory, which does indeed support the idea of a "Lloyd Webber show," defined through its overwhelming sense of the musical as a form for self-expression by the musical dramatist. The linking factor truly is the unavoidable presence of Lloyd Webber, and his shows reflect his unique experience of life and his own eclectic interests: musical stylistic inclusion, from his own background in which classical music clashed with pop and rock; the broad ballad and the intense dramatic structuring, from his own bright intellect, whose analysis fights with driving emotions (which ultimately win out); and principal char-acters questing for their own identity in antagonistic societies, from his own introversion and self-exploration, whose expression has been sought through such a public medium. There is a strong sense of biography in the totality of the repertory, and the complexity of the man is reflected in his works.

Thus it has also become a repertory of reinvention in which Lloyd Web-ber's own developing approaches to life have been expressed in shifting per-spectives and attitudes toward the genre. In turn, this process has been inter-nalized through the searching central characters themselves—Jesus, Evita, the Phantom. Reinvention has also been internalized in the repertory's own reincarnations, as with the reflexivities between the central figures of *The Phantom of the Opera*, *Sunset Boulevard*, and *Whistle Down the Wind*. The conjunction on screen of *Evita* and Madonna, herself an iconic reinventor par excellence, adds an additional awareness of self-reflection to this equa-tion. Such a process of reevaluation and consequent change has been exter-nalized in the music through its appropriation of a wide variety of genres, modes, and registers. It has also been seen in Lloyd Webber's changing col-laborations with writers and the rejection of the conventional assumption of the need for a single, sustained creative relationship; in this light, the move apart from Tim Rice after *Evita* seems to have been more a symptom of an underlying desire which only later became apparent than a hiatus in a necessary style of partnership which has ever since demanded replacing.

If Lloyd Webber is viewed from within the restrictive genre box, then his work is threatening to the genre identity; those who value the canon sense the otherness of Lloyd Webber's work and respond accordingly. Seen from without, it has created relevance in musical theater for many people who otherwise would not have taken notice of the genre. Unconcerned with the canon, the communicative appeal of each work has been allowed to make its own mark. And most demonstrably Lloyd Webber has touched the nerve of popular appeal and sparked off an enthusiastic response in people around the world: his work has inspired a visceral response to be praised for itself, and the enjoyment in the dramatic moment or the phrase that catches the ear so effectively is not to be lightly dismissed. This, after all, is fundamental to the greatest of musicals composers and the most long-lived of shows.

There is no doubt that the effects of Lloyd Webber will be around for a long time, through particularly famous numbers, through long-running shows alongside tours and revivals, and through the gradual move into the amateur repertory for selective works. Indeed, the primary test for some of the works will be in how they can be re-presented to overcome the strong impressions of their original and familiar "authorized" productions. *Joseph and the Amazing Technicolor Dreamcoat* has shown itself as appealing and flexible a work as its creative history of gradual evolution and expansion would suggest. *Jesus Christ Superstar* and *Evita* have entered the amateur repertory, their bold characters retaining a dramatic fascination and their musical styles so varied as to prevent their becoming solely and inextricably of their period of creation. The complete social worlds and their rich portrayals in music should ensure that *The Phantom of the Opera*, *Sunset Boulevard*, and *Whistle Down the Wind* will attract future amateur and professional productions, although *Phantom*, with its rich intertextual tapestry, seems the one most assured of a place in the canon. As to *Cats*, not all its licensed professional productions have been replicas of London and New York, and something of its infectious nature will be conveyed wherever there is energy and enthusiasm to match its concept.

Where Lloyd Webber's interest has been most broadly felt is in its demonstration of the openness of the form of the musical, revealing its chameleon-like properties at a time when the weight of the genre's own recent history (that "golden age") threatened to limit its horizons. Even in his support for the unashamed show song through a period when strophic melody seemed almost a guilty indulgence, to be consumed in private and not exploited in public, he kept prominent a quality of supreme importance to so many of the ticket-buying public in this most commercial of theatrical forms. In fact, through his continued direct appeal to a broad public, Lloyd Webber has upheld a fine tradition of "popular musical theater." The designation should still count for something, and commercial success should not be anathema to a form aware of its heritage.

The journey through Lloyd Webber's works is a fascinating one, revealing a world of connections and concepts, images and ideas, references and reworkings, all of which have come together in works of rich potential for study alongside great and varied enjoyment in performance. Lloyd Webber's challenges for the musical have created a unique repertory, vibrant in effective theatricality, and of importance not just in what it has already achieved but in what it has yet to achieve both in future performance and in the developing understanding of its significance. From whatever perspective— embraced or rejected, praised or denounced—Lloyd Webber's repertory is seminal to the understanding of the musical of the past twenty-five years. In the way that his works have prompted and provoked an awareness of musical theater across ages, across social groups, and across continents, Lloyd Webber has not only reached but maintained a position as a Broadway master.

Works by Andrew Lloyd Webber

Joseph and the Amazing Technicolor Dreamcoat

Cantata, after the book of Genesis
Lyrics: Tim Rice

1. March 1, 1968: Colet Court School, London; orch Andrew Lloyd Webber
2. May 12, 1968, revised: Central Hall, Westminster, London
3. August 21, 1972, revised: Edinburgh (as part of *Bible One: Two Looks at the Book of Genesis*)
4. November 8, 1972, revised: Roundhouse, London (with *Jacob's Journey*)
5. February 17, 1973, revised: Albery, London
6. 1999: film [video], Universal (dir. Stephen Pimlott and David Mallet)

OTHER PRODUCTIONS

American premiere: May 1, 1970, School of the Immaculate Conception, Douglastown, New York
Broadway premiere: January 27, 1982, Royale (previously off-Broadway at Entermedia, opening November 18, 1981)
West End revival: June 12, 1991, London Palladium
Broadway revival: November 10, 1993, Minskoff
Germany: December 5, 1996, Colosseum, Essen
Others include Australia, Austria, Canada, Hong Kong, Hungary, New Zealand, Singapore, Slovakia, South Africa

DISCOGRAPHY

1. Studio recording (The Joseph Consortium), January 1969: Decca KL4973 (mono LP); SKL 4973 (stereo LP); Deram 844 118-2 (CD)
2. Canadian recording (as *Joseph: A Rock Oratorio*), 1970: Rada RST 113 (LP)

3. London 1972 production, 1973: Polydor 2394 102/SPELP6 (LP)
4. First full-length studio recording (rec. autumn 1973), 1974: MCA MCF2544
    (LP); MCA MCLD 19023 (CD)
5. Broadway Cast, 1982: Chrysalis F2 21387 (CD)
6. London Cast, 1991 production: Polydor 511 130-2 (CD)

Jesus Christ Superstar

Rock opera, after the Gospels
Lyrics: Tim Rice
Orch Andrew Lloyd Webber
1. October 1, 1970: concept album, MCA MKPS 2011-2
2. October 12, 1971: stage premiere, Mark Hellinger, New York
3. 1973: film, Universal (dir. Norman Jewison)
4. 2000: film [video], Universal (dir. Nick Morris and Gale Edwards)

OTHER PRODUCTIONS

West End premiere: August 9, 1972, Palace, London
West End revival: November 19, 1996, Lyceum, London
Broadway revival: April 16, 2000, Ford Center for the Performing Arts
Others include Australia, Austria, Belgium, Brazil, Canada, Czech Republic, Denmark,
    Finland, France, Germany, Greece, Holland, Hungary, Iceland, Ireland, Israel, Italy,
    Japan (Kabuki-style production), Kenya, Malta, Mauritius, Mexico, New Zealand,
    Norway, Poland, Singapore, South Africa, Spain, Sweden, Switzerland, Trinidad,
    Uruguay, Yugoslavia, Zambia, Zimbabwe

DISCOGRAPHY

1. Superstar (Murray Head), 1969: MCA MCS 1164 (7″ single)
2. Concept album, 1970: MCA MKPS2011-2 (LP); MCA MCD00501-2 (CD)
3. Original Broadway cast, 1971: MCA STEREO DL7-1503 (LP)
4. Original London cast, 1973: MCA MDKS8008 (LP); DMCF2503 (CD)
5. Film soundtrack, 1973: MCA Records MCX 502 (LP)
6. 20th Anniversary Concert recording, 1992: First Night ENCORE CD 7 (CD)
7. Original London cast, 1996: Polydor 533735-2 (CD)

Jeeves/By Jeeves

Musical, after the novels of P. G. Wodehouse
Book and lyrics: Alan Ayckbourn
1. April 22, 1975: Her Majesty's, London; orch Don Walker, Andrew Lloyd
    Webber, Keith Amos, and David Cullen
2. revised as *BY JEEVES*: May 1, 1996; Stephen Joseph, Scarborough, England;
    orch David Cullen and Andrew Lloyd Webber
3. 2001: film (video), Universal (dir. Nick Morris and Alan Ayckbourn)

OTHER PRODUCTIONS, *BY JEEVES*

Sydmonton Festival, 1996
West End premiere: July 2, 1996, Duke of York's (transferred to the Lyric, October 3, 1996)
American premiere: October 17, 1996, Norma Terris, Chester, Conn. (Goodspeed Opera House)
Broadway premiere: October 28, 2001, Helen Hayes

DISCOGRAPHY, *JEEVES*

London cast, highlights, 1975: MCA MCF2726 (LP)

DISCOGRAPHY, *BY JEEVES*

1. Scarborough cast, live recording, highlights, 1996 (limited release): Polydor 531 723-2 (CD)
2. Original London cast, 1996: Polydor 533 187-2 (CD)
3. Film soundtrack, 2001: Really Useful Records 314 589 309-2 (CD)

Evita

Opera, after the life of Eva Perón
Lyrics: Tim Rice
1. 1976: concept album, MCA MCX 55031-2; orch Andrew Lloyd Webber
2. June 21, 1978: stage premiere, Prince Edward, London; orch Hershy Kay
3. 1996: film, Warner Bros. (dir. Alan Parker)

OTHER PRODUCTIONS

Sydmonton Festival, 1976: audio visual presentation of original recording
Broadway premiere: September 15, 1979, Broadway
Others include Australia, Austria, Belgium, Brazil, Canada, Denmark, Germany, Greece, Holland, Israel, Japan, Mexico, New Zealand, South Africa, Spain, Sweden

DISCOGRAPHY

1. Concept album, 1976: MCA MCX 55031-2 (LP); MCA DMCX503 (CD; 20th anniversary rerelease)
2. British studio cast, 1977: Polydor 2384 096 (LP)
3. Original London cast, 1978: MCA MCG3527 (LP); MCA DMCG3527 (CD)
4. Original Broadway cast, 1979: MCA 11007 (CD)
5. Film soundtrack, 1996: Warner Bros. 9362-46346-2 (CD)

Song & Dance

Tell Me on a Sunday ("Song")
Lyrics: Don Black
1. Sydmonton Festival, 1979
2. January 28, 1980: live performance, Royalty, London (BBC TV broadcast February 12, 1980)
3. April 15, 2003, revised: Gielgud, London

Discography

1. Original recording (Marti Webb), 1980: Polydor POLD 5031 (LP); Polydor 833 447-2 (CD)
2. London revision (Denive Van Outen), 2003: Polydor 076174-2

Variations ("Dance")
Sydmonton Festival, 1977

Discography

1. Original recording, 1978: MCA Records MCF 2824 (LP); MCA Records MCLD 19126 (CD); Universal MCLD 19396 (CD) (25th anniversary remastered release)
2. Symphonic recording (with William Lloyd Webber's *Aurora*), 1986: Philips 420 342-2 (CD)

Song & Dance
1. April 7, 1982: Palace, London
2. April 28, 1984: single performance staged at the Palace, London (recorded for album release and TV broadcast)
3. September 18, 1985, revised: Royale, New York (book and lyrics revised by Richard Maltby Jr.)

Other Productions

Others include Australia, Hong Kong/Singapore, Germany, Hungary, many U.S. stock productions and European tours

Discography

1. Original London cast (Marti Webb), live recording, 1982: Polydor PODV4 (2LP); Polydor 843 617-2 (2CD)
2. London cast (Sarah Brightman), live recording, 1984: RCA BL70480 (2LP); RCA BL 70480-2 (2CD)
3. Original Broadway cast (Bernadette Peters), song section only, 1985: RCA Victor 09026-68264-2 (CD)

Cats

Musical, after T. S. Eliot, *Old Possum's Book of Cats*
Orch David Cullen and Andrew Lloyd Webber
  1. May 11, 1981: New London, London
  2. October 7, 1982, revised: Winter Garden, New York
  3. October 1, 1998: film (video), Polygram (dir. David Mallet)

OTHER PRODUCTIONS

Sydmonton Festival: 1980
Austria: November 1983, Theater an der Wien, Vienna
Australia: July 27, 1985, Theatre Royal, Sydney
Germany: April 18, 1986, Operetten Haus, Hamburg
Others include Argentina, Belgium, Canada, Finland, France, Holland, Hong Kong,
  Hungary, Japan, Mexico, Norway, Russia, Singapore, South Korea, Sweden,
  Switzerland

DISCOGRAPHY

  1. Original London cast, 1981: Polydor CATX1 (LP); Polydor 817 810-2 (CD,
     digitally remastered)
  2. Original Broadway cast, 1982: Decca 521463 (CD)

Starlight Express

Musical
Book and lyrics: Richard Stilgoe
Orch David Cullen and Andrew Lloyd Webber
  1. March 27, 1984: Apollo Victoria, London
  2. March 15, 1987, revised: Gershwin, New York
  3. November 23, 1992, revised: Apollo Victoria, London

OTHER PRODUCTIONS

Sydmonton Festival: 1982
Germany: June 7, 1988, Starlight, Bochum
Las Vegas: September 14, 1993, Hilton Hotel
London, refurbished production: May 17, 2001, Apollo Victoria
Others include Australia, Japan, Mexico

DISCOGRAPHY

  1. Original London cast: Polydor LNER1 (LP)/Polydor LNERC1 (CD); Polydor
     821 597-2 (CD)
  2. Original cast Germany (Bochum), live recording, 1989: CBS 462585 2 (CD)
  3. Revised London Production, highlights, 1993: Polydor 519 041-2 (CD)

Cricket

Musical
Lyrics: Tim Rice
June 18, 1986: Windsor Castle (private performance)

OTHER PRODUCTION

July 5, 1986: Sydmonton Festival

The Phantom of the Opera

Musical, after the novel by Gaston Leroux
Book: Andrew Lloyd Webber and Richard Stilgoe
Lyrics: Charles Hart, with Richard Stilgoe
Orch David Cullen and Andrew Lloyd Webber
    1. October 9, 1986: stage premiere, Her Majesty's, London
    2. (forthcoming 2004): film, Warner Bros. (dir. Joel Schumacher)

OTHER PRODUCTIONS

Sydmonton Festival: 1983 (Andrew Lloyd Webber and Richard Stilgoe)
Broadway: January 26, 1988, Majestic
Japan: April 22, 1988, Nissei, Tokyo
Austria: December 12, 1988, Theater an der Wien
Canada: September 20, 1989, Pantages, Toronto
Germany: June 29, 1990, Neue Flora, Hamburg
Australia: December 8, 1990, Princess, Melbourne
Holland: August 15, 1993, Circustheater, Schveningen
Mexico: December 16, 1999, Teatro Alameda
China: 2004-5 (provisional)
Others include Denmark, South Korea, Spain, Sweden, Switzerland

DISCOGRAPHY

Original London cast, 1986: Polydor PODV9 (LP); Polydor 831273-2 (CD)

Aspects of Love

Musical, after the novella by David Garnett
Lyrics: Don Black and Charles Hart
Book adaption: Andrew Lloyd Webber
Orch David Cullen and Andrew Lloyd Webber
April 17, 1989: Prince of Wales, London

OTHER PRODUCTIONS

Sydmonton Festival: 1983 (as a cabaret by Andrew Lloyd Webber and Trevor Nunn)
Sydmonton Festival: 1988
Broadway: April 8, 1990, Broadhurst, New York
Germany: May 18, 1997, Stadtsoperette, Dresden
Others include Australia, Denmark, Finland, Hungary, Ireland, Japan, New Zealand,
   Switzerland

DISCOGRAPHY

Original London cast, 1989: Polydor 841 126-2 (CD)

Sunset Boulevard

Musical, after the film (1950, dir. Billy Wilder)
Book and lyrics: Don Black and Christopher Hampton
Orch David Cullen and Andrew Lloyd Webber
   1. July 12, 1993: Adelphi, London
   2. December 9, 1993, revised: Shubert, Los Angeles

OTHER PRODUCTIONS

Sydmonton Festival: 1991 (as a cabaret by Andrew Lloyd Webber, Don Black, and
   Amy Powers)
Sydmonton Festival: 1992
London relaunch (incorporating American revisions): April 7, 1994
Broadway: November 17, 1994, Minskoff
Germany: December 8, 1995, Rhein Main, Frankfurt   .
Others include Australia, Canada

DISCOGRAPHY

   1. Original London cast recording (1993): Polydor 519 767-2 (CD)
   2. Original Los Angeles cast recording (1994): Polydor 523507-2 (CD)

Whistle Down the Wind

Musical, after the novel by Mary Hayley Bell and the film (1961; dir. Bryan Forbes)
Lyrics: Jim Steinman
Book: Patricia Knop, Gale Edwards, and Andrew Lloyd Webber
Orch David Cullen and Andrew Lloyd Webber
   1. December 12, 1996: National Theatre, Washington, D.C.
   2. July 1, 1998, revised: Aldwych, London

OTHER PRODUCTIONS

Sydmonton Festival: 1995, Andrew Lloyd Webber, Jim Steinman, and Patricia Knop
U.K. tour (minor revisions): September 10, 2001

DISCOGRAPHY

1. Original London cast, 1998: Polydor 547 261-2 (CD)
2. Cover album *Songs from Whistle Down the Wind*, 1998: Polydor 559
    441-2 (CD)

The Beautiful Game

Musical
Book and lyrics: Ben Elton
Orch Andrew Lloyd Webber and David Cullen
September 26, 2000: Cambridge, London

DISCOGRAPHY

Original London cast, 2000: Telstar Records TCD3160 (CD)

Other

Requiem
Orch David Cullen and Andrew Lloyd Webber
February 24, 1985: St. Thomas Episcopal Church, New York; Decca 448 616-2 (CD)
Film: *Gumshoe*, 1971, Columbia (dir. Stephen Frears)
Film: *The Odessa File*, 1974, Columbia (dir. Ronald Neame); MCA MCF 2591 (LP)

Notes

CHAPTER 1. Aspects of Life

1. It is necessary to go back to a previous generation to find others who can approach Lloyd Webber's serial success: John Kander (born 1927), Charles Strouse (1928), Cy Coleman (1929), Jerry Herman (1932), and especially Stephen Sondheim (1930), the only other composer of musicals active at the same time who can match Lloyd Webber in his range of stylistic investigation. Some may find it portentous that Lloyd Webber, born March 22, 1948, shares a birthday with Sondheim.

2. Technicolor is a registered trademark of the Technicolor Group of Companies.

3. 1991: *Joseph and the Amazing Technicolor Dreamcoat*, *Jesus Christ Superstar* (in a kabuki version performed by a visiting Japanese company), *Cats*, *Starlight Express*, *The Phantom of the Opera*, and *Aspects of Love*. 1997: *Jesus Christ Superstar*, *Cats*, *Starlight Express*, *The Phantom of the Opera*, *Sunset Boulevard*, and *By Jeeves*.

4. See the List of Works for an indication of the worldwide dissemination by country for each show.

5. Bill Lloyd Webber was born in Kensington, London, on November 3, 1914, his wife on March 30, 1922, in Eastbourne, Sussex; they married in Kensington on October 3, 1942. From the single common final name it can be seen that Webber is their legal surname, and thus that of any offspring. Bill adopted the double-barreled *Lloyd Webber* when at the Royal College of Music in order to distinguish himself from a fellow student named William Webber. The Lloyd Webber appellation was continued by Bill for his work, and he had both his sons, Andrew and Julian (born April 14, 1951), christened with the middle name of Lloyd so that they could adopt the same form as he had if they wished. Andrew used a hyphenated form as a pretension for part of his adolescence but kept to the unhyphenated full form of his name from the start of his professional work; Julian has adopted a similar form. Thus they are William Lloyd Webber, Andrew Lloyd Webber, and Julian Lloyd Webber. With Andrew's elevation to the peerage through a baronetcy in The Queen's New Year's Honours list of 1997, he was invested into the House of Lords on February 26 of that year as the Baron Lloyd-

Webber of Sydmonton. The hyphen becomes essential in such circumstances to guard against the (admittedly unlikely) possible confusion with a future and concurrent ennobled Webber with the given name of Lloyd. Throughout this book the professional name form Andrew Lloyd Webber—unhyphenated—is adopted unless the reference is specifically in the context of the baronetcy, for which the customary, more general, designation *Lord* will also be used.

6. A facsimile of the letter of April 21, 1965, is in Walsh, *Andrew Lloyd Webber*, 32. Of the various biographies of Lloyd Webber, Walsh's remains the most comprehensive and insightful. For a detailed insight into the background and life of Tim Rice (born November 14, 1944) see his own *Oh, What a Circus.*

7. For example, he wrote a homemade book, *Ancient Monuments in the Home Counties*, in late 1959; the introduction to this, along with a letter sent in 1961 to the Ministry of Works deploring the state of several national monuments, are presented in facsimile in Walsh, *Andrew Lloyd Webber*, 27–28.

8. The domestic arrangements were fluid, with the family and attendant guests spread through next-door flats (10 and 2a) in Harrington Court, South Kensington, connected via a balcony. At the time of his arrival, Rice describes himself as living in no. 2a with Granny Johnstone and John Lill, with Bill, Jean, Andrew, and Julian in no. 10 (*Oh, What a Circus*, 102).

9. *Come Back Richard* received a single performance in oratorio form at the City of London School in 1969, directed by Alan Doggett (ibid., 427).

10. See Chapter 3 for the previous heritage of *Come Back Richard*'s "Those Saladin Days" and its later use in *Jesus Christ Superstar.*

11. Rice, *Oh, What a Circus*, 232. Stigwood first bought out Myers's controlling share of New Theatrical Management Ltd in November of 1970 and the remaining shares owned by David Land in May of the following year, renaming the company Superstar Ventures Ltd. The property had become too big for Myers (who had become ill) and Land.

12. See extracts from reviews in Suskin: *More Opening Nights*, 487–92. The growing popularity of the album was such that the impetus for a stage production in America had come from illegal concert versions of the show that had begun playing throughout the country. An official staging made sure that the money poured into the right coffers and that copyright was reasserted. This was akin to Gilbert and Sullivan's earlier copyright problems in America: *The Pirates of Penzance* was officially premiered in New York in a move to undercut the unauthorized productions in the United States from which they received no royalty payments.

13. Elliman was one of the few performing constants in the early life of the work. She appeared on the original concept album (1970), in the New York world premiere production (1971), in the Universal City restaging (1972), and in the film (1973).

14. Although the opening was later in coming, the show lasted in London for much longer than on Broadway—until August 1980, some 3,358 performances compared with New York's 711. It played at the Palace Theatre, one which Lloyd Webber later bought as his interests expanded into wider theatrical concerns. The London cast featured Paul Nicholas (Jesus), Stephen Tate (Judas), and Dana Gillespie (Mary).

15. They married on July 14, 1971. As Lloyd Webber described it, their honeymoon in Vienna was marred by, among other things, major roadworks in the city and his

"worrying about what they were doing to *Superstar* in New York so it was quite a relief to get home again" (*Evening Standard*, November 15, 1973).

16. Monica Mawson, *Evening News*, October 17, 1972.

17. Even before the release of the recording, however, in early summer, Lloyd Webber and Rice had visited the director Hal Prince with the unfinished tapes to talk about bringing *Evita* to the stage in anticipation of a similar trajectory to that of *Jesus Christ Superstar*. Prince had, in fact, previously approached the two with a view to the stage rights for *Jesus Christ Superstar*, but his message was passed on too late to be accepted.

18. Lloyd Webber attributed the long period from album to stage of *Evita* to the unavailability of Hal Prince to direct; summer 1978 was his first available slot. See John Higgins: "The Music Drama of Lloyd Webber," *The Times*, June 17, 1978.

19. There were two pre–New York tryouts, in Los Angeles (from May 8) and San Francisco (from July 17). The New York opening was at the Broadway Theatre on September 25, 1979; it eventually closed on June 5, 1983.

20. In 1986 there was one other private work, a commission from Prince Edward, The Queen's youngest son, as a present to his mother. This short musical drama by Lloyd Webber and Rice was written at the behest of monarchy to pay tribute to another national institution: *Cricket*. With a plot revolving around the trials of love and a cricket match at the Headingley Cricket Club, the brief work was given a private performance on June 18 at Windsor Castle as part of celebrations for The Queen's sixtieth birthday. (As Edward Windsor the prince worked from the beginning of 1988 to summer 1990 for the Really Useful Group as a production assistant in order to gain experience in the entertainment industry, in which he saw himself playing some kind of role.) *Cricket* received a performance at the Sydmonton Festival (which from its inception had featured a cricket match as part of its events) in July, and another later that year for the Lord's Taverners, the charitable cricketing organization of the show business world in the United Kingdom. The piece is of significance in yielding a few musical ideas reworked for later Lloyd Webber shows: there are connections between "All I Ask of Life" (*Cricket*) and "Anything But Lonely" (*Aspects of Love*), and between "All One Hot Afternoon" (*Cricket*) and "As If We Never Said Goodbye" (*Sunset Boulevard*).

21. Black has been the lyricist of many now-standard numbers, such as the film title songs for *To Sir with Love*, *Born Free*, *Ben* (an early solo hit for Michael Jackson), and the James Bond films *Thunderball*, *Diamonds Are Forever*, and *The Man with the Golden Gun*.

22. Black was also lyricist for *Bombay Dreams*, a Bollywood-influenced musical with music by A. R. Rahman and a book by Meera Syal, from an idea of Lloyd Webber's and the film director Shekhar Kapur. In spring 2002 it took over London's Apollo Victoria, recently vacated by *Starlight Express*. The production was by Lloyd Webber through his Really Useful Group. "Bollywood" refers to the genre of the Indian film musical, its name formed through combining Hollywood and Bombay, the former name for Mumbai.

23. Brightman had previously been a member of the television dance troupe Hot Gossip, which performed weekly on the long-running chart show *Top of the Pops*, and had achieved a minor hit in 1982 with a pop number, "I Lost My Heart to a Starship Trooper." She had appeared in *Cats* as Jemima, but Lloyd Webber's particular interest

in her arose from a later moment when he saw her perform in the premiere professional staging of Charles Strouse's *The Nightingale*, at the Lyric Theatre in Hammersmith, London.

24. The increasing media interest and celebrity status of the couple were shown in such press incidentals as the report *(The Guardian)* on March 2, 1984, that Lloyd Webber and Brightman had returned home early after visiting the Boston version of *Cats* because Lloyd Webber had a toothache. It was during his marriage to her that he acquired a duplex at Trump Tower in New York, a villa in the south of France, and a private jet, for example.

25. In response to other memories of the young Lloyd Webber printed in a newspaper, a neighbor of the Lloyd Webbers in Kensington for more than thirty years wrote, "I remember an Easter party that Bill Lloyd Webber, Andrew's father, gave just after Andrew moved out to his first flat. Andrew suddenly appeared at Harrington Court and totally disrupted what was an extremely pleasant evening. We could all hear a heated discussion about money in another room and Billy turned to me and said: 'Pam, I've bred a business man first and a musician last'" *(The Standard*, November 9, 1994).

26. Michael Owen, *The Standard*, March 2, 1984.

27. Quoted in David Lister, "The Cloning of Andrew Lloyd Webber," *The Independent*, February 11, 1995.

28. At intermission of the 1988 Sydmonton performance, Lloyd Webber went so far as to serve appropriately regional wine, produced in the area by Pau in the Pyrenees, the location of George's villa in the story.

29. Quoted in Coveney: *Cats on a Chandelier*, 135.

30. Margarette Driscoll, *The Sunday Times*, July 8, 1990.

31. There were several all-too-public delays to the London premiere, as the stage machinery took on a life of its own to dangerous effect: the electronics in the hydraulic system of the vast set were affected by mobile phone signals, which made them move unpredictably. This gave a sense of technical déjà vu, for local taxi messages had interfered with the sound system on the opening night of *Starlight Express*.

32. Quoted in Walsh, *Andrew Lloyd Webber*, 274.

33. Interview, Baz Bamigboye, "Why I Face the Future on a High Note, by Webber," *Daily Mail*, March 31, 1995.

CHAPTER 2. Telling Tales

1. The song was recorded by Wes Sands and can be heard on disk 5 ("The Vaults") of the collection *Now and Forever* (Polydor 589 393-2). This disk also includes other little-known and early works referred to in later chapters.

2. Quoted in Walsh: *Andrew Lloyd Webber*, 38.

3. Single releases have been associated with almost all the Lloyd Webber shows and with many of their regional productions, and to mark significant cast changes. Among the original casts and associated "name" recordings used in promotions for new shows, major revivals, and film versions have been:

Joseph: 1969—"The Coat of Many Colours/Close Every Door" (the Joseph Consortium); 1971—"Jacob and Sons/Any Dream Will Do" (the Joseph Consortium); 1991

London revival—"Any Dream Will Do" (Jason Donovan), "Song of the King" (David Easter);

Jesus Christ Superstar: 1969 trial single—"Superstar" (Murray Head);

Evita: album—"Don't Cry for Me, Argentina" (Julie Covington), "Another Suitcase in Another Hall" (Barbara Dickson); premiere stage show—"Don't Cry for Me, Argentina" (Elaine Paige), "Oh What a Circus/High Flying Adored" (David Essex); film—"You Must Love Me," "Another Suitcase in Another Hall," and "Don't Cry for Me, Argentina" (Madonna);

Cats: premiere stage show—"Mr Mistoffolees/Old Deuteronomy" (Paul Nicholas), "Memory" (Elaine Paige);

Starlight Express: premiere stage show—"AC/DC" (Jeffrey Daniel), "Only He" (Stephanie Lawrence), "I Am the Starlight" (Lon Satton and Ray Shell); revised London stage show—"Next Time You Fall in Love" (Reva Rice and Greg Ellis);

Phantom: premiere stage show—"The Phantom of the Opera" (Steve Harley and Sarah Brightman), "All I Ask of You" (Cliff Richard and Sarah Brightman), "The Music of the Night" (Michael Crawford), "Wishing You Were Somehow Here Again" (Sarah Brightman);

Aspects of Love: premiere stage show—"Love Changes Everything" (Michael Ball), "The First Man You Remember" (Diana Morrison and Michael Ball), "Anything But Lonely" (Sarah Brightman);

Sunset Boulevard: premiere stage show—"With One Look" and "As If We Never Said Goodbye" (Barbra Streisand), "Sunset Boulevard" (Michael Ball), "The Perfect Year" (Dina Carroll), "The Perfect Year" (Glenn Close);

Whistle Down the Wind: 1996 version—"When Children Rule the World" (the Red Hill Children); 1998 version—"Whistle Down the Wind" (Tina Arena), "No Matter What" (Boyzone), "A Kiss Is a Terrible Thing to Waste" (Meat Loaf);

The Beautiful Game: premiere stage show—"Our Kind of Love" (Hannah Waddington).

4. Goronwy Rees, *Sunday Telegraph*, July 30, 1972.

5. See Chapter 3 for details of this thematic reuse.

6. Mark Steyn, "Towards a New Intimacy," *The Independent*, April 8, 1989.

7. As Michael Billington wrote: "What is depressing is that the disaster was so foreseeable; for anyone with the slightest feeling for Wodehouse's work would know that he created a totally innocent, fairytale world untranslatable into flesh-and-blood terms and that his humour depends on his literary style. On the page one might well chuckle over a line like 'At the mere sight of a Wooster, her fetlocks quiver'; but, as delivered by David Hemmings [Bertie Wooster], the laughter died on one's lips. Indeed the worst thing one can say about this musical . . . is that it may convince people who have never read any Wodehouse that he was a painfully unfunny writer with an elephantine humorous style; and that I would never have thought possible" ("Jeeves," *The Guardian*, April 23, 1975).

8. Sydney Edwards, "Lessons of a West End Flop," *Evening Standard*, May 30, 1975.

9. Derek Jewell, *Sunday Telegraph*, November 14, 1976.

10. See, for example, Swain, "History as Musical."

11. Quoted in Joan Goodman and Mike Bygrave, "Presenting the Che and Eva show," *The Observer*, June 11, 1978.

12. Michael Billington, "For Evita a Prince of Quicksilver Fluency," *The Guardian*, June 22, 1978.

13. Milton Shulman, "The Very Best of British . . . ," *Evening Standard*, June 22, 1978.

14. John Barber, "*Evita:* A Musical Extraordinary," *Daily Telegraph*, June 23, 1978.

15. Michael Coveney, "*Evita*," *Financial Times*, June 22, 1978.

16. *The Sunday Times*, July 30, 1978.

17. *Evita* was in fact designated an opera, but its place within the rock opera subgenre is clear.

18. Michael Billington, "A Phantom Backs into the Future," *The Guardian*, May 12, 1986.

19. Robert Cushman, "The Cat's Whiskers," *Sunday Observer*, May 17, 1981. Additional drama attended the opening when Judi Dench, the original Grizabella the Glamour Cat, injured herself in rehearsals only a few weeks before opening. At a very late stage she was replaced by Elaine Paige, who thus got to create the role and be the first to sing "Memory" in the show, a number with which she has become especially identified.

20. The song has such lines as: "Come on and heat me up the way you do / And I can keep it going longer than you / Don't stop now . . . ya gotta keep it going all night."

21. Steve Walsh, *The Observer*, April 14, 1985.

22. Quoted in John Barber, "The Romance of the Opera," *Daily Telegraph*, June 25, 1986.

23. Quoted in Michael Billington, "A Phantom Backs into the Future," *The Guardian*, May 12, 1986.

24. Quoted in Sheridan Morley, "The Success Story So Far," *The Times*, August 20, 1988.

25. Barber, "Romance of the Opera."

26. Mark Steyn, "Limelight Express," *The Independent*, November 15, 1986.

27. Indeed, in 1987 the Really Useful Group won a Queen's Award for Export in Britain.

28. The "American invasion" of the West End beginning with the arrival of *Oklahoma!* in 1947 has gained the status of myth: often repeated, seldom challenged, and of questionable accuracy. See John Snelson, "We Said We Wouldn't Look Back," in *The Cambridge Companion to the Musical*, ed. William A. Everett and Paul R. Laird (Cambridge: Cambridge University Press, 2002), 101–19; John M. Snelson, "The West End Musical, 1947–54: British Identity and the 'American Invasion,'" Ph.D. diss., University of Birmingham, 2003.

29. Frank Rich, *New York Times*, April 9, 1990; rpt. in Rich, *Hot Seat*, 728–30.

30. Clive Barnes, *New York Post*, November 4, 1990.

31. Charles Bremner, *The Times*, April 10, 1990.

32. Coward's revue *This Year of Grace* and operette (his preferred term) *Bitter Sweet* were well received on Broadway in 1928 and 1929, respectively; indeed, Coward's was the only face of the British book musical on Broadway in the 1920s. But his later shows on Broadway fared less well, with *Conversation Piece* (1934) lasting 55 perfor-

mances and *Sail Away* (1961) 167 (admittedly longer than *Bitter Sweet's* 157, but set against very different expectations more than forty years later). None of the intervening shows seen in London, including *Pacific 1860* (1946), *Ace of Clubs* (1950), and *After the Ball* (1954), were successes.

33. Coward's profile was raised significantly by his "rediscovery" toward the end of his life, helped in musical theater terms by the successful London compilation show *Cowardy Custard* (1972), seen on Broadway as *Oh Coward!* (1973).

34. After a jury trial, a final judgment in favor of Lloyd Webber was entered on December 23, 1998; an appeal by Repp was not finally dismissed until October 27, 1999.

35. Other legal matters made spectacular news for Lloyd Webber, most notoriously in June 1994, when Faye Dunaway was dismissed from the role of Norma Desmond in the Los Angeles production of *Sunset Boulevard*, allegedly for being unable to sing satisfactorily. Although the case was finally settled out of court in January 1995, the increasingly personal statements from both sides reported in the press reinforced the widespread impression that Lloyd Webber's treatment of his stars was high-handed.

36. Michael Billington, "Wilder's Wit Turned to Romanticism in Lloyd Webber's Hollywood Dream," *The Guardian*, July 13, 1993.

37. Malcolm Rutherford, "Sunset Boulevard," *Financial Times*, July 13, 1993.

38. Andrew Lloyd Webber, "Whistle While You Work," *The Sunday Times*, June 28, 1998.

39. Quoted in Simon Fanshawe, "Raising His Game," *The Sunday Times*, September 17, 2000.

40. Christopher Hassall, *Edward Marsh: Patron of the Arts* (London: Longmans, Green, 1959), 587.

CHAPTER 3. Pop, Rock, and Classical

Epigraph: Alan Franks, "Royally Useful," *The Sunday Times* [magazine], June 19, 1993.

1. For a complete listing of pop songs written and/or produced by Tim Rice, in collaboration both with Lloyd Webber and with others, see Rice, *Oh, What a Circus*, 429–36.

2. The same "Buenos Aires" melody appears as the song "I Can't Go On" on the album *Ten Songs* (1974), recorded by Maynard Williams.

3. The increasingly florid eighth- and sixteenth-note elaborations of the harpsichord are texturally very much of the late 1960s, referencing such contemporary recordings as "Session Man," from the 1966 album *Face to Face* by the Kinks.

4. Paul Raven was incarnated variously in pop as Paul Munday, Rubber Bucket, and—finally and most successfully—the glam rock performer Gary Glitter. He sang the role of Priest on the original *Jesus Christ Superstar* album, also released in 1970.

5. The Eurovision Song Contest was established in 1956 through the auspices of the European Broadcasting Union. Each country submits one performer or group and new song which, after being presented in a single concert in a host country, is voted on by judges representing each of the countries. The contest, broadcast live across Europe, thus gives access to a large and potentially lucrative market of record buyers. In the

contest's early years the successful middle-of-the-road numbers could indeed achieve Europe-wide success; for example, the Italian entry of 1958, "Volare (nel blu dipinto di blu)," was third in the competition but has since become an international hit. Even recently, Europe-wide hits have been achieved in the face of a commercial pop market that increasingly caters to a club sound, as with Dana International's "Diva," Israel's winning entry of 1998.

6. The lyrics for "Try It and See" begin: "Try it and see, won't you try it with me / You could be so good for me—I could give you energy / Oh, love is for free, won't you try it and see / I could be so good for you too." The essence of Eurovision as it has come to be understood over its nearly half-century of existence can be seen in the 1979 winner, the gloriously kitsch "Hallelujah" from Israel, sung by the group Milk and Honey. It is as uplifting and infectious in its effect as it is banal and trite in its content.

7. The rules of contest had made no allowance for a tie; the four winners were United Kingdom (Lulu, "Boom-Bang-a-Bang"), Netherlands (Lennie Kuht, "De troubadour"), Spain (Salome, "Vivo cantando"), and France (Frida Boccara, "Un Jour un enfant"). In 1970 only ten countries entered the competition, largely as a result of the voting debacle of 1969.

8. The Palladium production opened on June 12, 1991, and closed on January 15, 1994; a U.K. tour of this production ran from December 10, 1993, through June 8, 1996. The London production opened in Los Angeles on February 25, 1993, before a Broadway opening at the Minskoff on November 10, 1993, where it ran until May 29, 1995; the U.S. tour of the same production began at West Point, New York, on January 13, 1995, and ended on December 8, 1996, in Toledo, Ohio.

9. David Whelton, managing director of the Philharmonia Orchestra in London, said of accusations of plagiarism: "What [Lloyd Webber] has is a feel for the moment, and for the use of an orchestra. There is also an ability to absorb stylistic trends and metamorphose them into his own language. . . . [It is] unfair to argue that the tunes are not his own. . . . In every age you have tonal composers whose own ideas must have an awareness of the ideas of others. As Elgar said of the process: 'It is in the air, all around me.'" Quoted in Franks, "Royally Useful."

10. The links to one particular Manfred Mann song, "Pretty Flamingo," are discussed in Chapter 6.

11. The lyrics of "Any Dream Will Do" still defy comprehension without the most torturous of metaphorical gymnastics.

12. "From the first rehearsal it was clear that 'Song of the King' would be a show stopper the only problem being that none of Alan's [Doggett] unbroken voices were ideal Presley impersonators. Consequently my vocal demonstration of the song to the boys won me the part for March 1, with the choir given an equally crucial role during the number—the bup-bup-shoo-waddy-wahs." (Rice, *Oh, What a Circus*, 136). Rice also relates how Presley recorded the Rice and Lloyd Webber song "It's Easy for You," which became in the process the last track on his last album, *Moody Blue* (1976).

13. "Don't Be Cruel" was released in 1956; "All Shook Up" and "Teddy Bear" (the latter a virtual alter ego of "Don't Be Cruel") are both from 1957. The "uh-uh-huh" of "All Shook Up" provided a quick aural "fingerprint" for referencing Presley's style; it was adopted a year before *Joseph* by the Bonzo Dog (Doo Dah) Band in "Death Cab for

Cutie" on their first album, *Gorilla* (1967). The Bonzo song bears several similarities with "Song of the King," parodying, as it does, the same source.

14. This epic film section is used earlier, for the entrance of Potiphar into his wife's chamber, when he discovers her seducing Joseph. Again, there is an abrupt change of style, here moving to epic film from 1920s softshoe. This ersatz 1920s sound is typical of that created by the Bonzo Dog (Doo Dah) Band in the late 1960s in such numbers as "Button Up Your Overcoat," "I'm Going to Bring a Watermelon to My Girl Tonight," and "My Brother Makes the Noises for the Talkies," released as singles in 1966.

15. Earlier examples of this type of "pop cantata"—*The Daniel Jazz* and *Jonah Man Jazz*—and later examples such as *Captain Noah and His Floating Zoo* failed to capture the contemporaneity of *Joseph*.

16. Such a context for *Joseph* was made explicit in the staging of the 1991 production with a seated narrator and a book, and amplified in the setting of the video production (1999) within Colet Court School at a school assembly, with the staff as the performers of the drama.

17. M. Harron, "McRock: Pop as a Commodity," in *Facing the Music: Essays on Pop, Rock, and Culture*, ed. S. Frith (London, 1990), 209–10.

18. Jon Lord (organ) and Ritchie Blackmore (guitar) often swapped classical references in their cadenza improvisations. For example, in their rendition of "Wring That Neck," performed at the same 1969 Albert Hall concert as Lord's *Concerto* (see below), allusions are made by Lord to J. S. Bach's Toccata in D minor, BWV 565, and Liszt's *La campanella*, while Ritchie quotes the "Gavotte en rondeau" from the Bach Partita no. 3 in E, possibly as a sly reference to the then-popular classical guitar recordings of John Williams. For further discussion of the influences of classical music on rock, see chapter 3, "Eruptions," in Robert Walser, *Running with the Devil: Power, Gender, and Madness in Heavy Metal Music* (Hanover, N.H.: University Press of New England, 1993).

19. It was written and orchestrated by the group's classically trained organist, Jon Lord, and recorded live at the Royal Albert Hall by Deep Purple and the Royal Philharmonic Orchestra, conducted by Malcolm Arnold.

20. "Shadows" was an outtake from the same album, *Shades of Deep Purple* (1968; released on CD in 2000).

21. From *Led Zeppelin* (1969).

22. Herod was sung by Mike d'Abo, a former lead singer with Manfred Mann.

23. The Mellotron is a keyboard instrument developed in Birmingham, England, during the early 1960s that produces sounds—most commonly of strings or voices—through analogue (tape) methods, rather than electronic synthesis.

24. Disk notes, *Deep Purple in Live Concert at the Royal Albert Hall*, EMI (CDP 7 94886 2).

25. Irregular meters or chords used as rhythmic punctuation were also widespread in popular-music forms beginning in the mid-twentieth century—the former, for example, in the popular jazz pieces of Dave Brubeck, and the latter in be-bop pieces, big band arrangements by Nelson Riddle for Sinatra, and Bernstein's music for *West Side Story*.

26. In the re-presentation of the overture material in "The Trial Before Pilate," the chords are shown to be the punctuation of what is essentially a recitative.

27. Penderecki's *Threnody to the Victims of Hiroshima*, for fifty-two strings (1960), is possibly the most familiar example.

28. See Chapter 5, "The Opera of the Phantom."

29. Tauber's diary describes events at a Nazi concentration camp in Riga, and prompts the journalist Peter Miller to search for the former Nazi commandant, Roschmann. The first statement of Miller's theme is a short and quiet one, which occurs as Miller has just finished reading the diary; his wife, Sigi, asks "Are you all right?" and he replies "No, I have a job to do."

30. Rice, *Oh, What a Circus*, 313; "Wooden Heart" was featured in Presley's 1960 film *GI Blues*.

CHAPTER 4. "Who Are You, Strange Angel?"

1. A restored version of the film including original tints and color sections was completed as part of the Channel 4–Photoplay Productions silents restorations (1996) and can be seen on the British Film Institute video BFIV 021. The influence of certain aspects of the film design, such as the Red Death costume and the arched passageways under the stage, can be seen in Maria Björnson's design for Lloyd Webber's stage version.

2. The NBC miniseries used a screenplay by Arthur Kopit, based on his and Maury Yeston's stage musical version, at that point unproduced. For a detailed treatment of Leroux's original novel and its many adaptations see Jerrold E. Hogle, *The Undergrounds of the Phantom of the Opera: Sublimation and the Gothic in Leroux's Novel and Its Progeny* (New York: St. Martin's, 2002).

3. See the foreword by Peter Hanning to *The Phantom of the Opera* (London: W. H. Allen, 1985), 26–30. The prologue to the musical fulfills the same purpose as that in the novel by creating a similar temporal distancing device for the main story.

4. Ibid., 49.

5. Quoted in Jeremy Kingston, "Going Cuckoo for the Phantom," *The Times*, November 9, 1995.

6. The former category includes such Gothic tales as Matthew Lewis's *The Monk*, Ann Radcliffe's *The Mysteries of Udolfo*, William Beckford's *Vathek*, and Horace Walpole's *The Castle of Otranto* (all to be parodied by Jane Austen in *Northanger Abbey*). These led to classic horror tales beginning with Mary Shelley's allegory on the advances of science in *Frankenstein* (with its own spur also from the first London performances of Mozart's *Don Giovanni*) and culminating in the Gothic excesses of Bram Stoker's *Dracula*. In respect of the latter category, for example, an appendix (pp. 263–64) to the 1985 edition of Leroux's novel includes a short letter from the *Devon County Chronicle* of 1965 headed "Holmes and the Opera Ghost." The writer speculates that Sherlock Holmes may have been familiar with the story of the Opera Ghost and the personal history of Erik. Leroux's approach to mystery, its solution, and its explanation is similar to that adopted by Conan Doyle.

7. The idea for such a list of references comes directly from Leroux, who adopted it in his programming for the gala concert at the Opéra. The use of the lot number for the chandelier, the symbol of the Phantom's diabolic side, is a bit of camp black humor: 666 is the mark of the antichrist in Revelation 13:18, although it is more recently famil-

iar from its appearance for shock value in heavy metal lyrics or as tattooed on the head of Damien in the *Omen* films.

8. It has actually appeared before in the show, during one of the later sections of "Prima Donna," sung by Firmin and Richard to the lines "Who'd believe a diva happy to relieve a chorus girl, / Who's gone and slept with the patron? / Raoul and the soubrette, / Entwined in love's duet! Although he may demur, / He must have been with her." Among the contrapuntal lines of this number the new musical idea does not register as an independent theme, associated with the "chorus girl." But we eventually hear, prominently and in public, this chorus girl's own voice.

9. The way in which the arrangement and orchestration of this section parallel the lyrics is something with which David Cullen—Lloyd Webber's co-orchestrator— was particularly pleased. It starts with high strings as though focused on the world of Christine; but as the lyrics darken, the pitch and texture increasingly descend to the lower sounds (especially pedal notes) appropriate to the Phantom.

10. Maybe an alternate universe in which Christine falls for the Phantom and aids him on a path to glorious artistic triumph in public would put a nice spin on *Phantom II*.

11. The same minor = past and major = present symbolism is used in Christine's act II song at the grave of her father, "Wishing You Were Somehow Here Again." More generally, the linking of minor-past and major-present has a long musical heritage; Broadway precedents from Cole Porter in particular are outlined in Geoffrey Block, *Enchanted Evenings: The Broadway Musical from Show Boat to Sondheim* (New York: Oxford University Press, 1997), 58, 184–85.

12. The novel describes the Angel most lyrically in chapter 5: "No one ever sees the Angel; but he is heard by those who are meant to hear him. He often comes when they least expect him, when they feel sad or discouraged. Then their ears perceive celestial harmonies, a divine voice, which they remember all their lives long. Persons who are visited by the Angel quiver with a thrill unknown to the rest of mankind. And they cannot touch an instrument or open their mouths to sing without producing sound that puts all other human sound to shame. Then persons who do not know that the Angel has visited these persons say that they have 'genius.' Little Christie asked her father if he had heard the Angel of Music, but Daddy Daaé shook his head sadly; and then his eyes lit up, as he said: 'You will hear him one day my child! When I am in heaven I will send him to you.'"

13. The same device of descending tones is used in *Sunset Boulevard* when Joe Gillis first comes across Norma Desmond's mansion, to the words "Christ, where am I? I had landed in the driveway of some palazzo." Again, the descending theme suggests a regression to a different world, in this case one of faded 1920s Hollywood splendor.

14. The novel describes the father's history in chapter 5, "The Enchanted Violin," linking father and the Angel of Music in the mind of the young Christine.

15. In the act II opera *Don Juan Triumphant*, a similar announcement is made to the same musical theme, referring again to the environment of the Phantom, but in this case the onstage world of his own opera: "You have come here in pursuit of your deepest urge, in pursuit of that wish, which till now has been silent . . . silent . . ."

16. Indeed, with the organ prominent in the Phantom's lair, his evening dress and black cloak, the young virginal sacrifice lying unconscious nearby, the guttering can-

delabras, and the decaying decadence of the decoration, there is as much Transylvania and Dracula in this imagery as Paris and Phantom.

17. Distorted as minor 2nd and a tritone, these intervals are to constitute the musical basis of the Phantom's own music, in his opera *Don Juan Triumphant.*

18. At one performance in London I was initially amused to hear a neighbor exclaim, "How did they get up there so quickly?" after Christine and the Phantom had descended through a trap in the floor at the front of the stage, to appear only moments later at the top of the moving platform, high at the back of the stage. Doubles are of course used, disguised by their position at the back of the stage and in low light, and aided by the cloaks of their costumes. But then that audience member experienced surprise at something I could appreciate only through a deliberate and knowing suspension of disbelief; she responded instinctively to the theatricality of Hal Prince's staging and got the more genuine thrill.

19. Gaston Leroux, *The Phantom of the Opera* (London: W. H. Allen, 1985), 142.

20. The works are apt for a story set in 1881: *Faust,* 1859; *Roméo et Juliette,* 1867; *Coppélia,* 1870; *Funeral March of a Marionette,* 1872, orchestrated 1879; *Danse macabre,* 1874; *Rêverie orientale,* 1879 (but more recently considered of doubtful attribution). As to the performers, there is a strong element of internationalism in Leroux's choice of a Spanish diva in La Carlotta and an Italian tenor in Piangi, while Christine has a Swedish father and eventually marries into French nobility. The modern reader can make an additional connection not in the mind of Leroux with Gounod's *Funeral March:* it is most familiar today from its adoption as the lugubrious, loping theme tune to Alfred Hitchcock's television series of suspense stories.

21. But *Dracula* and *Beauty and the Beast* provide equally strong antecedents.

22. See especially the incident of the safety pin, chapters 14 and 17. The managers provide parodic reference to the Phantom in the act II opening of the musical, when they appear dressed as skeletons for the masqued ball. (The printed libretto has both dressed as skeletons; currently in the London production only Firmin appears in a skeleton costume.) Skeleton imagery is part of the Phantom myth: in the novel he is described as very thin, with a skull-like head and sunken eyes (chapter 1), while as the Red Death (chapter 9), "a skeleton hand shot out of the crimson sleeve and violently seized the rash one's wrist; and he, feeling the clutch of the knuckle-bones, the furious grasp of Death, uttered a cry of pain and terror." In the musical, the face that Christine reveals to the audience at the end of "The Point of No Return" is that of a "horrifying skull."

23. See Walsh, *Andrew Lloyd Webber,* 180, and Coveney, *Cats on a Chandelier,* 136.

24. Wagner's *Rienzi* falls into such a category. It is worth noting that Halévy's *La Juive* is mentioned several times in Leroux's story.

25. The aria reminded Walsh more of Balfe than Meyerbeer, though the notion of a pastiche source is even less relevant for this number than the earlier chorus. *Andrew Lloyd Webber,* 180.

26. Christine's version is lowered in key to D major from Carlotta's F♯ major.

27. Quoted in Perry, *Complete Phantom of the Opera,* 73. Brightman, of course, made a similar career move, from dancer to singer.

28. Quoted ibid., 72. The composer also believed in the voice of the young singer,

Lloyd Webber having said of Brightman in a recent interview, "She was responsible for my writing the biggest musical that I will ever write." Quoted in Elizabeth Grice, "'I've Got More New Tunes Than Ever,'" *Daily Telegraph*, November 26, 2001.

29. In the orchestral score and vocal score the original couplet for Christine remains: "Flowers fade, the fruits of summer fade,/ They have their seasons, so do we." In its own way this couplet also references the historical framing of the plot by the prologue, mirroring it by projecting forward to the future.

30. John M. Clum identifies Lloyd Webber's evocation of Lehár in the backstage scenes of *The Phantom of the Opera. Something for the Boys: Musical Theater and Gay Culture* (New York: St. Martin's, 1999), 17. The Hamburg cast is heard on Polydor GMBH 847 514-2.

31. Madame Giry (referring to Christine): "She has heard the voice/ of the Angel of music"; André/Firmin (to Carlotta): "Those who hear your voice/ liken you to an angel!"

32. The allocation of this theme to the character of Madame Giry and its placing within the ensemble were indicated by Lloyd Webber on his manuscript to David Cullen, originally four bars earlier and with its usual tritone. The shifting of the exact position and alteration of the tritone to a 6th were made by Cullen to suit his arrangement. Despite this change in detail, Lloyd Webber clearly intended from the start that Madame Giry would represent the Phantom musically in the ensemble.

33. The last line is not always included in performance. Given the length of run of the London and New York productions, there is a nice contemporary twist in finishing with reference to the old audience, many of whom are not seeing the show for the first time.

34. Artistic arguments based on a France-Italy opposition were a theme of French opera in the 1700s, first with Lully-Rameau, then the Querelle des Bouffons, and later still with Rameau-Piccini.

35. The end of the 1925 film is particularly gruesome, as the mob corner the Phantom on the bank of the Seine, beat him to death with great relish, and throw his body unceremoniously in the water. It is a bleak and unforgiving view of the treatment of the outsider which, despite the appearance of the mob, the musical's enigmatic (and redemptive?) interpretation seeks to defuse.

36. Hal Prince saw the story as a representation of the myth of the impotent murderer, and artistic impotence is obviously a fundamental motivation for the Phantom's need to present himself through Christine and to destroy creativity in others. Is Carlotta really a bad performer or is the Phantom just a prejudiced critic?

37. Layers of meaning are given physical form in these characters. The Phantom at this point, for example, is a man in a mask representing the Angel and the Phantom, disguised as Don Juan (the lover), pretending to be his own servant, Passarino. And has the Phantom written Raoul into his opera as Passarino—the route to the object of his desire and whose character, including music, he adopts for the deceptive seduction? Or is Passarino the Phantom's alter ego, signifying—because the duplicitous Don Juan always takes precedence over Passarino—that his intent was evil from the start? Furthermore, with the Don Giovanni–Don Juan and Leporello-Passarino parallels, Lloyd Webber is simultaneously suggesting a modernist mirroring in a musical of a Mozart opera. The show constantly plays such games.

38. In a more romantic reading, it is also possible to see Christine as appealing to the highest side of his nature, in the belief that the "Angel" in him will triumph over his diabolic side.

39. Walsh, *Andrew Lloyd Webber*, 179–80.

40. Rich, *Hot Seat*, 576, 579.

41. At first presenting both plays and opera, His Majesty's Theatre (the personal pronoun varies according to the ruling monarch's sex) gradually became established in the 1920s as a leading London venue for musicals (mostly American); this has continued essentially unbroken since. The theater has hosted, among others, *Brigadoon* (1949), *West Side Story* (1958), *Bye Bye Birdie* (1962), *Fiddler on the Roof* (1967), and *Company* and *Applause* (both 1972).

42. Pepper's Ghost is a system of sheet glass and light which can reflect an image from, for example, the orchestra pit onto the stage to create a ghostlike effect.

43. Coveney, *Cats on a Chandelier*, 136.

44. Quoted in Walsh, *Andrew Lloyd Webber*, 179.

CHAPTER 5. "I'm Ready for My Close-Up"

Epigraph: Walsh, *Andrew Lloyd Webber*, 274.

1. Jon Ashworth, "Composer in Harmony with Corporate Captain," *The Times*, April 1, 1995.

2. For example, in June 1990 a cartoon version of *Cats* was announced with Steven Spielberg as director, and such names as Marlon Brando, Barbra Streisand, and Billy Joel mentioned as potential voices. In 1992—the same time as a film version of *The Phantom of the Opera* had ground to a halt at Warner Bros.—the plans had not been finalized. Almost exactly two years later a deal was announced with Universal and Spielberg for the cartoon to be filmed with a script by Tom Stoppard.

3. Baz Bamigboye, "Why I Face the Future on a High Note, by Webber," *Daily Mail*, March 31, 1995.

4. Quoted in Perry, *Sunset Boulevard*, 93.

5. See Perry, *Sunset Boulevard*, 91, for background to the development of the presentation of the car chase on stage.

6. For the whole of the scene in which Joe meets Norma for the first time the dialogue is taken straight from the screenplay.

7. A third, structural, advantage is found in the reprise of the music with altered lyrics to suit the astrologer, the analyst, and the beauticians in act II; this ties together musically the only visiting groups, all tradespeople in their own fields, selling to Norma, and carries through a point of reference from act I to act II.

8. In the stage musical, this moment (act I, scene 5) also brings with it a musical change of tone: "Christ, where am I?/I had landed/In the driveway of some palazzo/ Like an abandoned movie set." The lyric was changed for the Los Angeles version of the show to "In the garden of some palazzo," bringing it closer to the image of that moment in the film. The distinctive musical quality of the first phrase of the passage is achieved through a whole-tone descent underpinning the melody, a device which also marks Christine's expression of a retreat to the Phantom's world. The phrase seems to evoke

for Lloyd Webber a sense of being pulled, almost seduced, into a world of a different reality. (See the Regression theme, music example 4.5.)

9. The last line is set to a descending phrase that has its roots in *Evita:* "A New Argentina," with the lines "Don't close doors / Keep an escape clause" and following sections; and "Rainbow Tour," with the lines "Let's get this show on the road / Let's make it obvious."

10. Television documentary *"Sunset Boulevard,"* Omnibus, BBC-TV, 1994.

11. The stress on the first beat of each bar does cause problems for the word underlay, with some lines distinctly uneasy in this stress pattern; this is especially so on the rising sequences whose end rising tone gives an unfortunate accent at the very end of each phrase. The descending sequences work much better, notably in the reprise of the music toward the end of act II as Joe shows Betty the mansion with its numerous images of its owner. His emphatic phrase "That's Norma Desmond," sung four times in succession to the falling pattern of sequences, matches the stresses and structure of the melody while catching the mood of the moment. A lyrical case of "less is more."

12. In the film, the single silent title in the sequence that shows Norma's character praying reads "Cast out this wicked dream which has seized my heart." The line equally applies to the older Norma and the living dream that keeps her trapped in a lost past. The dream imagery is used in both film and stage show; but Joe's warning, voiced in the musical as "You don't yell at a sleepwalker / Or she could fall and break her neck," is ultimately what he ignores himself, precipitating his own death and her complete retreat into her memories.

13. Another example of the musical drawing attention to a brief but significant film moment through a complete number is found in "The Lady's Paying." This comes directly from the insinuating, sly aside of the shop assistant in the gentlemen's clothes shop: "Well, as long as the lady's paying for it, why not take the vicuna?"

14. For a musical sign of Max's more explicit emotions on stage, witness his organ solo, curtailed by Norma. In the film, he sits at the organ and plays J. S. Bach's Toccata in D minor, BWV 565, the classic piece of music for Dracula, the mad scientist, or any other horror film villain of evil intent; and it is, of course, the music behind the organ figurations that announces the Phantom of the Opera in the Lloyd Webber musical. The image in Wilder's film—surely done with a wry smile on the part of director and performer—is also of the black-suited Max at an ancient organ filmed with a close-up of his white-gloved hands. In the stage version this becomes a spirited rendition of the toccata finale to Widor's Organ Symphony No. 5 in F, a piece known in the United Kingdom as a common exit voluntary for weddings: a most unlikely choice for the Max of the film, and surprising for the more overtly expressive Max of the stage show.

15. The full credit for the musical: "Based on the original novel by Mary Hayley Bell and the film produced by Richard Attenborough and directed by Bryan Forbes from a screenplay by Keith Waterhouse and Willis Hall."

16. Quoted in an unsigned report, *Standard*, August 23, 1995.

17. Typically, the U.K. touring version of the show, which opened in September 2001 at the Theatre Royal, Plymouth, included a new song, "The Gang," with lyrics by Don Black rather than Steinman. Replacing the enigmatic (or just unclear) "Annie Christmas," it is a list song of the members of Jesus's "gang," a strange assortment of bib-

lical, contemporary, and fictional characters, which includes, among others, Solomon, David, Goliath, Perry Como, James Dean, Godzilla, Yin, and Yang. A jazzy tune in the minor with simple strophic repetitions, it is much more accessible than "Annie Christmas" and lacks the disturbing instability of the earlier number. The inability of the Man to provide a moral for his strange tale of Annie to satisfy the children's needs for absolutes and answers provokes the children's sympathy toward him (in "No Matter What"). They provide the certainty which he could not. The prompting of the children's sympathy after "The Gang" by an inability to reprise the number dilutes the dramatic point but is more immediately understandable than "Annie Christmas." ("Charlie Christmas" in act II was necessarily cut in the tour version to match the change in act I.) The touring version was a nonreplica production—that is to say, not a copy of the West End staging or designs—produced by Bill Kenwright, noted for his long-running U.K. tours of *Joseph and the Amazing Technicolor Dreamcoat* and *Blood Brothers*.

18. Walsh, *Andrew Lloyd Webber*, 271. The novel is set on a farm in Sussex, but the film is actually set in (and made in) Lancashire, though admittedly near its northernmost extreme, bordering on Yorkshire. The Lancashire setting is reinforced by such references as those to the Mayor of Burnley. Walsh's error is an unfortunate one given both the legendary animosity between Lancashire and Yorkshire, the source of many regional jokes, and Walsh's own subsequent (and accurate) attack on the spurious American geographical placings of the musical.

19. Hayley Mills made her screen debut two years earlier in *Tiger Bay* (1959), playing opposite her father. *Whistle Down the Wind* offers parallels with the earlier film: *Tiger Bay* portrays the growing relationship between a young girl and a seaman she has witnessed commit a murder, and her attempt to help him escape the police inspector (John Mills) illuminates the clash of values between the worlds of the adult and the child. Hayley Mills's appearance in *Tiger Bay* led to her portrayal of the ever-optimistic Pollyanna for Disney in the 1960 film of that name, for which she won a special miniature Academy Award. (This category had been invented for Shirley Temple in 1934, but infrequently awarded; Mills was its last recipient.) Decades later, Sir John Mills, almost blind by this time, played Gus the Theatre Cat in the 1998 video of *Cats*; Lord Attenborough took the role of Jacob in the 1999 video of *Joseph and the Amazing Technicolor Dreamcoat*.

20. The musical opened at George Square Theatre; performances were also given that August at the Adam Smith Theatre in nearby Kircaldy.

21. Andrew Lloyd Webber, "Whistle While You Work," *The Sunday Times*, June 28, 1998.

22. Andrew Lloyd Webber, foreword to Mary Hayley Bell, *Whistle Down the Wind* (London: Hodder and Stoughton, 1997), vii.

23. Bell, *Whistle Down the Wind*, 15. Bette Davis is a pet dog who will defecate only on newspaper.

24. An explanation of the holes in the stranger's feet is provided later in the novel: the man shot himself in his feet in 1942, the inference being that he was trying to escape active military service in World War II. In the musical this becomes the deliberate spearing of his feet with a pitchfork in order to gain access to the infirmary of the penitentiary, from where it would be easier to escape.

25. The design of the poster for the London production also used the cruciform

image, with a man holding a rifle over his shoulders to create the cross, standing next to a motorbike, all set off by a red sky. The James Dean overtones were here appropriate to elements of the plot, neatly summarizing the tension between sacred and secular, conformity and rebellion. Although apt, the design did not have the same impact as the earlier posters for *Cats* (silhouetted dancers in a pair of cat's eyes) or *The Phantom of the Opera* (a white mask and red rose).

26. This ending from the film was added to the musical for the 2001 U.K. tour version.

27. Mrs. Lodge (the Sunday school teacher): "Well, Jesus has never really left us. He's with us all the time, he's never really left us." Kathy: "What would they do to him if he did come back? . . . Would they crucify him?" Mrs. Lodge: "Well, I suppose some of the bad people might try, but this time all the good people would have to try even harder to stop them. We know what we'd do, don't we, if Jesus came back on earth. What would we do? We'd praise him."

28. The idea for the kittens in the film probably comes from this passage in the novel: "'Here's Elizabeth,' cried Poor Baby suddenly. And there she was. She had a sack she was humping along. Looked like a dead cat in it or something." Bell, *Whistle Down the Wind*, 66. The sack in fact contains foodstuffs for the supposed Jesus.

29. The character of Raymond was developed from the novel's Amos Nodge, a spoiled child with his own nanny, physically excluded from the social circle of the children. At one point the children sit on a trapdoor in a farm building to prevent him getting to them and their Jesus, whom the children have moved from the barn for safety. In the film the child outsider became the aggressive bully Raymond, whose anti-social traits were developed further in the musical as a disenfranchised teenager with experience of reform school. The restoration of the biblical name Amos was eminently suitable for the Louisiana setting of the musical, although in the novel Amos Nodge, who gives away the big secret to the adults, is explicitly compared to Judas.

30. The novel includes illustrations by Ōven Edwards which show the man as physically slight with a bit of facial stubble, but not a familiar representation of Christ. By contrast, publicity stills for the stage musical of Davis Gaines (Washington) and Marcuss Lovett (London) show the Man—long hair, rough moustache, and beard—as physically interchangeable with the usual images of Jesus in productions of *Jesus Christ Superstar*.

31. A major change in the 2001 U.K. touring version was that the lines formerly allotted to Boone in the final reprise of "Whistle Down the Wind" were given to the disembodied voice of the Man, as a bright beam of light illuminated Swallow from above. The reuniting of the family became one of a solely visual image in the final tableaux, not given verbal expression. As with the substitution of "The Gang" for "Annie Christmas," the effect was powerful in its theatrical moment, but not necessarily of dramaturgical benefit, as the supernatural took precedence over the human.

32. This also suggests just why *The Beautiful Game* followed *Whistle Down the Wind*. It has at its heart the same themes of opposing societal forces that take the innocent child only to produce the distorted and dangerous adult.

33. "When Children Rule the World" has its antecedent in an exchange from the novel, not present in the film: "'When we run the world there'll be a purpose,' said Swallow. 'No schools,' said Susan. 'Or policemen,' said Crikky. 'Or caning,' said Andrew.

. . . 'No death or dustbins, eh, Brat? What a great world you'll all make it. I'd like to be here then. P'raps there won't be any more wars, or passports, misery, or starvation, or fear, or shame. I shall look forward to your world.'" Bell, *Whistle Down the Wind*, 105–6. "No Matter What" has its origins in the presentation of gifts by the children to "Jesus" in the film. This is one of a sequence of short scenes of biblical parallel in the film; in another, the bully Raymond and the child Jackie reenact in the school playground Peter's triple denial of Christ. The gentle allusion of the film becomes more direct in the musical, which not only sets the story at Christmas time but also allocates a song to the giving of presents to Jesus in the barn (picking up on the "We Three Kings" reference from the film) and pushes further the strange role reversal created by the adult Man and the Magi children.

34. At one point before it was staged, a move directly from album to film was considered. Joan Goodman and Mike Bygrave, "Presenting the Che and Eva show," *The Observer*, June 11, 1978.

35. Perversely, it is like the approach to the opening of the film of *The Sound of Music*.

36. Russell was able to impose a whole series of additional meanings and references onto the story of *Tommy*. This strategy was not as accessible to Jewison, dealing with a story that already had accreted so many layers of symbolism through two millennia, to the point where such references had to be scaled down rather than expanded. In the Crucifixion sequence, Jewison included images of historic iconography in a montage of paintings and frescoes of Christ on the Cross, but his concern was to provide contemporary links as with the references to the Arab-Israeli conflict through the tanks and fighter planes, and through the framing device of the acting troupe that blurs the boundary between reality and reenactment. Russell piled on all sorts of additional resonances to the vague symbolism of *Tommy* in an attempt to make it more coherent as a symbolic narrative than it actually was, or was originally intended to be on the concept album. He drew on established Christian imagery with Tommy as a crucified Christ during his trip induced by the Acid Queen, and presented subversions of organized religion in "Eyesight to the Blind," "Sally Simpson," and "Tommy's Holiday Camp." Russell also included symbolism specific to the film—the constant reappearance, for example, of the metal spheres first seen as ball-bearings at the factory where Tommy's pregnant mother receives the news that her unborn child's father is missing in action. Used as a running image throughout the film, the spheres are later seen, for example, as part of the Doctor's diagnostic machine, and finally become huge versions that make up the holiday camp terrain, atop one of which Tommy sits teaching, gurulike.

37. Quoted in Goodman and Bygrave, "Presenting the Che and Eva Show."

38. There is something irresistible in Tim Rice's original lyrics for the album, describing Juan Perón's role in the army: "He began his career in the army overseas / Teaching all the other soldiers all he knew about skis," which leads to the classic Rice payoff: "Great men / Don't grow on trees / I'm one / I ain't gonna freeze / Dictators / Don't grow on skis." The incongruent playfulness of the lines is bizarre but great fun. However, this number also includes the introduction of Che Guevara as a scientist with a new fly-killing formula, Eva's lack of support for which becomes the final straw in Che's decision to oppose the military regime.

39. The end of this sequence does, however, point to a weakness that the film

shares with the film of *Jesus Christ Superstar*: in neither case is the title role played by someone compelling enough to make the character believable. Ted Neeley had been chosen as Jesus following his appearance on stage in the role, so at least he came with the right vocal potential (if not always utilized). The choice of Madonna as Eva Perón seems more a case of biographical wish fulfillment than an appropriate choice of performer. Madonna did not have the vocal range, technically or emotionally, to deal with the role. Consequently, many sections were transposed down to suit her more limited range, so that the edge of the original writing—that sense of effort and thrill of the female voice high on the break or right down at the lower limits—was ironed out. On the original recording just after the end of "Don't Cry for Me, Argentina," the Eva of Julie Covington revels in the sentiments behind the lines "Just listen to that!/The voice of Argentina!/We are adored! We are loved!" She is strident and triumphant in tone, ending right at the top of the belt voice range on a high E, as in the stage show. The lowering of the phrase by a tone for Madonna, along with the close-miked, safe but always underpowered delivery, castrates the effect of the original writing: the vocal energy of the original conception is never manifested through the central characterization, and the hypnotic fascination of the character from youthful aspiration to hard-driven politico to eventual self-justification in final illness never really materializes.

CHAPTER 6. "Memory"

1. Michael Feingold, *Village Voice*, quoted in Walsh, *Andrew Lloyd Webber*, 207.

2. J. Peter Burkholder, *All Made of Tunes: Charles Ives and the Uses of Musical Borrowing* (New Haven: Yale University Press, 1995), 416–17. For extended discussions of the issues surrounding borrowing in music, ones which have significantly informed this chapter, see Burkholder's thorough application of such ideas to a single composer ibid. and his lengthy article "Borrowing" in *The Revised New Grove Dictionary of Music and Musicians* (London, 2000).

3. Harold Bloom, *The Anxiety of Influence* (New York: Oxford University Press, 1973).

4. Walsh, *Andrew Lloyd Webber*, 13–14.

5. Coveney, *Cats on a Chandelier*, 199.

6. Quoted ibid., 197.

7. Shared knowledge between composer-lyricist and audience is essential to pastiche, and the location of that connection and the degree of emphasis it is given mark the territory where pastiche slips into parody. When the audience is invited to respond to particular heightened features of the style being pastiched with the intent of subverting the integrity of the original, the result is parody. Thus "U.N.C.O.U.P.L.E.D." is parody, as the laconic delivery is matched to the spelling of the unspeakable word, extended by two syllables from its "D.I.V.O.R.C.E." origins just enough to drive home the point. The effect of parody in "U.N.C.O.U.P.L.E.D." is achieved through its text, whereas the music is a well-observed but ordinary country-and-western tune; the words, not the music, elevate the song from pastiche to parody. A comparison could be made with Mary Rodgers and Stephen Sondheim's *The Boy from . . .* in which either lyrics or music on their own contain parody: the lyrics in the ridiculously long name, the

music in its unexpected disruption of the neat four-bar phrases, harmonically and rhythmically treading water, so pointing up the cadence when it finally happens. By way of contrast with "U.N.C.O.U.P.L.E.D.," the song "Next Time You Fall in Love," with lyrics by Don Black, was added in the revamp of *Starlight Express* for London (opened November 23, 1992) and still stands out as the most genuine number of the score amid the plethora of stylistic clichés elsewhere.

8. Subtly implied on the original recording, this became explicit in the 1996 London cast recording.

9. The last three notes of the anacrusis phrase (the paused phrase) at the start of "On This Night of a Thousand Stars" are mitigated in their resemblance to the equivalent phrase in "Cherry Pink and Apple Blossom White" on the film soundtrack of *Evita*, in which Jimmy Nail's rendition replaces the descending three-note scale with a descending three-note arpeggio.

10. As a young child Lloyd Webber was apparently soothed by the playing of recordings of the bands of Edmondo Ros, who in the late 1940s and 1950s was the most prominent of British Latin-American bandleaders, responsible for popularizing samba and rhumba styles in Britain.

11. It is also a distinctly nonauthentic, Latin musical view, using the sound of Latin filtered through Western popular music. Some effort to counteract this was made in the film version, in which the orchestration of the club performance was given a more authentic instrumental arrangement and tonal coloring, especially through the use of the piano accordion.

12. Bagatelle in A minor, Woo59.

13. Op. 95 in E minor, the fifth symphony under the old numbering system.

14. Rice, *Oh, What a Circus*, 125.

15. Emerson, Lake, and Palmer's self-titled first album (1970) contains "The Barbarian," after Bartók's *Allegro barbaro*, and "Knife-Edge," after Janáček's *Sinfonietta*; their arrangement of Mussorgsky's *Pictures from an Exhibition* was recorded as a live performance and released the following year.

16. I love the Kansas morning / Kansas mist at my window / Kansas winds shift and sigh / I can see you now / We're flying high / Kansas, love of mine.

17. Coveney, *Cats on a Chandelier*, 199.

18. Howard Kissel, *Women's Wear Daily*, quoted in Suskin, *More Opening Nights on Broadway*, 273–74.

19. Of course, the device is not solely Puccini's: for example, the same effect of a distant high note was used by Verdi for Nanetta in *Falstaff*.

20. The use of distinctive patterns of chords as a motivic representation of something strange, exotic, or mysterious is a musical commonplace. In opera, examples can be found in such diverse places as the end of Strauss's *Der Rosenkavalier* and the sequence of contrasting major and minor chords used by Britten in *Billy Budd* to express the things spoken between Vere and Billy but never revealed.

21. See Citron, *Sondheim and Lloyd Webber*, 333–35. The same point was demonstrated by Billy Crystal's character in *Forget Paris* (1995).

22. "Una gioia / strana, una nova pace / che dir non so!"

23. Could this also be a shadow behind Frederick Loewe's melody for his song with Lerner, "Come to Me, Bend to Me"? Attention has been drawn elsewhere to the

similarity between the opening of the verse to "With a Little Bit of Luck" in *My Fair Lady* with Tosca's act I aria "Non la sospiri la nostra casetta." (For example, see Geoffrey Block, *Enchanted Evenings: The Broadway Musical from Show Boat to Sondheim* [New York: Oxford University Press, 1997], 380, n. 46.) A few lines later in the same aria ("pien d'amore e di mister?") a theme emerges that is very similar to the opening of the title chorus of *Paint Your Wagon*.

CHAPTER 7. "Now and Forever"

1. See Geoffrey Block, "The Broadway Canon from *Show Boat* to *West Side Story* and the European Operatic Ideal," *Journal of Musicology* 11 (1993): 525–44. Block's "Canonic Twelve" for the period he investigates include *Show Boat* (1927), *Porgy and Bess* (1935), *Pal Joey* (1940), *Oklahoma!* (1943), *Carousel* (1945), *Kiss Me, Kate* (1948), *South Pacific* (1949), *Guys and Dolls* (1950), *The King and I* (1951), *My Fair Lady* (1956), *The Most Happy Fella* (1956), and *West Side Story* (1957).

2. It is worth remembering that *Oklahoma!* can be read as a compendium of musically clichéd popular styles—the two-step, the rousing chorus, the romantic waltz, and so on—and it generated its own popular hits, sung by people on the way into the theater (as the by-now proverbial phrase has it). Furthermore, if the influence of the innovative long-playing recording is included alongside the exposure of the public to its melodies through radio, dance arrangements, and so on, the publicity machine was vast. It was certainly the case that the storming public response to the opening of the show in London in 1947 was severely "hyped" by the expectation generated through an awareness of the show in advance: bringing back an LP of *Oklahoma!* from America was high on the list of acquisitions for British visitors after the war and even those from farther afield, such as South Africa. In this sense, Lloyd Webber's works have carried on the "tradition."

3. *Sweeney Todd* has, for example, been presented by the New York City Opera, the Lyric Opera of Chicago, and the Royal Opera, Covent Garden. Of Block's canonic twelve shows, at least six have appeared on the professional operatic stage: *Show Boat, Kiss Me, Kate, West Side Story, Porgy and Bess, Carousel,* and *The Most Happy Fella* to this author's knowledge; no doubt others have too.

4. Ethan Mordden, *Coming Up Roses: The Broadway Musical in the 1950s* (New York: Oxford University Press, 1998), 3, 27.

5. Such a reevaluation is behind the "discovery" of works from the past, an active archaeology of musical theater much in evidence in concert versions and specialist re-released recordings. In London there has been the long-running Lost Musicals series, while Encores! in New York was in part sponsored by Lloyd Webber and the Really Useful Group.

6. An interesting parallel can be found in the serious study by the academy of Puccini, whose work has been much less represented than its popularity and canonical import to opera would tend to suggest. As William Drabkin has observed: "In most discussions of opera composed in the century or so leading up to Puccini—say from Mozart to late Wagner and Verdi—an important criterion of excellence has been demonstrability of some sort of *unity*, a system or method operating over the entire range of a score. . . . Studies sympathetic to Puccini may have fallen into the unity trap

by praising his music not for its sheer verve, as Debussy is said to have put it, but for qualities which have conferred the halo of classicism upon early composers: motivic economy and total unity." "The Musical Language of *La bohème*," in *Giacomo Puccini: La bohème*, ed. Arthur Groos and Roger Parker (Cambridge: Cambridge University Press, 1986), 81–82.

7. Walsh, *Andrew Lloyd Webber*, 173.

8. Clive Barnes, "Andrew and Aspects of Hate," *New York Times*, April 11, 1990.

9. Two of Ivor Novello's plays were performed on Broadway, with him in the cast: *Suite in Two Flats* (Shubert Theatre, September 16, 1930) and *The Truth Game* (Ethel Barrymore Theatre, December 27, 1930).

10. The importance of general social distinctions, in effect a less specifically British form of class observation, has nonetheless retained its place in the Lloyd Webber works. Apart from the formal class structure of *The Phantom of the Opera*, there are other forms of social division evident, as in the significance of religious affiliation in *Whistle Down the Wind* and *The Beautiful Game*. Dividing up society in whatever way still seems to be a strong feature of British concerns in the musical.

11. It is unfortunate in this respect that the third edition (2000) of Steven Suskin's invaluable reference work *Show Tunes* has removed the second edition's category of "Notable Imported Shows"—as Suskin acknowledges, "half of them by Lloyd Webber." While Suskin has defined his focus as strictly on Broadway-generated shows, a casual perusal of the chronological listings of Broadway productions in appendix 1 can lead to misinterpretation from 1971 onward when the Lloyd Webber repertory is removed. A similar but reversed situation has existed in relation to the British musical immediately postwar, with the stressing of American imports disproportionate to the home-grown, considerable successes. For example, the chronological listing for the West End in Stephen Citron's *Sondheim and Lloyd Webber*, a table substantially reprinted from two of the author's earlier comparative biographies, significantly distorts the emphasis of the West End immediately after World War II by adopting the commonly held but fallacious assumption of immediate and overpowering American success followed by British collapse in the face of it. The American musicals that "took London" in 1947 had a serious rival in Vivian Ellis's *Bless the Bride*—a major hit—while the poor reception of the unmentioned *Finian's Rainbow* in the same year (61 performances) does not fit the conveniently assumed pattern of the success of all things American. Similarly, in 1948, an "American invasion" would hardly have been furthered by the ill-received 48 performances of *Lute Song*, for the West End was more strongly influenced by the 337 performances of *Cage Me a Peacock* or the 466 performances of *Carissima*, which opened in the same year. Similarly, in 1950 the "American hit" *Carousel* (566 performances) ran for less time than did the home-grown musical *Blue for a Boy* (664 performances). Such figures are not necessarily a reflection on the lasting theatrical value of these lesser known works—anyone today would almost certainly find more to enjoy in a revival of *Carousel* than one of *Blue for a Boy*—but they are important in assessing the theatrical scene and mood of the time. It is through such retrospective interpretations that canonical values are additionally bolstered and the list of its works reinforced.

12. Clive Barnes, *New York Times*, quoted in Suskin, *More Opening Nights on Broadway*, 489.

13. "Those shallow mean pretenders to your throne / Will come to learn ours is the upper hand / For I do not accept this is not known / In rich established parcels of our land / To face the storms so long and not capsize / Is not the chance achievement of a fraud / Conservatives are kings of compromise / It hurts them more to jeer than to applaud / And I shall have my people come to choose / The couple who shall wear their country's crowns / In thousands in my squares and avenues / Emptying their villages and towns / Where every soul in home or shack or stall / Knows me as Argentina — that is all." Rice's lyrics are in Shakespearean sonnet form: lines of ten syllables, two parts of eight lines (the octave) and six lines (the sestet), and a rhyming scheme of ABABCDCD EFEFGG. In the stage version just the sestet was retained, leaving only a shadow of the number's origins through the characteristic, closing rhymed couplet. In addition, for the stage show, the phrase "The couple" was replaced with "Two Peróns."

14. This is especially so when *Superstar* is considered in the context of Broadway in 1971, the year of its first staging there. Rock had reached Broadway with *Hair* in 1968, also the year of the pop of Bacharach and Hal David in *Promises, Promises*; the long runs of each ensured that they were still playing in 1971, when *Godspell* — which also brought pop and religion together — opened in May, five months before *Superstar*. They all established pop and rock in the musical theater world, but none brought so many stylistic elements together in so forceful a way as did Rice and Lloyd Webber's creation.

15. Jesus' address to God in Gethsemane makes it clear why this particular dimension among others is so central: "Show me there's a reason for your wanting me to die / You're far too keen on where and how and not so hot on why."

16. Quasi-philosophical in that there is no sustained argument but only the articulation of a set of varying standpoints: the result is disjointed rather than sustained, interrogative but not conclusive.

17. *Aspects of Love* is an exception in its amorality. That the drama stops when it does seems arbitrary, for there is no obvious point of resolution, just another stage in the sequence of "change partners and dance."

18. Liner notes, "The Vaults," *Andrew Lloyd Webber: Now and Forever*, 2001 (Polydor 589 393-2).

19. Martin Kettle, "Phantom of the Opera House," *Guardian*, May 20, 2000.

20. The other contemporary working of Gaston Leroux's tale, Yeston and Kopit's *Phantom*, makes considerably less comment on the musical-opera relationship in its musical style and dramatic structure than does Lloyd Webber's.

21. By contrast, when the Beatles recorded Meredith Willson's "Till There Was You" from *The Music Man*, it required no such alteration of its implied dramatic context.

22. *Whistle Down the Wind*, Polydor (559 441-2).

23. One has to go back to such a number as Gloria Gaynor's high-energy disco version of Jerry Herman's "I Am What I Am" (from *La Cage aux Folles*) in the 1980s to find a comparable successful high-profile shift of a repackaged show song to suit a dance category of the popular musical charts. In that particular case, even the lyrics needed no adaptation: its manifesto for homosexual and transvestite acceptance was effortlessly appropriated from the musical by gay disco.

24. An overture was prepared for *Aspects* but not used. Other features of the presentation of this bold opening number create the feeling of a manifesto for the show to

come. These include the gradual introduction of the chamber instrumentation to the piano, which provides an orchestral slow build in which the string basis of the ensemble is first established. By the third verse, marked by an abrupt semitone shift upward in key to B♭ major, the high set chordal writing of the upper strings provides an intensity but not weight to the melody, while the insistent, quasi-martial nature of the accompaniment is conveyed through horn fanfare figures and the use of timpani to mark the tune's periodicity.

25. The lyrics of the radio song represent Alex, by paralleling his condition: he wants to talk to someone who is not eager to talk back. As the radio plays "Speak to Me," Alex asks Rose what he should order for her to drink, but her single-word reply, "Armagnac," is curt and barely conversational. A similar parallel occurs at the end of the first full refrain. In the second refrain, as Rose warms more toward Alex's presence, the parallel works the other way: as the radio plays "Tell me true" Rose asks Alex to promise to answer truthfully how old he is.

26. The scene has just Alex and Rose, alternately sleeping then both awake on a train journey, sharing with the audience their mutual attraction. This song is marked *andante con moto* at the start and *non sentimentale* against the solo violin. A sense of impetus through the *più mosso* section ("Whatever happens, one thing is certain . . .") and the more animated accompaniment of Rose's section prevents the song becoming too indulgent.

27. Both are big emotive ballads with broad melodies on the theme of love; each is harmonically assertive in its conventionality; each features a descending scale as its most prominent melodic feature; each in its arrangement features an abrupt key change before the last verse. Also, each wants to climax on the tonic at the high octave at the end for that final closure, but only "Seeing Is Believing" is allowed to do so. "Love Changes Everything" is completed in this fashion only for the end of the first act.

28. Although it was a sung reprise for the London opening, later scores have this section as instrumental, not vocal, though still to be understood as a thematic reprise and concluding coda. Indeed the whole of scene 6 is redundant: scene 7 shows George in Paris cursing Alex and reading a telegram that conveys all necessary information ("Nephew Alex break in, stop . . . / Stealing household supplies, stop. / Living in sin, stop. / Please advise, stop"). But whether sung or played, the reprise restating of the theme uninterrupted allows the number a sense of completeness denied to "Love Changes Everything" or "Parlez-vous Français?"

29. The motif is clearly related to the *Benedicte* sung at the blessing service for Lloyd Webber's third wedding, and to "Surrender" and "The Lady's Paying" in *Sunset Boulevard*.

30. Such a figure is also part of the musical vocabulary of *The Phantom of the Opera* (Regression theme, see example 4.5) and *Sunset Boulevard* (Joe's first sight of the mansion).

31. The words are slightly altered in the third verse: "Love will never, never let you be the same." There is one other occurrence of the descending scale motif, for a single but important line between verses two and three. Alex sings, "Why did I go back to see her?" which is met with a balancing sense of "when" as Giulietta (as we later learn her to be) speaks the reply, "Alex, it's all in the past." Those two lines neatly and immediately arouse questions of identity, motivation, relationships, and purpose. Their

concision is set off by their placing within the context of the ballad. As the title says, it is concerned with love and relationships right from the outset.

32. The change begins as Rose contemplates her own position, with her line of explanation "I'm resting again"; Rose feels that she ought to give Alex some token explanation of her tetchiness. The orchestra underscores this with the introduction of a new lyric motif, heading much more toward melody than the earlier fragmented musical ideas, but as yet not fully formed. A descending scale begins in the flute, countered by a rising scale in violin II, and is developed into a much more tender and calm melodic statement, amplified by an orchestration relying on clear solo tones. It is Rose who now leads Alex with her questions, and the downward scalic movement of the accompanying orchestral phrase is answered by a rising phrase from Alex: "I'm travelling through France / Until my call-up" (thus Alex is, like Rose, between engagements). The further evolution of these two phrases is shortly to create "Seeing Is Believing." The next development of the unifying scalic descent comes as Alex asks, "May I ask a stupid question?"; in this form the scale later turns up as the main theme of the fairground song "Everybody Loves a Hero" (act I, scene 14) and the circus number "Journey of a Lifetime" (act II, scene 18).

33. Quoted in Mark Steyn, "Towards a New Intimacy," *The Independent*, April 8, 1989.

Bibliography

Citron, Stephen. *Sondheim and Lloyd Webber: The New Musical.* Oxford: Oxford University Press, 2001.

Coveney, Michael. *Cats on a Chandelier: The Andrew Lloyd Webber Story.* London: Hutchinson, 1999.

Gänzl, Kurt. *The British Musical Theatre.* Vol. 2, 1915–1984. London: Macmillan, 1986.

————. *The Complete Aspects of Love.* London: Aurum, 1990. Includes libretto.

————. *The Music of Andrew Lloyd Webber.* New York: Harry N. Abrams, 1989.

Lloyd Webber, Julian. *Travels with My Cello.* London: Pavilion, 1984.

Mantle, Jonathan. *Fanfare: The Unauthorised Biography of Andrew Lloyd Webber.* London: Michael Joseph, 1989.

McKnight, Gerald. *Andrew Lloyd Webber: A Biography.* London: Granada, 1984.

Morley, Sheridan. *Spread a Little Happiness: The First Hundred Years of the British Musical.* New York: Thames and Hudson, 1987.

Nassour, Ellis, and Richard Broderick. *Rock Opera: The Creation of Jesus Christ Superstar, from Record Album to Broadway Show and Motion Picture.* New York: Hawthorn, 1973.

Parker, Alan. *The Making of Evita.* London: Collins, 1996.

Perry, George. *The Complete Phantom of the Opera.* London: Pavilion, 1987. Includes libretto.

————. *Sunset Boulevard: From Movie to Musical.* New York: Holt, 1993. Includes libretto.

Prece, Paul, and William A. Everett. "The Megamusical and Beyond: The Creation, Internationalisation, and Impact of a Genre." In *The Cambridge Companion to the Musical,* ed. William A. Everett and Paul Laird, 246–65. Cambridge: Cambridge University Press, 2002.

Rice, Tim. *Oh, What a Circus: The Autobiography, 1944–1978.* London: Hodder and Stoughton, 1999.

Rice, Tim, and Andrew Lloyd Webber. *Evita.* London: Elm Tree, 1978.

Rich, Frank. *Hot Seat: Theater Criticism for the New York Times, 1980–1993*. New York:
    Random House, 1998.
Richmond, Keith. *The Musicals of Andrew Lloyd Webber*. London: Virgin, 1995.
Seeley, Robert, and Rex Bunnett. *London Musical Shows on Record, 1889–1989*. Har-
    row: General Gramophone, 1989. Discography.
Steyn, Mark. "The Maximalist." In *Broadway Babies Say Goodnight: Musicals Then
    and Now*, 273–86. London: Faber, 1997.
Suskin, Stephen. *More Opening Nights on Broadway: A Critical Quotebook of the
    Musical Theatre, 1965–1981*. New York: Schirmer, 1997.
———. *Show Tunes, 1905–1991: The Songs, Shows, and Careers of Broadway's Major
    Composers*. 2d ed. New York: Limelight, 1992.
Swain, Joseph P. "History as Musical." In *The Broadway Musical: A Critical and Musi-
    cal Survey*, 293–307. New York: Oxford University Press, 1990.
Walsh, Michael. *Andrew Lloyd Webber: His Life and Works*. London: Viking, 1989;
    2d ed. New York: Abrams, 1997.
www.reallyuseful.com (official website of The Really Useful Group).
www.tiretracks.co.uk (extensive site on the musicals of Andrew Lloyd Webber).

Permissions

La bohème
MUSIC: Giacomo Puccini
LIBRETTO: Giuseppe Giacosa and Luigi Illica
Reproduced by kind permission of G. Ricordi and Co. Ltd.

"Cherry Pink and Apple Blossom White"
MUSIC: Louiguy
LYRICS: Marcel Ageron
TRANSLATION: Mack David
© Copyright Sidomusic B Liechti and Cie
Warner Chappell Music Ltd., London W6 8BS
Reproduced by permission of International Music Publications Ltd.
All rights reserved.

"Christmas Dream" from *The Odessa File*
WORDS AND MUSIC: Andrew Lloyd Webber and Tim Rice
© copyright 1974 (renewed 2000) Screen Gems–EMI Music Ltd.
All rights in the U.S. and Canada Controlled and Administered by Colgems–EMI
Music Inc.
All Rights Reserved. International Copyright Secured. Used by permission.

"Cold" from *Whistle Down the Wind*
MUSIC: Andrew Lloyd Webber
LYRICS: Jim Steinman
© Copyright 1996, 1998 The Really Useful Group Ltd., Songs of PolyGram International, Inc., and Lost Boys Music
All Rights for The Really Useful Group Ltd. in the United States and Canada Administered by PolyGram International Publishing, Inc.
International Copyright Secured. All Rights Reserved.

Evita
MUSIC: Andrew Lloyd Webber
LYRICS: Tim Rice
© copyright 1976 Evita Music Ltd. Administered by Universal–MCA Music
Publishing, Inc.
All Rights Reserved. Used by permission.

La fanciulla del West
MUSIC: Giacomo Puccini
LIBRETTO: Geulfo Civinini and Carlo Zangarini
Reproduced by kind permission of G. Ricordi and Co. Ltd.

Gavotte from Prokofiev "Classical" Symphony
© Copyright 1926 by Hawkes and Son (London) Ltd.
Reproduced by permission of Boosey and Hawkes Music Publishers Ltd.

"Go, Go, Go Joseph" from *Joseph and the Amazing Technicolor Dreamcoat*
MUSIC: Andrew Lloyd Webber
LYRICS: Tim Rice
© copyright 1969 The Really Useful Group Ltd. Copyright renewed.
All Rights for North America Controlled by Williamson Music Co.
International Copyright Secured. All Rights Reserved.

"Goodbye Seattle"
MUSIC: Andrew Lloyd Webber
LYRICS: Tim Rice
© copyright 1970 The Really Useful Group Ltd. Copyright renewed.
International Copyright Secured. All Rights Reserved.

Jesus Christ Superstar (except "King Herod's Song")
MUSIC: Andrew Lloyd Webber
LYRICS: Tim Rice
© copyright 1969 Universal–MCA Publishing, Inc. on behalf of MCA Music Ltd.
All Rights Reserved. Used by permission.

"Kansas Morning"
MUSIC: Andrew Lloyd Webber
LYRICS: Tim Rice
© copyright 1966 Tim Rice and Andrew Lloyd Webber
All Rights Reserved. International Copyright Secured.

"King Herod's Song" from *Jesus Christ Superstar*
LYRICS: Tim Rice
MUSIC: Andrew Lloyd Webber
© copyright 1971 Norrie Paramor Music Ltd. Copyright renewed.
All Rights Administered by Chappell & Co.
International Copyright Secured. All Rights Reserved.

"Love Changes Everything" from *Aspects of Love*
MUSIC: Andrew Lloyd Webber
LYRICS: Don Black and Charles Hart
© Copyright 1988 The Really Useful Group Ltd.
International Copyright Secured. All Rights Reserved.

"Masquerade" from *The Phantom of the Opera*
MUSIC: Andrew Lloyd Webber
LYRICS: Charles Hart
ADDITIONAL LYRICS: Richard Stilgoe
© Copyright 1986 The Really Useful Group Ltd.
All Rights for the United States and Canada Administered by Universal–PolyGram
International Publishing, Inc.
International Copyright Secured. All Rights Reserved.

"Poor, Poor Joseph" from *Joseph and the Amazing Technicolor Dreamcoat*
MUSIC: Andrew Lloyd Webber
LYRICS: Tim Rice
© copyright 1969 The Really Useful Group Ltd. Copyright renewed.
All Rights for North America Controlled by R&H Music Co.
International Copyright Secured. All Rights Reserved.

Starlight Express
MUSIC: Andrew Lloyd Webber
LYRICS: Richard Stilgoe
© copyright The Really Useful Group Ltd.
All Rights Reserved. International Copyright Secured.

"Sunset Boulevard" from *Sunset Boulevard*
MUSIC: Andrew Lloyd Webber
LYRICS: Don Black and Christopher Hampton, with contributions by Amy Powers
© Copyright 1993 The Really Useful Group Ltd.
All Rights for the United States Controlled by Famous Music Corporation.
International Copyright Secured. All Rights Reserved.

"Think of Me" from *The Phantom of the Opera*
MUSIC: Andrew Lloyd Webber
LYRICS: Charles Hart
ADDITIONAL LYRICS: Richard Stilgoe
© Copyright 1986 The Really Useful Group Ltd.
All Rights for the United States and Canada Administered by Universal–PolyGram
International Publishing, Inc.
International Copyright Secured. All Rights Reserved.

Tosca
MUSIC: Giacomo Puccini
LIBRETTO: Giuseppe Giacosa and Luigi Illica
Reproduced by kind permission of G. Ricordi and Co. Ltd.

"Try It and See"
MUSIC: Andrew Lloyd Webber
LYRICS: Tim Rice
© copyright 1969 The Really Useful Group Ltd. Copyright renewed.
International Copyright Secured. All Rights Reserved.

"With One Look" from *Sunset Boulevard*
MUSIC: Andrew Lloyd Webber
LYRICS: Don Black and Christopher Hampton, with contributions by Amy Powers
© Copyright 1993 The Really Useful Group Ltd.
All Rights for the United States Controlled by Famous Music Corporation.
International Copyright Secured. All Rights Reserved.

General Index

Page numbers in *italic type* refer to images.

Ace of Clubs (Coward), 189, 227n.32
After the Ball (Coward), 189, 227n.32
"All Shook Up" (Blackwell, Presley), 60, 228n.13
Anderson, Carl, 7
Anderson, Kevin, 16
Andrews, Julie, 124
Annie (Strouse, Charnin, Meehan), 124, 125
Anything Goes [revised] (Porter, T. Crouse, Weidman), 32, 33
Applause (Strouse, Adams, Comden, Green), 234n.41
Arena, Tina, 199, 225n.3
Aspects of Love (novella: Garnett), 15
Attenborough, Richard, 135, 154, 236n.19
"Avalon" (Rose, Jolson), 171
Ave Maria (Bach-Gounod), 174–75
Awdry, Rev. W., 13
Ayckbourn, Alan, 9, 18, 26, 162

Balfe, Michael W., 232n.25
Ball, Michael, 45, 199, 225n.3
Banderas, Antonio, 146, 152
Barber, John, 28
Barnes, Clive, 46, 188, 190
Bart, Lionel, 47, 188–89
Bartók, Béla, 64, 171, 240n.5

Bates, Alan, 135
Batt, Mike, 78
The Beatles, 59, 60, 67, 68
Beauty and the Beast (Menken, Ashman, Rice, Woolverton), 34
Berlin, Irving, 123
Billington, Michael, 28, 225n.7
Billy Budd (Britten, Forster, Crozier), 240n.20
Binge, Ronald, 60
Bitter Sweet (Coward), 188, 189, 226–27n.32
Björnson, Maria, 15, 40, 119, 230n.1
Black, Don, 10, 15, 16, 31, 44, 127, 223nn.21–22; on "Sunset Boulevard," 129
Blane, Ralph, 126
Bless the Bride (Ellis, Herbert), 242n.11
Blood Brothers (Russell), 188
Blue for a Boy (Parr Davies, Purcell), 242n.3
La bohème (Puccini, Giacosa, Illica), 177–78, Ex. 6.5
Bolero (Ravel), 173–74
Bolton, Guy, 47
The Bonzo Dog (Doo Dah) Band, 228–29n.13, 229n.14
"Boom-Bang-a-Bang" (Warne, Moorhouse), 58
Boublil, Alain, 41
The Boy Friend (Wilson), 47, 162, 188

"The Boy from . . ." (M. Rodgers, Sond-
    heim), 239n.7
Boy George, 199
Boyzone, 199, 225n.3
Bragg, Melvyn, 25
Brando, Marlon, 234n.2
Bremner, Charles, 46
Brett, John, 181
Brigadoon (Lerner, Loewe), 234n.41
Brightman, Sarah, 36, 223–24n.23, 225n.3,
    232n.27; marriage to Lloyd Webber, 11–12,
    13, 15–16, 224n.24; and The Phantom of
    the Opera, 38–39, 109, 126, 225n.3
Britten, Benjamin, 27
Brolly, Brian, 22
Brooks, Mel, 126
Brubeck, Dave, 229n.25
Butler, Gerard, 126
Bye Bye Birdie (Strouse, Adams, Stewart),
    123, 125, 234n.41

Cabaret (Kander, Ebb, Masteroff), 124, 145,
    185
Cage Me a Peacock (Lynd, Langley), 242n.11
Caird, John, 33
Camelot (Lerner, Loewe), 123
La campanella (Liszt), 229n.18
Candide (Bernstein, Wilbur, Hellman), 198
Caprice in A minor (Paganini), 9, 171
Carissima (May, Maschwitz), 242n.11
Carousel (Rodgers, Hammerstein), 123,
    241nn.1,3, 242n.11
Carroll, Dina, 225n.3
Carsen, Robert, 53
The Castle of Otranto (Walpole), 230n.6
La Cava (O'Keefe, Keeling, Clafin and
    Broccoli), 198
Chaney, Lon, 78, 78
"Cherry Pink and Apple Blossom White"
    (Louiguy), 167–68, 169, Ex.6.2
Chicago (Kander, Ebb, Fosse), 124
Chitty Chitty Bang Bang (R. M. and R. B.
    Sherman, Sams), 34, 126
A Chorus Line (Hamlisch, Kleban, Kirk-
    wood, Dante), 124, 185
Christie, Tony, 146, 161
Cinderella (Prokofiev), 70
"The Circle of Life" (John, Rice), 124

Close, Glenn, 17, 225n.3
"Clotho" (Emerson), 64
The Code of the Woosters (Wodehouse), 9
Coleman, Cy, 221n.1
Collins, Joan, 154
"Come to Me, Bend to Me" (Lerner and
    Loewe), 176, 240–41n.23
Como, Perry, 72
Company (Sondheim, Furth), 234n.41
Concerto for Group and Orchestra (Deep
    Purple), 64, 68
"Congratulations" (Coulter, Martin), 58
Conversation Piece (Coward), 189
Cooper, Alice, 68
Coppélia (Delibes), 106, 232n.20
"Could It Be Magic" (Manilow, Anderson),
    171
Coveney, Michael, 28
Covington, Julie, 9, 225n.3, 239n.40
Coward, Noël, 47, 125, 188–89, 226–27n.32,
    227n.33
Crawford, Michael, 13, 126, 225n.3
Cullen, David, 159, 231n.9, 233n.32
Cushman, Robert, 32

D'Abo, Mike, 229n.22
Daltrey, David, 59
Dance, Charles, 80
"Dance of the Knights" (Prokofiev), 70
Daniel, Jeffrey, 225n.3
Danse macabre (Saint-Saëns), 95, 106,
    232n.20
Days of Future Passed (Moody Blues), 68
Dean, James, 143
"Death Cab for Cutie" (Stanshall), 228n.13
Debussy, Claude, 104
Deep Purple, 7, 64–65, 229nn.19,20; classical
    references, 229n.18
Dickson, Barbara, 9, 225n.3
Distel, Sacha, 57
"D.I.V.O.R.C.E" (Braddock, Putnam), 161,
    239n.7
Divorce Me, Darling! (Wilson), 162
Doctor Dolittle (Bricusse), 126
Doggett, Alan, 6, 222n.9, 228n.12
Domingo, Plácido, 13
Don Giovanni (Mozart, Da Ponte), 114,
    230n.6, 233n.37

Donovan, Jason, 59, 61, 225n.3
"Don't Be Cruel" (Blackwell, Presley), 60, 228n.13
Dracula (Stoker), 230n.6
Dunaway, Faye, 227n.35

Easter, David, 225n.3
HRH Prince Edward, 223n.20
Edwards, Gale, 49, 134
8½ (Fellini), 126
Eliot, T. S., 11, 31, 39
Elliman, Yvonne, 7, 161, 222n.13
Elliott, Desmond, 6
Ellis, Greg, 225n.3
Ellis, Vivian, 125, 161, 188–89
Elton, Ben, 40, 51–52, 126
Emerson, Lake, and Palmer, 64, 171, 240n.15
Essex, David, 225n.3
Etude in E major, op. 10 no. 3 (Chopin), 171
Eurovision Song Contest, 57–58, 227–28n.5, 228nn.6,7
The Everly Brothers, 144, 199
Expresso Bongo (Heneker, More, Manko- witz), 125

Falsettos trilogy (Finn, Lapine), 193
Fame, 126
La fanciulla del West (Puccini, Civinini, Zangarini), 176–78, 180, Ex. 6.6 and 6.7
Fantasie Impromptu in C♯ minor, op. 66 (Chopin), 171
Le Fantôme de l'Opéra (novel: Leroux), 13, 79, 121; adaptation for the Lloyd Webber musical, 88, 104, 106, 230n.1, 230–31n.7, 232n.22; adaptations for film, 78–79, 80, 98, 106, 233n.35; comparison of style with the Lloyd Webber musical, 80–81; sources for the novel, 77
Fauré, Gabriel, 37
Faust (Gounod, Barbier, Carré), 77, 106, 232n.20
Fellini, Federico, 126
Fiddler on the Roof (Bock, Harnick, Stein), 124, 150, 195, 234n.41
Finian's Rainbow (Arlen, Harburg, Saidy), 242n.11
Finn, William, 194
Finney, Albert, 71

Forbes, Bryan, 135
42nd Street (Warren, Dubin, Stewart, Bramble), 126
Frankenstein (Mary Shelley), 230n.6
Frears, Stephen, 71
Friedman, Maria, 154
Frost, David, 7
The Full Monty (Yazbek, McNally), 136, 186
Funeral March for a Marionette (Gounod), 106, 232n.20
A Funny Thing Happened on the Way to the Forum (Sondheim, Shevlove, Gelbart), 125
Für Elise (Beethoven), 171

Gaines, Davis, 237n.30
Garnett, David, 44
Garnier, Charles, 77
Gay, Noel, 188
Gaynor, Gloria, 243n.23
Gershwin, George, 123
Gershwin, Ira, 123
Gillan, Ian, 7, 66
Gillespie, Dana, 222n.14
Grainer, Ron, 60
Gurdon, Madeleine Astrid, 15, 16
Guys and Dolls (Loesser, Burrows), 123, 241n.1
Gypsy (Styne, Sondheim, Laurents), 123

Hair (MacDermott, Ragni, Rado), 243n.14
Half a Sixpence (Heneker, Cross), 125, 188
Hamlet (Thomas, Barbier, Carré), 77
Hammerstein, Oscar, 2nd, 38, 40, 130, 187
Hampton, Christopher, 40, 127
Hannaman, Ross, 21, 56, 170
Harley, Steve, 13, 225n.3
Hart, Charles, 15, 40, 44, 78
Haworth, Jill, 124
Head, Murray, 7, 66, 225n.3
Hellé (Duvernoy, Du Locle, Nuitter), 77
Hello, Dolly! (Herman, Stewart), 124, 125
Hemmings, David, 225n.7
Heneker, David, 188
Herbert, A. P., 189
Herman, Jerry, 125, 186, 221n.1
"Hey Jude" (Lennon, McCartney), 67
"Hey There" (Adler, Ross), 171

Hill, Ken, 79
Holden, William, 131
Holt, Thelma, 15
How to Succeed in Business Without Really Trying (Loesser), 123
Hugill, Sarah Jane Tudor, 7, 11, 15

"I Am What I Am" (Herman), 243n.23
"I Could Change the World" (Davis), 171
"I Got You Babe" (Bono), 59
"I Lost My Heart to a Starship Trooper" (Hughes, Calvert), 223n.23
"I'm Always Chasing Rainbows" (Carroll, McCarthy), 171
Into the Woods (Sondheim, Lapine), 42

Janáček, Leoš, 64, 171, 240n.15
Jewell, Derek, 6, 22, 27
Joel, Billy, 171, 234n.2
Jolson, Al, 171
Jones, Tom, 199, 200
La Juive (Halévy, Scribe), 232n.24
Julian, Rupert, 78

Kanawa, Kiri Te, 54
Kander, John, 221n.1
Kapur, Shekhar, 223n.22
Kenwright, Bill, 59, 236n.17
Kern, Jerome, 123
The King and I (Rodgers, Hammerstein), 123, 241n.1
Kissel, Howard, 175, 176
Kiss Me, Kate (Cole Porter, B. and S. Spewack), 123, 241n.1, 241n.3
"Knights in White Satin" (Hayward), 68
Knop, Patricia, 134
Kopit, Arthur, 79, 230n.2

Land, David, 7, 222n.11
Lawrence, Stephanie, 225n.3
Led Zeppelin, 64, 66
Lennon, John, 22
Lerner, Alan Jay, 40, 240–41n.23
Levin, Bernard, 29
Lill, John, 5, 222n.8
The Lion King (John, Rice, Allers, Mecchi), 34

A Little Night Music (Stephen Sondheim, Wheeler), 125, 126, 185
Lloyd Webber, Andrew
—biography: awards, honours, and records established: 1–2, 6, 10, 11, 17, 18, 29, 41, 54, 221n.3, 221–22n.5, 226n.27, Table 1.1
—business and Really Useful companies: 9, 12, 13, 14, 17–18, 33, 125–26, 134, 223nn.20,22, 226n.27, 241n.5
—domestic life, 5–8 passim, 11–16 passim, 36, 222n.8, 222–23n.15, 224n.24, 240n.10
—education, 5–6, 21, 69
—personal interests, 8, 15, 18, 222n.7, Sydmonton Court House and Festival, 8, 9, 15, 16, 26, 31, 32, 36, 44, 49, 162, 181, 207, 223n.20, 224n.28
—works (*See also individual works in* Index of Lloyd Webber's Works)
  —borrowing in, 9, 36–37, 47–48, 155–82, 227n.34, 228n.9; and "Cherry Pink and Apple Blossom White" (Louiguy): 167–69, Ex. 6.2; and J. S. Bach, 67, 171, 174–75; and Mendelssohn Violin Concerto, 72–73; and Puccini, 37, 171, 176–80, 197–98, 240–41n.23, Examples 6.5, 6.6, and 6.7
  —critical response to, 15, 24, 27, 36–37, 119, 134–35; London: 22, 28–29, 32, 33, 48, 52–53, 225n.7; New York: 29, 41–43, 46, 119, 188
  —genre identity of, 20, 27–28, 32, 36, 37–38, 41, 46–47, 49–50, 73–75, 122, 183–207, 241nn.1,3, 241–2n.6, 242n.11, 243nn.13,14,21,23
  —Lloyd Webber's assessment of, 25, 31–32, 38–39, 40, 49, 51–52, 122, 136, 207
  —self-borrowing in, 16, 25, 27, 36, 37, 56–58, 73, 161, 172, 176, 223n.20, 231n.13, 234n.8, 244n.29
  —visualization of music in, 29–30, 146–54, 149, 238nn.35,36
Lloyd Webber, Julian, 5, 221n.1, 222n.8; as solo cellist, 25, 72; and Variations, 9
Lloyd Webber, William Southcombe, 5, 6, 13, 221n.5, 222n.8, 224n.25
Loesser, Frank, 171
Loewe, Frederick, 40, 240–41n.23

Lom, Herbert, 80
Lord, Jon, 68, 229nn.18,19
"Lost in His Arms" (Berlin), 194
The Loves of Ergasto (Greber), 120
Lovett, Marcus, 237n.30
Lulu, 58
LuPone, Patti, 16, 48
Lute Song (Scott, Hanighen), 242n.11
Lux aeterna (Ligeti), 70
Lynne, Gillian, 31, 32

Maazel, Lorin, 13
Mackay, Fulton, 71
Mackintosh, Cameron, 32, 33, 42
Madama Butterfly (Puccini, Giacosa, and
    Illica), 198
Madonna, 17, 209, 225n.3, 239n.40
Mame (Herman, Lawrence, Lee), 125
Mamma Mia! (Andersson, Ulvaeus, and
    Johnson), 186
"Mandrake Root" (Blackmore, Evans), 65
Manfred Mann, 59, 229n.22
Manilow, Barry, 171
"Maria" (Bernstein, Sondheim), 194
Marsh, Edward, 53
Martin, George, 68
Martin, Hugh, 126
Martin, Mary, 124
Mayall, Rik, 68
Mayor, Lottie, 199
Maytime (Romberg, Young), 123
McKenna, Patrick, 17, 125
Me and My Girl (Gay, Rose, Furber), 188
Meat Loaf, 225n.3
Meet Me in St. Louis (stage musical: Martin,
    Blane, Wheeler), 126
Messiaen, Olivier, 37, 64
Meyerbeer, Giacomo, 108, 232n.25
Miles-Kingston, Paul, 13
Mills, Hayley, 236n.19
Mills, John, 136, 154, 236n.19
Minnelli, Liza, 124
Les Misérables (Boublil, Shönberg,
    Kretzmer), 33, 41, 42, 197
The Mixed Bag, 6
Monckton, Lionel, 46
The Monk (Lewis), 230n.6

The Monkees, 60
The Moody Blues, 68
Moore, Roger, 45
Mordden, Ethan, 187
Morrison, Diana, 225n.3
The Most Happy Fella (Loesser), 198,
    241nn.1,3
The Music Man (Willson, Lacey), 123
Mussorgsky, Modest, 171
My Fair Lady (Lerner, Loewe), 32, 33, 123,
    241n.1
Myers, Sefton, 7, 222n.11
The Mysteries of Udolfo (Radcliffe), 230n.6

Nail, Jimmy, 240n.9
Napoleon (Williams, Sabiston), 198
Naughty Marietta (Herbert, Young), 123
Neame, Ronald, 71
Neeley, Ted, 7, 238–39n.40
Nicholas, Paul, 222n.14, 225n.3
The Nightingale (Strouse), 224n.23
Nights of Cabiria (Fellini), 126
Nine (Yeston, Kopit), 126
Norma (Bellini, Romani), 120
Northanger Abbey (Austen), 230n.6
Novello, Ivor, 53, 125, 188, 189, 242n.9
Le nozze di Figaro (Mozart, Da Ponte), 111
Nunn, Trevor, 13, 15, 33, 34, 39, 44, 127, 162,
    207

O'Horgan, Tom, 7, 25, 148
Oklahoma! (Rodgers, Hammerstein), 33, 123,
    125, 184, 193, 194, 241nn.1,2
Oliver! (Bart), 47, 125, 188
"One Hand, One Heart" (Bernstein, Sond-
    heim), 195
Organ Symphony No. 5 in F (Widor),
    235n.14
Osmond, Donny, 61, 154, 199, 200

Pacific 1860 (Coward), 227n.32
Paige, Elaine, 22, 154, 181, 199, 225n.3
Paint Your Wagon (Lerner, Loewe), 241n.23
The Pajama Game (Adler, Ross, Abbott,
    Bissell), 123
Partita no. 3 in E (J. S. Bach), 229n.18
Pavone, Rita, 58

Penderecki, Krzystof, 70
Peter Grimes (Britten, Slater), 117
Phantom (Yeston, Kopit), 79, 243n.20
The Phantom of the Opera (films),
—1925: 78, 98, 233n.35
—1943: 78, 98
—1962: 78, 80
—1990: 79, 80
The Phantom of the Paradise (film, 1984), 78
Piano Sonata no. 8 op. 13, "Sonata Pathé-
tique" (Beethoven), 171
The Pirates of Penzance (Gilbert, Sullivan),
222n.12
Plagiarism. *See* Lloyd Webber, Andrew:
works, borrowing in; self-borrowing in
Porgy and Bess (G. and I. Gershwin,
Heyward), 241n.1,3
Porter, Cole, 123
Prelude in C major, BWV 870 (J. S. Bach),
174
Prelude in C minor, op.28 (Chopin), 171
Presley, Elvis, 60, 72, 143, 228nn.12,13,
230n.30
"Pretty Flamingo" (Barkan), 169
Previn, André, 25
Prince, Hal, 16, 134, 223nn.17,18; and *Evita*,
28, 29, 151; and *The Phantom of the
Opera*, 38, 119, 121, 232n.18, 233n.36
The Producers (Brooks, Meehan), 126, 186
Prokofiev, Sergey, 27, 55, 70
Promises, Promises (Bacharach, David,
Simon), 243n.14
Puccini, Giacomo, 37, 241–42n.6
"Puppet on a String" (Martin, Coulter), 58

HM The Queen, 223n.20
Querelle des Bouffons, 113

Ragtime (Flaherty, Ahrens, McNally), 186,
198
Rahman, A. R., 223n.22
Raven, Paul, 57, 227n.4
The Red Hill Children, 225n.3
Rent (Larson), 193
Repp, Ray, 181, 227n.34
Rêverie orientale (Saint-Saëns), 106, 232n.20
Rhapsody on a Theme of Paganini, op.43
(Rachmaninoff), 171

Rice, Reva, 225n.3
Rice, Timothy Miles Bindon, 6–10 passim,
30, 38, 39, 40, 161–62, 209, 223n.20;
and *Evita*, 9, 10, 28–29, 30, 190, 223n.17,
238n.38, 243n.13; and *Jesus Christ Super-
star*, 7–8, 22, 24–25, 145, 172; and *Joseph
and the Amazing Technicolor Dreamcoat*,
6–7, 21–22, 55, 228n.12; and pop songs: 21,
56–58, 72–73, 161, 170–71, 172
Rich, Frank, 46, 119
Richard, Cliff, 13, 58, 225n.3
Riddle, Nelson, 229n.25
Rienzi (Wagner), 232n.24
Rinaldo (Handel, Rossi), 120
Robert le Diable (Meyerbeer, Scribe), 81
Rodgers, Richard Charles, 38, 40, 123, 130,
187
The Rolling Stones, 64
Roméo et Juliette (Gounod, Barbier, Carré),
106, 232n.20
Ros, Edmondo, 240n.10
Rose-Marie (Friml, Harbach, Hammerstein),
123
"Rosemary" (Loesser), 194
Der Rosenkavalier (Strauss, Hofmannsthal),
240n.20
Rossum, Emmy, 126
Russell, Ken, 150, 151, 238n.36
Russell, Willy, 188

Le Sacre du printemps (Stravinsky), 70, 116
Sail Away (Coward), 227n.32
Salieri, Antonio, 111
Sands, Wes, 224n.1
Satton, Lon, 225n.3
Saturday Night Fever (B., M., and R. Gibb,
Knighton, Phillips), 126
Schoenberg, Arnold, 104
Schönberg, Claude-Michel, 41
Schubert, Franz, 109
La serva padrona (Pergolesi, Federico), 112
"Session Man" (Davies), 227n.3
Sharman, Jim, 7
Shaw, Sandie, 58
Shell, Ray, 225n.3
Shostakovich, Dmitry, 70
Show Boat (Kern, Hammerstein), 123,
241nn.1,3

Shulman, Milton, 28
Side by Side by Sondheim, 162
Simon, John, 29
Sinatra, Frank, 229n.25
Smiles of a Summer Night (Bergman), 126
"So Deep Is the Night" (Miller, after Marietti and Viaud, after Chopin), 171
"Some Enchanted Evening" (Rodgers, Hammerstein), 194
Sondheim, Stephen, 125, 186, 194, 221n.1
Sonny and Cher, 59
The Sound of Music (Rodgers, Hammerstein, Lindsay, R. Crouse), 26, 123, 144, 195
Sounds of Blackness, 199
"The South Bank Show," 9
South Pacific (Rodgers, Hammerstein, Logan), 26, 241n.1
Spielberg, Stephen, 73, 234n.2
A Star Is Born (film: Wellman), 126
Steiner, Max, 73
Steinman, Jim, 49, 134
Steyn, Mark, 25, 39
Stigwood, Robert, 7, 222n.11
Stilgoe, Richard, 33, 40, 78
Stoppard, Tom, 234n.2
Stravinsky, Igor, 27, 55, 70
Streisand, Barbra, 199, 225n.3, 234n.2
Strouse, Charles, 125, 221n.1
Sullivan, Arthur Seymour, 46
Sunset Boulevard (film), 127–33
"Supercalifragilisticexpialidocious" (R. M. and R. B. Sherman), 124
Swanson, Gloria, 131, 133
Sweeney Todd (Sondheim, Wheeler), 186, 197, 241n.3
Sweet Charity (Coleman, Fields, Simon), 123, 126
Syal, Meera, 223n.22
Symphony in Three Movements (Stravinsky), 70
Symphony no. 1, the "Classical" (Prokofiev), 165, Ex. 6.1
Symphony no. 9, "From the New World" (Dvořák), 171

Tate, Stephen, 222n.14
"Teddy Bear" (Mann, Lowe), 60, 228n.13
"This Night" (Joel), 171

This Year of Grace (Coward), 226n.32
Thomas, Leslie, 6
Threnody to the Victims of Hiroshima (Penderecki), 230n.27
"Till There Was You" (Willson), 243n.21
"Till You" (Repp), 181
Toccata in D minor, BWV 565 (J. S. Bach), 229n.18, 235n.14
Tommy (Townsend, Entwistle, Moon), album, 65; film (1975), 150–51, 238n.37
Tosca (Puccini, Giacosa, Illica), 171, 179, Ex. 6.6
Tyler, Bonnie, 199, 200

Vathek (Beckford), 230n.6
Victor/Victoria (Mancini, Bricusse, Edwards), 125
Violin Concerto in E minor, op. 64 (Mendelssohn), 172–73

Waddington, Hannah, 199, 225n.3
Waxman, Franz, 128
Webber, Jean Hermione, 5, 221n.5, 222n.8
West Side Story (Bernstein, Sondheim, Laurents), 123, 229n.25, 234n.41, 241nn.1,3
Whelton, David, 228n.9
Whistle Down the Wind (film: Forbes) 134, 139–41; status of film, 135–36
Whistle Down the Wind (musical: Labey, Taylor) 136, 236n.20
Whistle Down the Wind (novel: Bell) 134, 138, 141; synopsis, 137–38
"Whistle While You Work" (Churchill, Morey), 124
Whitelaw, Billie, 71
"A Whiter Shade of Pale" (Brookes, Reid), 67, 171
The Who, 64, 150
Wilder, Billy, 127
Williams, John, 73
Williams, Maynard, 227n.2
Wilson, Patrick, 126
Wilson, Sandy, 47, 162, 188, 189
"With a Little Bit of Luck" (Lerner, Loewe), 241n.23
Wodehouse, P. G., 47

Xenaxis, Iannis, 70

"Yesterday" (Lennon, McCartney), 170
Yeston, Maury, 79, 230n.2
"You'll Never Walk Alone" (Rodgers, Ham-
    merstein), 195
Young, Roy, 72

"Younger Than Springtime" (Rodgers,
    Hammerstein), 193

Die Zauberflöte (Mozart, Schikaneder), 111

Index of Lloyd Webber's Works

Page numbers in *italic type* refer to images.

"AC/DC," 225n.3

"All I Ask of Life," 223n.20

"All I Ask of You," 13, 41, 90, 93, 115, 163, 198, 225n.3, Ex.4.2; and "Music of the Night," 98, Ex. 4.9; and Puccini, 180, Ex. 6.7

"All One Hot Afternoon," 223n.20

"And the Money Kept Rolling In (and Out)," 71, 74, 146, 153

"Angel of Music," 94, 117, Ex. 4.5

"Annie Christmas," 235n.17, 237n.31

"Another Suitcase in Another Hall," 9, 28, 75, 225n.3; and self-borrowing, 27

"Any Dream Will Do," 22, 60, 198, 208, 224–25n.3, 228n.11; and self-borrowing, 58, 176

"Anything But Lonely," 225n.20; and self-borrowing, 223n.3

"The Arrest," 67

"The Art of the Possible," 151; and self-borrowing, 73

"As If We Never Said Goodbye," 199, 225n.3; and self-borrowing, 223n.20

Aspects of Love, 2, 10, *44*, 50, 75, 193, 208, 221n.3, 243n.17, 243–44n.24, Table 1.1; and allusion, 165, Ex. 6.1; analysis of opening scenes, 200–207, Ex. 7.1; critical response, 46, 188; as film, 17, 125; genesis, 15–16, 37, 44; and genre, 46, 186–87, 197; and lyricists, 40, Ex. 6.1; musical structure, 27, 37–38, 45–46, 75, 186–87, 203–207, 245n.32; and pastiche, 163; premieres: 15, 45–46; and self-borrowing, 73; at Sydmonton, 44, 207, 224n.28

"Baby, You're Good for Me," 72

The Beautiful Game, 19, 26, 52, 76, 163–64, 208; dramatization in, 52–53, 193, 237n.32, 242n.10; effectiveness, 40, 53; genesis, 51–52, 126; and self-borrowing, 53–54

"Believe Me I Will," 57

Benedicite, 36, 244n.29

"Benjamin Calypso," 62

"Blood Money," 191

"Buenos Aires," 56, 227n.2

By Jeeves, 18, 19, 50, 161–62, 193, 208, 221n.3, Table 1.1; as revision of *Jeeves*, 18, 51; video, 154, 155

"Capped Teeth and Caesar Salad," 31

Cats, 11, 19, 38, 39, 40, 42, 50, 75, 189, 194, 221n.3, 225n.3; critical response, 32, 188; as film, 125, 155, 234n.2; genesis, 162; and genre, 32, 185–86; orchestration of, 31; and pastiche, 162; premieres, 11, 226n.19; revision, 28; structure, 31–32, 39, 162;

Cats (continued)
  success of, 1–2, 2, 11, 18, 32–33, 186, 210,
    Table 1.1; video, 154–55, 236n.19
"Chanson d'enfance," 45, 203
"Charlie Christmas," 236n.17
"Clean the Kit," 76
"Close Every Door," 60, 224n.3
"The Coat of Many Colours," 224n.3
"The Code of the Woosters," 161
"Cold," 141, 144, 163, 199
*Come Back Richard, Your Country Needs
  You*, 6, 57, 222n.9
"Could We Start Again Please," 146
"The Craic," 76
Cricket, 223n.20
"The Crucifixion," 70

"Damned for All Time," 191; use of rock riffs,
  65
"Dangerous Jade," 27, 74
"Don Juan Triumphant," 87, 91, 101, 104–5,
  113–15, 197, 231n.15, 231–32n.17, 233n.37,
  Ex. 4.11
"Don't Cry for Me, Argentina," 9, 28, 75,
  239n.39, Ex. 6.4; and borrowing, 174–
  76; promotional single, 198, 225n.3; and
  self-borrowing, 56; visualization of, 153
"Don't Like You," 76
"Down on the Farm," 27
"Down Thru' Summer," 21, 56, 171

"Eva and Magaldi," 73
"Eva's Sonnet," 190, 243n.13
"Every Movie's a Circus," 130
"Everybody Loves a Hero," 45, 245n.32
"Everything's Alright," 71, 191; analysis of,
  66–67
Evita, 22, 38, 39, 41, 50, 74, 145, 161, 189;
  and borrowing, 30, 167–68, 170; casting
  of Madonna in film, 209, 238–39n.39;
  characterization of Che in film, 146;
  comparison of concept album with *Jesus
  Christ Superstar*, 145–46; critical response,
  27, 28–29, 42, 188; film, 17, 125, 145, 151–
  54, 155–56; genesis, 9–10, 27–29, 38; and
  genre, 27, 73–74, 166, 190, 192–93; and
  pastiche, 30; revisions for stage, 151; and
  rock, 74–75; and self-borrowing, 27, 56,

73; structure of, 27, 30, 36, 145–46, 192–
  93; success of, 1–2, 10–11, 29, 41–42, 125,
  210, Table 1.1; visualization of music, 30,
  146–47, 151–54

"The First Man You Remember," 225n.3

"The Gang," 235–36n.17, 237n.31
"Gethsemane," 66, 67, 150, 243n.15
"Girl Meets Boy," 130
"Go, Go, Go Joseph," 59, 60, 63; and model-
  ing, 168–69
"God's Own Country," 167
"Goodbye Seattle," 57
"The Greatest Star of All," 133
Gumshoe, 8, 71–72; and self-borrowing, 25, 73

"Half a Moment," 161
"The 'Hallo' Song," 161
"Hannibal," 81, 88, 106–10, 107, 116, 197
"The Heart Is Slow to Learn," 53
"Heaven on Their Minds," 65, 69, 191; and
  visualization of music, 147–48
"Herod's Song," 57, 68, 147, 160–61; and
  self-borrowing, 57–58
"High Flying Adored," 27, 193, 225n.3
"Hosanna," 69, 70, 147

"I Am the Starlight," 225n.3
"I Can't Go On," 227n.2
"I Don't Know How to Love Him," 147, 198;
  and borrowing, 172–73
"I Fancy You," 58
"I Never Get What I Pay For," 144
"I'd Be Surprisingly Good for You," 75; and
  modeling, 170
"I'd Rather Die on My Feet Than Live on
  My Knees," 76
"If Only," 199
"Il muto," 85–86, 108, 111–13, 112, 116, 197
"I'll Give All My Love to Southend," 21, 56
"It's a Pig," 161
"It's Easy for You," 228n.12

"Jacob and Sons," 22, 61, 224n.3
Jacob's Journey, 8
Jeeves, 9, 29, 46, 161, 225n.7; genesis, 26–27,
  38; and self-borrowing, 161

Jesus Christ Superstar, 23, 26, 38–39, 50, 72, 161, 189, 208; comparison of concept album with *Evita*, 145–46; comparison of recordings, 67–68; concept album, 7, 22–23, 67–68, 145, 227n.4; critical response, 24, 188; dramatization in, 30, 191–92, 193, 243nn.15,16; film (1973), 7, 25, 125, 145–51, 149, 155–56, 238n.35; genesis, 7, 29, 64–65, 191; and genre, 24, 27, 190–91; modern classical influences, 69–70; musical characterization, 66, 165–66, 190; and orchestra-rock integration, 68–69; overture, 70; and pastiche, 30, 161; and rock, 55, 64–69, 74–75, 76, 191, 243n.14; stage show, 7, 25, 145; success of, 1–2, 2, 10, 192, 210, 221n.3, 222n.14, Table 1.1; video, 145, 154; visualization of music, 30, 146–51

"John 19:41," 22, 148

Joseph and the Amazing Technicolor Dream-coat, 26, 62, 70, 189, 221n.3, 229n.14; critical response, 22, 188; development of, 8, 58–59, 61–62, 229n.16; genesis, 6, 24, 29; and genre, 27, 36, 229n.15; and pastiche, 30, 60–63; and pop, 21, 55, 58–61, 63, 76; recordings compared, 59–64, 68; and self-borrowing, 57; success of, 1, 2, 10, 11, 33–34, 210, 228n.8, Table 1.1; video, 154–55, 229n.16; visualization of music, 30

"Joseph's Dreams," 59, 62

"Journey of a Lifetime," 245n.32

"Kansas Morning," 240n.16; and self-borrowing, 172

"A Kiss is a Terrible Thing to Waste," 75, 140, 144, 199, 225n.3

"The Lady's Got Potential," 74, 151–52, 238n.38

"The Lady's Paying," 128, 234n.7, 235n.13; and self-borrowing, 244n.29

"The Last Supper," 67–68, 165–66

"Let Us Love in Peace," 76

"Light at the End of the Tunnel," 195

The Likes of Us, 6, 161

"Little Lotte," 83, 102

"Lotta Locomotion," 57

"Love Changes Everything," 45, 193–94, 198, 201, 225n.3, 243–44n.24, 244n.27; and musical motifs, 201, 203

"Love Is Here," 161

"Magdalena," 161

"Make Believe Love," 5, 21, 224n.1

"Married Man," 71

"Masquerade," 80, 86, 86, 117–18

"Memory," 31, 39, 185, 198, 225n.3, 226n.19; and borrowing, 173–74, Ex. 6.3; revision of "One Star," 16; similarities with "Our Kind of Love," 53

"Mr. Mistoffelees," 31

"Music of the Night," 41, 84, 102, 104, 116, 163, 225n.3; and "All I Ask of You," 98, Ex. 4.9; concluding "mystic chords," 99, 118, Ex. 4.10; and Puccini, 176–79, Ex. 6.5 and Ex. 6.6

"Nature of the Beast," 144, 195–96

"A New Argentina," 74, 235n.9

"New Ways to Dream," 132

"Next Time You Fall in Love," 17, 225n.3, 240n.7

"1969," 56, 170–71

"No Matter What," 144, 225n.3, 236n.17, 238n.33; as pop single, 198–99

"Notes," 110, 208

The Odessa File, 8, 69, 72–73, 230n.29; and self-borrowing, 25, 73

"Off to the Party," 76

"Oh What a Circus," 56, 152, 225n.3

"Old Deuteronomy," 31, 225n.3

"On This Night of a Thousand Stars," 75, 146, 161, 170, 240n.11; comparison with "Cherry Pink and Apple Blossom White," 167–69, 240n.9, Ex. 6.2

"One More Angel in Heaven," 62

"One Star," 16

"Only He," 225n.3

"Our Kind of Love," 53, 174, 199–200, 225n.3

"Parlez-vous Français?" 163, 244n.25; and musical motifs, 201–3

"The Perfect Year," 225n.3

"Peron's Latest Flame," 152–53

The Phantom of the Opera, 26–27, 31, 36,
38, 46, 50, 77–122, 189, 209, 244n.30; and
the 1925 film (Julian), 78, 78, 98, 106,
230n.1; characterization of Christine, 84,
91–96, 102, 109, 115–18; characterization
of Raoul, 88–90, 97–99, 100; characterization of the Phantom, 96–105, 113–18,
120, 233n.36; critical response, 42–43, 119;
explanation of success, 41, 118–22; as film,
17, 125–26, 145, 234n.2; genesis, 15, 37–39,
79; and genre, 41, 122, 197–98; and historical context, 77–78, 106, 111–13, 119–21,
230n.6, 232n.20, 234n.41; and lyricists, 39–
40; musical language of Christine, 91–96,
102–3, 109, 115–18, 231nn.8,11, 234–35n.8,
Ex. 4.3 and Ex. 4.4; musical language
of Raoul, 88–90, 97, 117, Ex.4.2 and Ex.
4.9; musical language of the Phantom,
89–90, 93–105, 110–11, 113–18, 232n.17,
Ex. 4.1, Ex. 4.5–4.13; musical structure,
37–38, 75, 87–88; and the novel (Leroux), 77–78, 79–81, 88, 98, 101, 104, 106,
121; and opera, 105–15, 197–98 (*See also*
"Don Juan Triumphant;" "Hannibal;" "Il
Muto"); and operetta, 110, 113 (*See also*
"Prima Donna"); orchestration of, 89, 93,
95, 101–4, 107–8, 111, 113; and pastiche,
72, 163; the Phantom as operatic composer, 104–5; the Phantom compared to
Raoul, 97–99, 100; premieres, 13–15, 40–
41, 42–43, 43; and Puccini, 177–80, Ex.
6.5–6.7; and Sarah Brightman, 38–39, 41,
109; and self-borrowing, 37, 44, 242n.10,;
staging, 88–89, 90, 96, 101, 106–107, 108–
9, 119–21, 232n.18; success of, 1–2, 2, 19,
118–19, 190, 221n.3, Table 1.1; synopsis,
81–87, Table 4.1
"The Phantom of the Opera," 75, 83, 85, Ex.
4.7; and borrowing, 180–81; effectiveness,
99–101; promotional single, 13, 14, 225n.3
"Pie Jesu," 36
Play the Fool, 21
"The Point of No Return," 114–15, 117
"Poppa's Blues," 163
"Prima Donna," 90, 231n.8, 233nn.31,32;
analysis of, 110–11
"Probably on Thursday," 56–57, 59
"Pumping Iron," 163

"The Rainbow Tour," 146, 235n.9
Requiem, 13, 36–37
"Rolling Stock," 33, 226n.20
"The Rum Tum Tugger," 31

"Seeing Is Believing," 45, 207, 244nn.26–28;
and musical motifs, 202–3
"She Is a Diamond," 193
"Simon Zealotes," 66, 69, 148, 149
Song & Dance, 10–11, 12, 25, 28, 31. See also
Tell Me on a Sunday; Variations
"Song of the King," 60–61, 62–63, 164,
225n.3, 228n.12, 228–29n.13
Starlight Express, 19, 32, 33–36, 34, 35, 44,
75, 208, 221n.3, 223n.22; critical response,
33, 41–42; as film, 17, 125; genesis, 12–13;
and genre, 37–38, 185, 189, 197; lyrics of,
40; and pastiche, 162–63; premieres, 13,
15, 41, 224n.31; revision, 10, 41, 240n.7;
and self-borrowing, 57; success of, 1, 2, 33,
35–36, 38, Table 1.1
"Stone the Crows," 176
"Summer Day," 27
Sunset Boulevard, 18, 26, 33, 41, 42, 48,
50, 128, 156, 189, 197, 208–9, 221n.3,
225n.3, 227n.35; adaptation from film,
127–33, 144, 146; and the close-up, 131–
33; genesis, 16; lyricists of, 10, 40, 129;
musical effectiveness, 48–49, 70–71, 75;
musical language of Joe, 128–30, 166;
musical language of Norma, 128–32,
166, 231n.14; premieres, 17, 48, 224n.31;
prologue, 129–30; revision, 17, 28; and
self-borrowing, 25, 36, 73, 244nn.29,30;
success of, 1–2, Table 1.1; at Sydmonton,
16
"Sunset Boulevard," 225n.3, 235n.11; and
self-borrowing, 73
"Superstar," 22, 66, 191, 225n.3
"Surrender," 244n.29

"Take That Look Off Your Face," 31
Tell Me on a Sunday, 10, 31, 38. See also
Song & Dance
"The Temple," 71, 191
"Then We Are Decided," 146
"There's a Light at the End of the Tunnel,"
163

"Think of Me," 81–83, 109–10, 232n.26; and self-borrowing, 37
"This Jesus Must Die," 69
"This Time Next Year," 130
"Those Canaan Days," 62
"Those Saladin Days," 57
"Tire Tracks and Broken Hearts," 75, 142–43, 144, 199, 200
"Too Much in Love to Care," 71, 130, 194
The Toy Theatre, 5
"Travel Hopefully," 161
"The Trial Before Pilate," 70, 229n.26
"Try It and See," 57–58
"Try Not to Be Afraid," 144, 199
"Twisted," 91–92, 231n.9, Ex. 4.3

"U.N.C.O.U.P.L.E.D.," 160–61, 163, 239–40n.7
"Unsettled Scores," 144, 199

Variations, 9, 11, 25, 31, 69, 72, 73, 171; and genre, 27–28. See also Song & Dance
"The Vaults of Heaven," 144, 199, 200

"Waltz for Eva and Che," 146, 193; visualization of, 153–54

"What a Line to Go Out On," 161
"What's the Buzz?" 191
"When Children Rule the World," 76, 144, 199, 200, 225n.3, 237–38n.33
"When Love Arrives," 161
Whistle Down the Wind, 19, 50–51, 70, 76, 142, 146, 156, 189, 193, 196, 209, 237n.26, 242n.10, Table 1.1; adaptation from the film (Forbes), 134–37, 135, 139–42, 144; adaptation from the novel (Bell), 134, 136, 139–44; genesis, 49, 125, 134, 136–37; and genre, 50, 197; pop cover versions, 198–99; premieres, 17, 18, 26, 49, 134; revision of, 10, 18, 49–50, 237n.31; and rock, 75; at Sydmonton, 49
"Whistle Down the Wind," 144, 199, 225n.3
"The Wine and the Dice," 45, 71, 207
"Wishing You Were Somehow Here Again," 87, 225n.3, 231n.11; and self-borrowing, 37
"With One Look," 131–33, 225n.3
"Wrestle with the Devil," 199

"You Must Love Me," 17, 225n.3